D0935609

INSIDE

MAPLE LEAF
GARDENS

INSIDE

MAPLE LEAF GARDENS

THE RISE AND FALL OF THE TORONTO MAPLE LEAFS

WILLIAM
HOUSTON

McGraw-Hill Ryerson
Toronto Montreal

INSIDE MAPLE LEAF GARDENS
The Rise and Fall of the Toronto Maple Leafs
Copyright © 1989 William Houston

All rights reserved. No part of this publication may be reproduced, stored in a retrieval system or data base, or transmitted, in any form or by any means, electronic, mechanical, photocopying, recording, or otherwise, without the prior written permission of the publisher.

First published in 1989 by
McGraw-Hill Ryerson Limited
330 Progress Avenue
Scarborough, Ontario M1P 2Z5

ISBN: 0-07-549886-3

1 2 3 4 5 6 7 8 9 0   M   8 7 6 5 4 3 2 1 0 9

Canadian Cataloguing in Publication Data

Houston, William, date
Inside Maple Leaf Gardens

ISBN 0-07-549886-3

1. Toronto Maple Leafs (Hockey team)–History.
I. Title.

GV848.T6H68   1989   796.96′26   C89-095415-1

Design: Kirk Alexander Stephens

Printed and bound in Canada

CONTENTS

Acknowledgements

There are many to thank, but most notably David Johnston, who believed in the book and sold it; Glen Ellis at McGraw-Hill Ryerson, who was supportive and enthusiastic from beginning to end; Andrea Gallagher Ellis, whose editing improved the manuscript significantly; and Barbara Aarsteinsen, who helped in the research.

A special thanks to the many Leafs, past and present, who were interviewed, for their recollections and insights, and to the employees of Maple Leaf Gardens whose contributions must remain anonymous.

Thanks also to Linda Barnard, James DuPlacey, Benny Ercolani, Al Garner, Lenore Gray, Tom Hawthorn, Bud Jorgensen, David Langford, Mark Lee, Nancy Lee, Peter Livingston, Don Loney, Brian Milner, Paul Patton, Clive Powell, Joe Romain, Al Strachan, Dan Westell, Scott Young, and the reporters who chronicled the Leafs over the years.

Publications referred to in the text include Punch Imlach's two books on the Leafs, *Hockey Is a Battle* and *Heaven and Hell in the NHL*; autobiographies by Lanny McDonald (*Lanny*), Frank Selke Sr. (*Behind the Cheering*), and Conn Smythe (*If You Can't Beat 'em in the Alley*); Paul Kaihla's profile of Bill Ballard ("Like Father, Like Son?"), in *T.O. Magazine* (June 1987); Earl McRae's profile of Harold Ballard in the book *The Victors and the Vanquished*; John Melady's book on Bill Barilko, *Overtime, Overdue: The Bill Barilko Story*; and Scott Young's biography of Foster Hewitt, *Hello Canada! The Life and Times of Foster Hewitt*.

Finally, for the assistance of the *Globe and Mail*, particularly its library and clerical staff, a grateful acknowledgement.

INSIDE
MAPLE LEAF
GARDENS

1

BIG MAC

ATTACK

By early 1988 the decline of the Toronto Maple Leaf hockey club was almost complete. Once seen as the standard for sportsmanship and success, the club had deteriorated in the 1980s to a condition that provoked ridicule and contempt. The Leafs were regarded by almost everyone in the business as the most incompetently run organization in the National Hockey League. They had been consistent losers for years, and now there was a very real state of paralysis.

For three weeks during January and February while Harold Ballard, the 84-year-old Leaf owner and president, recovered from a heart attack in a hospital in Miami, Florida, the club was without anyone in charge. There was no chain of command, and as the team slipped deeper into a mid-season slide, tension increased between the coaching staff and the front office, headed by the general manager, Gerry McNamara.

With any other club the general manager would have been in control. But the Leafs were no ordinary operation; they hadn't been since Ballard had become principal owner in 1972. During his proprietorship, the loud, bombastic Ballard had kept a firm grip on all aspects of the company, but had been a failure in terms of putting a winning team on the ice.

McNamara was in many ways the ideal general manager for Ballard. He was submissive, acquiescent, and uncritical. He hovered over Ballard and catered to his every wish. He never questioned

Ballard's decisions, supporting him on every matter and spending as little of his money as was possible. Ballard appreciated that, too. Along with his firm grip, Ballard had a tight fist. The Leafs, although one of the league's most profitable teams, spent less than any NHL club. The team's player payroll was near the bottom of the league's scale and the hockey operations staff was an underpaid skeleton crew. Perhaps McNamara's greatest asset from Ballard's perspective was his relationship with the Toronto media. McNamara hated the media and for the most part the feeling was mutual. Ballard warmly endorsed this attitude, for, as much as the owner loved to promote himself, he despised those who criticized him, and by 1988 they were many. McNamara was never one to press for changes in the organization, to go to bat for those who worked under him, or to take a strong stand on any issue if it risked ruffling Ballard. In this way he had protected his job. But despite all this, McNamara was about to be fired.

The 1987-88 season, like so many, had started with optimism. There had been encouraging signs from the previous year, which had been John Brophy's first as head coach, when at the midway point the team had been only one game under .500. However, they slipped in the second half and finished in fourth place in the Norris Division. Only 4 teams in the 21-club league had poorer records. Still, by the modest standards established in Toronto over the previous years, this was viewed as somewhat satisfactory. The 32 victories, after all, were the most in a regular season in eight years. The 42 losses were 6 fewer than the previous season. And in the playoffs, they redeemed themselves by upsetting the St. Louis Blues and pushing the Detroit Red Wings to a seventh and deciding game.

As a result, many were anticipating a breakthrough in 1987-88. The team had had a year to get used to Brophy. The younger players, who had been acquired with high draft choices, were beginning to reach the age when they should blossom and lead the team–that is, if everything went as planned. And there had been a blockbuster trade in the summer: wingers Steve Thomas and Rick Vaive and defenceman Bob McGill had been sent to the Chicago Blackhawks for centre Ed Olczyk and winger Al Secord.

The merits of this trade were debated endlessly. Still, one senior hockey writer in Toronto was so certain of Leaf success that he predicted the team would finish first in the division and that Brophy would win the coach of the year award. The Toronto media always has been inclined to overrate the Leafs, particularly during training camp, but even this seemed extreme, and it quickly became apparent that the Leafs were not going to set the league on fire.

By early December they were in the midst of a five-game losing streak. For the remainder of the month, they held fast, neither gaining nor losing. Then, two days before Christmas, they defeated the Blues 5-1 in one of their rare regular-season victories in St. Louis. The Leafs cheered lustily in the dressing room after the win; it would be a merry Christmas indeed, if not a happy new year.

The losing streak started three days later with a Boxing Day loss to the Montreal Canadiens at Maple Leaf Gardens. The Leafs would continue to go winless for more than a month until the end of January when they would defeat the Los Angeles Kings at the Gardens. When that game ended, the players leapt off the bench, hugged one another, and shook their arms in the air. It was an odd sight, given the events that led up to the celebration. The Leafs had set a club record for futility by failing to get a victory in 15 consecutive games. They had been embarrassed time and again on home ice, including an 11-3 loss to the Calgary Flames. They had dropped to the bottom of their division and the league, and the jobs of Brophy and McNamara hung in the balance.

By this time, Ballard had been gone for several weeks. One of the last things he had done before leaving early in January for Florida with his companion, Yolanda, had been to grant an interview to his favourite sports writer, Milt Dunnell of the *Toronto Star,* in which he criticized his three children and said he was leaving his estate to charity. Ballard had said little about the team, other than to confirm his undying support of Brophy, whom he viewed as one of the best coaches in the league. Long before this, Ballard had cooled in his attitude toward McNamara, although he had never harshly criticized him publicly.

While in Florida, Ballard and his companion stayed at the home of Steve and Sally Stavro in Palm Beach. Stavro, a Gardens director, was a wealthy businessman and sportsman and owner of the Knob Hill Farms supermarket chain as well as a stable of thoroughbred horses.

But two days after arriving in Florida, Ballard, a diabetic, took sick. He was moved to the Miami Heart Institute on 10 January, where it was determined he had suffered a heart attack. His illness was first reported by Dunnell. Then, a little more than a week later, Ballard, feeling much better, telephoned Dunnell with the news that heads were going to roll when he got back to the Gardens.

"You could say something will be hitting the fan when I get back to the Gardens," Ballard said. "It'll be starting with the manager."

Not once during Ballard's absence had he called the Leaf hockey office to speak to McNamara. He had telephoned Brophy regularly, as he had others such as Dunnell, Gardens treasurer Donald Crump, and even McNamara's assistant, Gord Stellick. But the man who was supposed to be in charge, McNamara, was ignored–in the deep freeze, so to speak, a place habituated many times before by people Ballard was preparing to fire. To those close to the Leafs it was apparent that Brophy had won the power struggle.

The bitterness between manager and coach had started the previous March when the Leafs came perilously close to missing the playoffs. With the team in last place in the Norris Division, McNamara met with Ballard and other Leaf hockey people and suggested that Brophy be fired.

During the meeting, McNamara turned to Stellick, who was running the club's American Hockey League affiliate in Newmarket, and asked him to repeat what he had heard from Jerome Dupont, a fringe defenceman for the Newmarket team who had come down to Toronto and played some games with the Leafs. When Dupont returned to Newmarket, he told Stellick that the atmosphere in the Leaf dressing room had been oppressive. The players disliked Brophy and found it impossible to loosen up and play effectively under him. It was a hopeless situation. When Ballard heard the story, he said, "I guess we should have known something was wrong."

After a loss to the Blues at the Gardens, McNamara and Stellick met again, along with Floyd Smith, the club's chief scout and a former coach. Stellick happened to mention that the team had been unlucky in the game, hitting several goalposts. Impatiently, Smith said that they couldn't go on making excuses for Brophy. Later, Smith lost his zeal for a coaching change when he was told that he would be the replacement. There was really nobody else.

Smith's one season behind the bench in 1979-80 had been a disaster and had been cut short when he was hospitalized following a car accident near St. Catharines in which two people were killed. Smith suffered a broken leg and was charged with impaired driving and criminal negligence. He was later acquitted of the negligence charge.

Smith and Stellick kept waiting for McNamara to make a move. "I told Yolanda I wanted to talk to him [Ballard]," said McNamara, who then left the office apparently to fire Brophy. But a few minutes later he returned and said, "I couldn't do it without the old man."

The next morning Stellick went down to visit Brophy in the coach's office which is adjacent to the dressing room. When Brophy started talking about some of the ideas he had for the next game, Stellick said, "Why don't you go up and tell Gerry?"

Brophy immediately sensed something was wrong. "Am I getting fired?" he asked.

"Yeah, I think so," said Stellick.

Brophy's immediate response was, "Well, I'm not going back to Newmarket to sell advertising." As coach of the Newmarket team before taking over the Leafs, Brophy had helped promote the team and indeed sell ads. But as it turned out Brophy didn't need to worry. McNamara's request was denied. There would be no coaching change.

To those in the hockey office, the implication was clear. The balance of power had shifted. Brophy was secure, but time would quickly run out on McNamara unless the team started playing much better.

Even though the Leafs made the playoffs that spring, mainly because of a poor performance by the North Stars, who were able to pick up only two wins in their last 17 games, the relationship between Brophy and McNamara was permanently poisoned. Other coaches who had worked for McNamara felt they had received little or no support from McNamara in difficult times, and now Brophy was having the same experience.

But Brophy, unlike many, got along well with the owner. They genuinely liked each other. Both cursed a lot, liked to tell off-colour stories and jokes, and reminisce about the old days of hockey. Brophy was a tough guy and had a reputation as such: this impressed Ballard, who felt they were both men's men.

McNamara was different. He was a big man and had a hot temper, but he never swore. He was a devout Roman Catholic and a good family man. There was an air of self-righteousness about him, which sometimes irritated people. He and Ballard really had little in common except for a hatred of the media and a tendency toward pettiness when it came to people they thought were their enemies. Still, McNamara was viewed with a certain sympathy in the hockey office during the final weeks before his dismissal. Stellick felt that Brophy was really to blame for most of the team's troubles and should have been the first to go.

Stellick thought later that perhaps McNamara should have taken the initiative during the period of Ballard's hospitalization and fired Brophy. One can only guess at what would have happened if McNamara had done that. Ballard would have blown his top, of course. But if, by the time he returned, the team had won a few games with a new coach behind the bench, Ballard probably would have accepted the change and perhaps even spared McNamara. McNamara, however, was not prepared to make such a bold move. He had survived so far by doing nothing, and this strategy–or non-strategy–might continue to work.

After Ballard's remarks to Dunnell about holding his general manager accountable for the state of the team, McNamara said to one of the dwindling number of Toronto hockey reporters with whom he spoke: "I have to keep my chin up, the coach has to keep his chin up, and I've told the players to keep their chins up. Part of my job is not to figure out what Mr. Ballard is thinking of me. But I'm accountable. I'm the GM and I certainly hope to have some answers for him when he comes back."

In the Leaf hockey office it was a grim and uncertain time. When Brophy made an attempt to talk, McNamara ignored him. One day during this period Brophy walked over to where McNamara and Stellick were sitting in a hotel lobby–McNamara pointedly got up and left. That night, he refused to go to dinner with Stellick and the assistant coach, Garry Lariviere, when he learned that Brophy would be there. McNamara also became angry with Dick Duff, one of the Leaf scouts and a Leaf star from the late fifties and early sixties. Duff had been spending a lot of time in the hockey office and often watched games with Ballard. McNamara suspected Duff of attempting to undermine his position.

A few days before Ballard's return to Toronto, a second report appeared in a newspaper, this time the Toronto *Sun*. Even more than the earlier story, it indicated the dismissal of McNamara. Ballard was quoted as saying: "I owe it to Gerry to talk face-to-face, to let him defend himself. But he has lots of explaining to do." Ballard reiterated his contention that Brophy was "one of the best coaches in the league," and went on to say: "It's tough for Brophy not getting the co-operation from McNamara. If that's the case, I will find out why. I intend to talk to Gerry and give him a chance to defend himself."

As it turned out, Ballard had already made up his mind to get rid of McNamara before he spoke to him. In the past, Ballard had rarely mustered the courage to fire an employee personally. His two previous general managers, Jim Gregory and Punch Imlach, had learned of their dismissals through other channels. Ballard announced in the Toronto *Sun* that Imlach would not be returning as general manager for 1981–82. Imlach read the news while lying in a hospital bed, recovering from a heart attack. He said before his death in 1987, "It was like Ballard didn't have the guts to tell you to your face that you were fired." Gregory, the NHL's vice-president for hockey operations, says he learned he was fired in 1979 when Scotty Bowman, who had just left his post as coach of the Montreal Canadiens to seek a general managing position, called him to say he had been offered Gregory's job.

In McNamara's case, he was on the road with the team for games in Buffalo on Friday and Hartford on Sunday when Ballard arrived home at the Gardens, where he lives in a second-floor studio apartment. On Saturday, Toronto *Sun* columnist George Gross bumped into Ballard at a tennis tournament at the arena; they spoke and Gross reported the next day that barring a last-minute respite McNamara was finished.

The next morning Ballard put in a call to McNamara, who was at the Leafs' skate prior to the game that night. Ballard asked McNamara to resign; McNamara refused and so was fired. The call lasted 10 minutes. When it was over, McNamara walked over to Stellick, who was sitting in the empty stands, and said, "That's it. Can you get me outta here?"

During that final conversation, Ballard did his utmost to persuade McNamara to resign. He said, "Tell 'em I'm a miserable prick to work for and you decided to quit." McNamara refused, for obvious reasons. He had one and a half years to run on his contract, which paid him about $150,000 annually. If he quit he would forfeit more than 200 G's. Later in the day, Ballard called Stellick and implored him to convince McNamara that the best way out was to resign.

When McNamara arrived back in Toronto he told reporters: "My trouble started last year, when I decided we needed a change. I spoke up about it. As it turned out, it wasn't my job to do so. I'm not responsible for the club's record. I'm responsible for the people on the ice. I can't and won't take responsibility for the record. You have the job to pick and choose your coach. You have the authority. I didn't have anything to do with picking the coach."

McNamara had been denied his request to fire Brophy, although, on a recommendation from Floyd Smith, he had been responsible for bringing Brophy into the organization and appointing him head coach. And there was really only so much he could blame on Brophy, who had been head coach just a year and a half. McNamara was responsible for six abysmal seasons. His argument about Ballard's not giving him a free hand seemed a little self-serving. During his term as general manager he had gone out of his way to defend Ballard against criticism. He consistently had said that there wasn't a better man to work for than Harold Ballard. He had said Ballard never interfered in the running of the club. He had praised Ballard to friends as a smart hockey man, who had his finger on all aspects of the game. McNamara would say how amazed he was at what the owner knew about hockey. For six years he had been Ballard's biggest fan, and for six years he had presided over the most unsuccessful period in the history of the team.

The numbers were staggering. By far, he had the worst record of any Leaf general manager. In his five complete seasons, the team had finished 15th, 18th, 21st, 19th, and 16th in the 21-team league. In the 1987–88 season–McNamara was fired two months before its conclusion–the Leafs finished 20th. The team's winning percentage was .374 during McNamara's reign. The Leafs set club records for consecutive winless games (15), fewest wins (20), fewest points in a season (48), longest losing streak at home (7) and away (10), and most goals against in a season (386). As they say in the world of sports, his record spoke for itself. It spoke eloquently.

2

Canada's

Team

For years the Maple Leafs were a glittering national treasure, as Canadian as prairie wheat fields and lonely northern lakes. They epitomized excellence and a winning tradition. In English Canada, they were the country's most popular team–in any sport.

By 1951 the Maple Leaf empire, so-called because of the team's influence at all levels of hockey in Canada and its chain of minor-league hockey affiliates, could boast more Stanley Cups than any team in the NHL–significantly more than their chief rival, the Montreal Canadiens. When Bill Barilko scored the Stanley Cup winning goal in 1951, it gave Toronto nine championships compared to Montreal's six. In the 1960s, the prosperity continued with four more.

Of the 21 clubs in the NHL today, Toronto and Montreal are the only two that date back to the founding of the league. The NHL was established in 1917 and included three teams, the Toronto Arenas, the Montreal Canadiens, and the Ottawa Senators, although a team called the Montreal Wanderers were in for 6 of the 22 regular-season games. In 1919, the Arenas were renamed the St. Patricks, but the moniker did not attract spectators from Toronto's large Irish community, nor did it bring the team much luck. The St. Pats fared poorly in the 1920s, financially as well as on the ice.

When the owners decided to sell in 1926, a group from Philadelphia tried to buy the team for $200,000. It was at this point that

Conn Smythe, a young hockey man from Toronto, got involved. A few months earlier Smythe had been hired to manage the fledgling New York Rangers. He built the Rangers quickly with players such as Ching Johnson and Bill and Bun Cook from western Canada. The Rangers won their division in their inaugural year and finished third overall. The next season they won the Stanley Cup.

But Smythe was well out of the picture by then. He was strong willed and not at all diplomatic, and after disagreements over players with Colonel John Hammond, who operated Madison Square Garden, he was fired before the Rangers played their first NHL game. Back in Toronto, he managed and coached the Varsity Grads. They were graduates from the University of Toronto, and Smythe had coached them at the university, taking them to the Allan Cup final.

When Smythe heard the St. Pats were about to be sold, he launched a campaign to keep them in Toronto. He argued that if the city lost its NHL team it would be years before it would get another. He went to the newspapers, talked to businessmen, and did whatever he could to round up enough financial support to buy the team. With help from J. P. Bickell, a wealthy Toronto financier and part owner of the St. Pats, Smythe pulled together a group, headed by himself, to take control.

Smythe would become a national figure as a decorated hero of two wars and, of course, as the founder of two Canadian institutions, the Maple Leaf hockey club, and the club's Toronto home, Maple Leaf Gardens. Smythe was the son of poor immigrants from Ireland and England. His father, Albert, was a serious, religious man who worked as a journalist for the Toronto *World* newspaper. He covered almost everything, including sports. When he went to Woodbine race track, now called Greenwood, Conn would accompany him and run his copy back to the *World* offices. Conn developed a passion for horses, gambling, and most sports, especially hockey.

Conn grew up sturdy but short, no more than 5-foot-7. But he was tough, aggressive, and cocky. Others would describe him as egotistical, intolerant, and even bigoted. More praiseworthy were his patriotism and loyalty to king and country. In 1915, he enlisted in the 40th Battery, which was the Sportsmen's unit led by Major Gordon Southam of the family that owned the Canadian newspaper chain. In the First World War, he was awarded the Military Cross for rescuing prisoners and returning them to safety. Several months later he was captured and spent more than a year in prison camps.

Upon his return home he married his teenage sweetheart, Irene Sands, completed his degree at the University of Toronto, and started a contracting business specializing in sand and gravel. In the 1920s, three children were born to the Smythes, Stafford in 1921, Miriam in 1923, and Hugh in 1927.

Hockey was a large part of his life. He coached at various levels of amateur hockey through the 1920s and boasted of knowing every pro player in Canada during that time. Smythe's first moves after buying the St. Pats in 1926 were to change the team colours to blue and white from green and white and to give the team a new name, the Maple Leafs. In his memoirs (*Conn Smythe: If You Can't Beat 'em in the Alley,* with Scott Young, 1981), Smythe said he decided on the name Maple Leafs because the 1924 Canadian Olympic team had had a maple leaf logo on the chest of their sweaters, and during the war he had worn it on badges and insignias.

Joseph Romain, the archivist at the Hockey Hall of Fame, believes he has uncovered another origin. An old-time hockey player from pre-1927 days can remember a team in the east end of Toronto using the same name, Maple Leafs–not Maple Leaves–long before Smythe bought the St. Pats.

When Smythe took over, the team had two star players, Irvine (Ace) Bailey, a right winger who would win the scoring championship in 1928-29, and Clarence (Happy) Day, a defenceman and winger who would become Smythe's closest friend and perhaps the most important man in the Leaf organization for the next 30 years. Day had attended the Ontario College of Pharmacy in Toronto in the 1920s before deciding on a career as a professional hockey player. A non-smoker and non-drinker, Day would set a standard for the Leafs in the years to come. In the summer of 1927, he became Smythe's business partner by purchasing 16 per cent of the sand and gravel business called C. Smythe Ltd.

Smythe, as coach and manager, began a major overhaul of the Leafs that summer. He sold off several of the players to Detroit, Chicago, and New York, and brought in new people, the most important of whom was Joe Primeau. Primeau was a quiet man, a graceful skater and a clean player. His nickname was Gentleman Joe. During Smythe's brief period with the Rangers, he had signed Primeau, a young centre with the senior Marlboros, an amateur team in Toronto, to a personal contract rather than a team contract. When Smythe was fired, he brought Primeau back to Toronto with him. Primeau played little that season and returned to the Marlies for a couple more years before making it to the Leafs on a permanent basis in 1929. He quickly became a star, winning the Lady Byng Trophy as the league's most gentlemanly player in 1932 and twice finishing second in the scoring race.

An incident in the 1928 playoffs helped Smythe in acquiring a top-flight goaltender. In a game against the Montreal Maroons, Lorne Chabot of the Rangers was hit in the left eye by a shot from Nels Stewart. Teams didn't carry two goaltenders in those days, and when the Rangers were refused permission to bring in a substitute, 44-year-old Lester Patrick, the coach and manager, strapped on the pads. The Rangers won the game 2–1 in overtime, and went on to win both the series and the Stanley Cup. Patrick was hailed as a hero, but Chabot never played for the Rangers again.

After Chabot's injury there were rumours that his eye had been permanently damaged. The Rangers themselves wondered if he would ever be the same, and when an offer came from Smythe, they traded him for the Leafs' goalie, John Ross Roach. Chabot would become the first of many great Leaf goaltenders.

George (Red) Horner, a young hard-rock defenceman from the Marlies was added for 1928–29, as was Andy Blair, a slick centre from Winnipeg. Next came left winger Harold (Baldy) Cotton from Pittsburgh for cash. Cotton, who was brave and tough, became the team's leading scorer in 1929–30.

Perhaps Smythe's most fortuitous acquisition was not a player but a man who could help him in the front office, Frank Selke. During the late 1920s, Selke kept telling Smythe to bring in more young players. Selke, an electrician by trade, but a first-rate hockey manager, had been running the Marlies for several years. On 7 September 1929, Selke went to work for Smythe full-time as his assistant. He brought with him two more Marlboros, Charlie Conacher, a big right winger, and left winger Harvey (Busher) Jackson. Jackson was only 18 years old when he joined the team. He was brash and a jokester, but extraordinarily gifted. Of the two, Conacher was more reserved, and he had a thunderous wrist shot.

Before Christmas in 1929, with the team playing poorly, Smythe moved Primeau onto Conacher's line with Cotton. When an injury kept Cotton out of a game against Chicago, Jackson took his spot. In that game, Primeau set up the cocky Jackson for a goal, and then did the same for Conacher. Mike Rodden, the sports editor for the Toronto *Globe*, wrote that the "youthful triumvirate" had been impressive. Lou Marsh, the sports editor at the *Star*, noted that "the kid line showed well." Thus was born the famous Kid Line. They were colourful, sometimes controversial, and always exciting. Primeau would say in the years that followed that his biggest problem was keeping his two linemates happy. If he passed too often to Jackson, Conacher would curse him on the ice. If the puck went the other way, Jackson would do the same. The Kid Line would lead the Leafs to their first Stanley Cup in 1932 and continue to carry the banner well into the 1930s, with Jackson winning the scoring championship in 1932, and Conacher in 1934 and 1935.

But before that happened, there was one more addition. His name was Francis Michael (King) Clancy, colourful, exciting, and one of the best defencemen in the league. In the summer of 1930, with the country at the beginning of the Great Depression, the Ottawa Senators were in serious financial difficulty. The owners felt that one way out was to sell their best player. The price for Clancy was $35,000, a huge sum in those days and one Smythe didn't think his directors would agree to pay.

Smythe owned a filly called Rare Jewel, which he had bought for $250. Until the Coronation Futurity, a race for two-year olds, Rare Jewel hadn't done anything. But in the week leading up to the race, she started to show better times. To help her along in the race, the trainer and his partner, each unaware of what the other was doing, both fed her a half flask of brandy just minutes before the start.

Smythe had already put money on Rare Jewel. But at the last minute he decided to hedge his bet by placing a $60 wager on the favourite, Frothblower. Smythe was at the pari mutuel window and had taken out his money when the Leafs' former team doctor, a man he disliked, came along, slapped him on the back, and said, "Frothblower all the way, eh, Connie?"

Smythe wasn't about to show a lack of confidence in his own horse, so he said boldly, "Sixty across on Rare Jewel." And of course Rare Jewel, moved by the spirits perhaps, took the lead in the home stretch and held on to win. Smythe ended up pocketing about $15,000, which was enough, combined with the amount the directors put up, to buy Clancy. "Now we're going to win the Stanley Cup," he kept saying to himself.

There was, however, some uneasiness over the Clancy deal–

Clancy had had terrible feuds with Leaf players over the years, particularly Day, and he was something of a wild man on the ice. But when Selke went to Ottawa, the man he met at the Chateau Laurier was gentlemanly and enthusiastic about playing in Toronto. He said he would be happy to play in a Leaf uniform with such a good man as Hap Day. "Don't mind my battling everybody in Toronto," he told Selke. "I just go there to win. And George Boucher [the Ottawa team captain] and I, being Catholics, like to take a reef out of those hard-headed Protestants."

Clancy would bring the Stanley Cup to Toronto but not before a new arena was built. The Leafs had been playing in the Mutual Street Arena which seated fewer than eight thousand. Because of the team's popularity, more than nine thousand were jammed in on most nights. But the Leafs weren't making enough money from gate receipts to compete with the salaries that the American teams, playing in larger arenas, were paying their players. Smythe wanted a new building that would seat at least twelve thousand. He told Greg Clark of the *Star,* "We need a place where people can go with evening clothes, if they want to come there from a dinner or party. We need . . . everything new and clean, a place that people can be proud to take their wives or girlfriends to."

Because of the Depression, few believed Smythe would pull it off. Money was tight, and construction of the proposed Maple Leaf Gardens would cost well over a million dollars. But a Maple Leaf director and good friend of Smythe's, Larkin Maloney, who was the general manager of Canada Building Materials, liked the idea and suggested they talk to the Montreal architectural firm of Ross and MacDonald, which had built the Royal York Hotel. In Montreal, Ross and MacDonald recommended Sun Life Assurance Co. of Canada for financial backing. Sun Life came in for $500,000.

Several sites were considered. The first was on the waterfront and owned by the Toronto Harbour Commission. Another was on Spadina Avenue north of College Street. The site finally settled on, at Carlton and Church, was owned by the T. Eaton Company. Eaton's sold it to Maple Leaf Gardens Ltd., which was incorporated in February 1931, for $350,000, some of which was accepted as Gardens stock. The Eatons had invested heavily in a new store at College and Yonge, just west of the Gardens site, and an arena nearby would be good for business.

But when the bids for construction opened, Smythe discovered that his company was $200,000 short, a problem that was solved by persuading labour unions to allow members to take stock in lieu of wages. To set an example for the unions, Selke, a member of the Electricians Union, mortgaged his house to buy stock.

So, during the Depression, and over a period of five months, Maple Leaf Gardens was built at a cost of $1.5 million. On opening night, 12 November 1931, the bands of the 48th Highlanders and the Toronto Irish Regiment marched onto the ice and played "Happy Days Are Here Again" as 13,542 spectators, most in evening dress, assembled to watch the first hockey game at the Gardens. The Leafs lost that night, 2-1 to Chicago, but it was a memorable season, one that set the tone for an exciting decade. Over the next 10 years the Leafs became Canada's most popular team. It was an era of success and class.

For the 1931-32 season, Smythe removed himself as coach. Art Duncan, who had been a Leaf defenceman, was appointed his successor. But it wasn't long before Smythe became unhappy with Duncan, who he felt was too easy on the players. They were "flabby" according to Smythe, who thought that Conacher and Jackson were spending too much time in their new cars "chasing women." With only two ties to show for the first five games, Smythe started looking for a replacement.

The man he had in mind was Dick Irvin, a former centre in the NHL who had coached the Chicago Blackhawks the previous season and had taken them to the Stanley Cup final. Surprisingly, the Blackhawks fired Irvin. He was coaching in Regina when the call came from Smythe. The Leafs were in last place when Irvin took over. But he turned them around quickly by driving the players, punishing the partiers, and setting high standards. As a result of the efforts of the coach and management, the Leafs were a spartan outfit in those days. Smythe, Selke, Irvin, and Day, the team captain, neither drank nor smoked. The players had to dress well on the road. Moustaches and beards were not allowed, which is a rule that still stands, and the players were not allowed to play poker on the trains, only rummy, with a limit of a penny a point.

The Leafs were a hungry and aggressive team that season. Big Conacher got into fights. Horner, the toughest of them all, was an intimidator and a hitter on defence. The beetle-browed Chabot, at 6-foot-1, was an imposing and sometimes frightening figure in goal. In addition to the muscle there was talent. Conacher, Jackson, and

Clancy were all-stars. Primeau and Bailey weren't far behind. By the time March arrived, the Leafs were sure they could win the Stanley Cup.

In those days, the playoff quarter-finals and semi-finals were two-game series determined by total goals. The Leafs easily swept aside both Chicago and the Montreal Maroons to get to the final, where they met the Rangers. For Smythe there was a certain poetic justice to this. Smythe had been fired by the New York management, but the team he had assembled was still pretty much in place. Then there had been the big swap of goaltenders, with Chabot joining the Leafs and Roach going to the Rangers.

But the best-of-five final wasn't even close. The Leafs won it in three straight games. In his memoirs, Smythe gloated: "Rangers were never in it. We scored six goals a game against old Roachy, to win the Cup three straight, 6-2, 6-4, 6-2. Like a tennis match."

Lou Marsh wrote: "The Flying Frenchmen? Don't even talk about the Flying Frenchmen in the same breath as the Toronto Tornados after a night's exhibition of sustained speed, courage, endurance and strategy. Saturday night's torrent of speed would have left even the cyclonic Canadiens hogtied and helpless." Several newspapers called it "Toronto's greatest hockey season." Not only had the Leafs captured the Cup, but the top senior team from Toronto, the National Sea Fleas, which included 28-year-old Harold Ballard as the team's business manager, had won the Allan Cup.

The success of the Leafs in the 1930s would fire the imagination of the nation for years to come, though there was little enthusiasm for them in Quebec where French Canadians cheered for the Canadiens, the Maroons being the province's anglo team. But west of the Ontario–Quebec border and in the Maritimes, the Leafs were supreme.

This never would have happened without Foster Hewitt, who became the country's first media star, and, as Scott Young noted in his biography, the most famous Canadian of his time. Hewitt was the son of William A. Hewitt, who in the 1920s was the sports editor of the *Toronto Star* and the secretary of the Ontario Hockey Association. He became known as Mr. Hockey in Ontario. Foster became interested in broadcasting as a young man. When the *Star* started its own radio station in Toronto, Foster, a cub reporter at the newspaper, worked part-time as an announcer on various shows. The first hockey game he called was played at the Mutual Street Arena in 1923.

Smythe quickly saw that radio could be an effective marketing and promotional tool for his team, and soon Hewitt's play-by-play of the Leaf games was broadcast every Saturday night. When the Gardens was built, Hewitt advised the contractors where his broadcast booth, which became known as the gondola, should be situated, and he was there for opening night in November 1931. The following season, his Leaf broadcasts were aired nationally. The Leafs became an institution, and Hewitt a national celebrity.

Howie Meeker, who grew up in Kitchener, Ontario, and won the Calder Trophy as the league's top rookie in 1946-47 with the Leafs, can remember sneaking downstairs late at night, long after being sent to bed by his mother, to listen to Hewitt on the radio. "I remember in 1933, my mother had girls over to play bridge and I turned on the DeForest-Crosley radio real, real low and heard Ken Doraty get that goal at about 1:30 in the morning," Meeker says.

That was one of many memorable games at the Gardens and it was among Hewitt's most famous broadcasts. It had been a bitter best-of-three semi-final between the Leafs and the Boston Bruins, and the series was tied 2-2 entering the fifth and deciding game. After three scoreless periods, the game went into overtime. It stayed deadlocked after two, three, four, and then five 20-minute over-time periods.

As the night wore on, Hewitt mentioned over the radio that some fans had left but that others had shown up to watch. When people started flocking to the arena to witness the historic event, Smythe gave instructions to let them in. After the fifth overtime period, league president Frank Calder called Smythe and Boston Bruins president Art Ross together to see if another means could be found for deciding the game. Apparently a coin toss and even playing without goaltenders were discussed. The final against the Rangers was set to start later the same day in New York, and the Rangers refused to postpone.

But the two teams opted for another overtime period and what Meeker and others heard at about 1:55 in the morning was the following:

There's Eddie Shore going for the puck in the corner beside the Boston net! Andy Blair is on for the Leafs now—he hasn't played as much as the others and seems a little fresher than some. He's moving in on Shore in the corner. Shore is clearing the puck–Blair intercepts! Blair has the puck! Ken Doraty is dashing for the front of the net! Blair passes! Doraty takes it! He shoots! He scores!

Hewitt's ringing announcement of a goal–"He Shoots! He scores!"–became part of the game's lexicon. And so did the gondola. Today, for example, the Canadian edition of *Funk and Wagnalls Standard College Dictionary* lists gondola, along with the word's usual definitions, as "Canadian informal–a broadcast booth commanding a view of an arena, stadium, etc."

The name was coined by C. M. Passmore, who was co-director of radio for MacLaren Advertising, which purchased the rights to Leaf games and then sold the air time. When Passmore, who produced hockey games for 18 years in the 1930s and 1940s, saw the broadcast booth from rink level, it looked to him like a long thin tube hanging in the air. "Why," he said to Hewitt, "it looks just like the gondola on an airship."

So Hewitt's booth became the gondola–the control centre on a ship that was the Gardens. It was 56 feet (17 metres) straight up from the ice level and accessible only by a catwalk that did not have a guardrail or handrail. On Hewitt's first trip, he refused to walk the distance, choosing instead to make his way across on his hands and knees. Later, side cables were added, but they provided only marginal comfort for the uninitiated. Conn Smythe, Frank Selke Sr., and Hewitt's father, W.A., for example, never visited the booth, despite repeated invitations.

Once, actor George Raft, who usually portrayed a tough guy in Hollywood movies, was asked to be Hewitt's guest, he was warned that the height might be a problem. The star of gangster films just laughed it off. About half-way across the catwalk, however, Hewitt looked behind him and saw Raft frozen in his tracks and obviously terrified. Hewitt told Scott Young: "When I looked back there was Raft, about a third of the way across, hanging on to the wire for dear life. I had an awful job getting him to let go."

When radio was joined by television, Hewitt and later his son Bill continued the broadcasts in both media. Foster became a multimillionaire through the ownership of his Toronto radio station CKFH (now CJCL), which was founded in 1951, and also his investment in John W. Bassett's Toronto television station, CFTO.

Hewitt had always been friendly with Harold Ballard, but his decision to sell his Gardens shares in 1971, after Ballard and his partner Stafford Smythe had been charged with fraud and theft, cooled the relationship. In 1978, Ballard severed Hewitt's connection with the Gardens by selling the radio rights to Leaf games to CKO, an FM station. Then, a year later, Ballard trashed the gondola to make way for private boxes. A piece of the game's history, which the Hockey Hall of Fame had hoped to keep, had disappeared. When Hewitt was told, he wept. Ballard just laughed about it, and said that Hewitt could build himself a new gondola. "I'll pay for the nails," he said.

For the Leafs of the 1930s, the most heart-breaking incident involved Bailey and occurred at the Boston Garden on 12 December 1933. Bailey was 30 years old, and his career was coming to a close. But it ended sooner than he had anticipated, and typically, the result of a cheap shot by Eddie Shore, the Bruins' intimidating defence-man, who was called the "Edmonton Express." As the play developed, Horner body-checked Shore, sending him sliding into the boards. As Horner moved up ice, Bailey stayed back to cover.

Bailey, who was one of the Leafs' cleanest players, was leaning forward, resting on his stick, when Shore charged up from behind in full flight and drove Bailey's kidneys with his shoulder, sending the slightly built forward up into a backward flip and then down to the ice on his head. The crowd roared, but then it fell silent. Bailey wasn't moving. His head was twisted at a cruel angle and his legs started to twitch. Horner immediately went to him and attempted to straighten his neck. Then Horner, the toughest of the Leafs, went after Shore.

"Why did you do that, Eddie?" he said.

Shore just smiled and said nothing. With that, Horner threw off his gloves and slammed Shore on the jaw with a blow that sent him straight back and bounced him off the ice.

In his memoirs, Selke wrote: "It was a right uppercut which stiffened the big defence star like an axed steer. As he fell, with his body rigid and straight as a board, Shore's head struck the ice, splitting open. In an instant he was circled by a pool of blood about three feet in diameter."

Immediately the Bruins leapt off the bench to get at Horner, who was by himself for a few seconds. But suddenly big Conacher was beside him. Together they extended their sticks. Conacher said, "Which one of you is going to be the first to get it?"

Doctors operated on Bailey's fractured skull that night. Then a second operation was needed. Shore, who had not been seriously injured, apologized, and the league suspended him for 16 games, but Bailey never played again.

In February, the league held a benefit game in Toronto between the Leafs and a group of NHL all-stars to pay for Bailey's medical expenses and to set up a trust fund for him. This was the league's first all-star game, although it did not become an annual event until 1947. The Leafs that night wore sweaters with "Ace" emblazoned across the front along with the maple leaf. Before the game, which was won 7–3 by Toronto and raised $23,000, Bailey and Shore met at centre ice. It was the first time they had faced each other since the night of the accident. The arena fell silent, but when they hugged, there was a huge cheer.

After his injury, Bailey asked the league if he could work as a linesman, but he was turned down because officials in those days were not allowed to wear helmets. Bailey coached the University of Toronto Blues for 12 years and took them to three Canadian Interuniversity Athletic Union championships. In 1938, he was hired by the Gardens as a penalty timekeeper, a position he held until 1985 when he received a letter signed by Harold Ballard telling him he was being replaced. There was no special sendoff for the old Leaf and he has never been honoured by the club.

In the 1930s, the Leafs had great success, finishing first in the Canadian Division four times and advancing to six Cup finals, but they never won another championship in that decade. Some have speculated there was a lack of commitment from some of the players. Certainly, Jackson's drinking was widely known, and Conacher was a notorious partier. Bailey can remember Charlie Conacher and his brother Lionel, Canada's greatest ever all-round athlete, operating a bootleg joint above a garage in Toronto. Charlie was a ladies' man, too, whose conquests were the subject of countless locker-room stories.

Bailey thinks the team did not attach enough importance to defence. Frank Selke, Jr., questions Irvin's coaching; even though Irvin is considered one of the great coaches of all time, Selke Jr. feels that Irvin wasn't at his best in the big games.

"My father always felt that in the clutch, Irvin was not a good coach," Selke says. "He would beat himself with his strange ways of doing things. It cost him his job in Toronto. When Smythe found out Montreal was looking for a coach, he forced Dick to go there."

Even if the Leafs didn't dominate hockey in the thirties, it was in that decade that they became a part of the national lore, their appeal cutting across all economic and cultural lines. From coast to coast Saturday night truly was hockey night in Canada as Canadian families huddled around their radios to hear Hewitt's Maple Leaf Gardens broadcasts from the gondola. Arguably no other professional sports team in North America and perhaps the world has had the support of an entire nation as the Leafs did in English Canada in the 1930s and 1940s, and even later. They had become far more than Toronto's team–they had become Canada's team.

3

THE

GLORY YEARS

As the 1930s drew to a close, so too did an era in the history of the Maple Leafs. In 1936, Joe Primeau retired at the relatively young age of 30. Without Primeau, the little workhorse, Charlie Conacher and Harvey Jackson were not as effective, and both were eventually traded, Conacher to Detroit, Jackson to the New York Americans.

The most difficult trade Conn Smythe would ever make came in 1937 when he sent King Clancy and Hap Day to the Americans for 18-year-old Wally Stanowski. In Stanowski, he received a talented young defenceman, but he lost his two oldest and most loyal friends. Clancy chose to retire immediately following the trade; Day played one year in New York before returning to Toronto to work in Smythe's business and to coach at the amateur level.

Day says he was bitter about the trade, but understood why it was made. "I resented it," he says, "after being there 13 years. But I'd say it was a pretty good trade—a couple of old men, who were finished, for a kid who went on to become an all-star."

Red Horner, who followed Conacher as captain, was the last from the 1932 championship team to go when he retired in 1940. The most significant change yet occurred in 1940 also, when Day replaced Dick Irvin behind the bench. The team had lost too many big games under Irvin to satisfy Smythe, and Irvin was given no choice but to leave; he accepted the coaching job with the Canadiens.

So began a new period for the Toronto Maple Leafs, one that

would prove to be their most successful. There would be six Stanley Cups in 10 seasons. There would be new names and new heroes–Syl Apps, Max Bentley, Turk Broda, and others–but the three people at the top remained the same. They were Smythe, Frank Selke, and Day, who would make his mark as one of the finest coaches ever to work in the NHL. When the best are mentioned, the names that usually come up are Dick Irvin, Scotty Bowman, Punch Imlach, Toe Blake, and Al Arbour. But what Day did in the 1940s with some average teams was quite remarkable.

Frank Selke, Jr., who was around the Leafs with his father in the early 1940s, says of Day: "He made a lot of ordinary and mediocre players into–if not superstars–certainly good journeymen guys who could more than carry their own weight. He did it by the sheer force of discipline. The Leafs in the 1940s were the best-disciplined team probably in the history of the game."

Day was tough and exacting but he wasn't abusive. He didn't scream or attempt to intimidate. Ted Kennedy, one of the heroes of that era, likens him to a Tom Landry, the stalwart and stoical coach of the Dallas Cowboys of the National Football League for 27 years. "A lot of guys made him out to be a tyrant," Kennedy says. "But he wasn't. He was a good guy. He loved to win, and as long as you played hard for him, you didn't have any problems with Hap."

The Leafs in those days were often called Hap Day's "clutch and grabbers" because of their close checking. If they scored the first goal, they often would sit on it and win. Meeker played for Day in the postwar 1940s and years later was a popular analyst on "Hockey Night in Canada." On television Meeker would stress the importance of defensive play, of playing your position and "finishing your check." These, of course, were things that Day had taught Meeker 30 years earlier.

Meeker says, "First of all, he demanded discipline and got it. And he had a system, and it was very simple–you played to the system or you didn't play. Those were his rules and regulations, and he demanded hard work. And if you did those things he kept you there."

In practices Day sometimes would make the team work on the same drill for an hour. It might have been faceoffs or a checking system. Occasionally he would run scrimmages in which one side used sticks and the other didn't. The Leafs were taught how to play with their bodies, how to manipulate their arms in certain ways, how to interfere without taking penalties. In Day's defensive system, usually one man, the centre, forechecked. The two wingers stayed back near the blueline with the defencemen to pick up the advancing forwards. In those days, the centre as a rule carried the puck through the middle and then passed off to a winger. But with four men protecting the blueline, this became impossible.

To counteract this strategy, the Red Wings became the first team to consistently shoot the puck into the attacking zone and chase it. Other teams copied them. And for better or worse, the dump and chase, coupled with strong defence, became the trademark of the NHL game for decades to come.

Day's conservative style of hockey, as well as the discipline, determination, and toughness of the Leafs in the early 1940s, very much reflected the personality of the country at that time. Canadians had endured the Depression, and now their young men were being sent overseas to fight in the Second World War. In Toronto, the populace was still archly conservative, "more British than the King," as it was sometimes described. In this context, the Leafs embodied all that was commendable and good. Many of the team's stars neither drank nor smoked, and, of course, Day was a "milkshake and ice-cream man." Coupled with this pristine image was the intense patriotism of Smythe and the symbolism of his team wearing the Canadian emblem.

In the late 1930s and 1940s, no one player epitomized Smythe's idealistic vision of the perfect Leaf more than Charles Joseph Sylvanus (Syl) Apps, a 6-foot centre from Paris, Ontario, who joined the team in 1936. Apps was not only an abstainer and non-smoker, but he played cleanly and never swore. He once considered the ministry. He received his degree from McMaster University before joining the Leafs, and during his 10 years was considered the team's best player. He was an extraordinary talent who some believe has never been given his due. Kennedy says the two best players he has ever seen are Apps and Gordie Howe, in that order.

"He has never gotten the credit," Kennedy says. "People who played with him or against him knew how great he was. He could take the puck and roll with it. He was a great skater, he could score goals. He'd make things happen. There weren't all that many players in the league who could make things happen. Syl was one."

Apps was an all-round athlete. He had been an outstanding halfback in football and was sought by the Hamilton Tigers. He had played third base for Paris in the Inter-county Baseball League. He golfed in the low 70s, although he had never taken a lesson, and he had participated in track and field. Before joining the Leafs, he represented Canada at the 1936 Summer Olympics in Berlin in the pole vault, finishing sixth with a vault of 13 feet, 1½ inches.

The acquisition of Apps and later Stanowski began a rebuilding process for the Leafs. Gordie Drillon, a big right winger, joined the team in 1937 and a year later won the scoring championship with 52 points in 40 games, with Apps, his centre, collecting a league-leading 29 assists. Other key players were Billy Taylor, a slick little centre, and left winger Sweeney Schriner, a veteran picked up from the Americans, who in the 1944-45 season streaked toward 50 goals in 50 games at a faster pace than the Canadiens' Rocket Richard before being injured. Most important, perhaps, was a goaltender purchased from the Detroit organization. Walter (Turk) Broda tended toward corpulence and sometimes wasn't sharp in the regular season, but he was a money player and at his best in the big games. He would become the greatest Leaf goaltender to that time.

By 1941-42, the NHL had been reduced from ten to seven teams. The Depression killed off three, the Ottawa Senators, the Montreal Maroons, and Philadelphia, and one more, the Americans, would fold the next year. The Leafs had fared well in the regular season, finishing second overall to the Rangers. Apps, who was the captain by this time, was a first-team all-star. Drillon, defenceman Wilfrid (Bucko) McDonald, and Broda made the second team. In the semi-final, the Leafs got past the Rangers in six games. Over in the other semi-final the Red Wings, an unimpressive team with a losing record, had beaten the Bruins.

In the final, another upset seemed a certainty. The Leafs lost the first game at the Gardens 3-2. Then they were defeated in the second, 4-2. In Detroit, it was 4-3 for the home team. Toronto was on the brink, one game away from elimination, humiliated by a team that had finished fifth in the standing.

It was then that a letter arrived from a 14-year-old girl named Doris Klein, who lived in Detroit but cheered for the Leafs. She said she was heartbroken over the three losses. In a very emotional appeal she implored her heroes to fight their way back and win the Cup. The letter was given to Day and he decided to read it to his players before the fourth game at the Olympia. "Gentlemen," said Day. "Here's how a little 14-year-old girl feels about our situation tonight."

Day said later he had never sensed so much tension in the dressing room. Today, Day's motivational tactic probably would be viewed as corny and evoke little more than a few snickers. But in a more innocent time, the Leafs went out, and backed by some magnificent goaltending from Broda, fought back from a two-goal disadvantage, scored twice in the third period, and defeated the Red Wings 4-3.

Thus began the greatest comeback in the history of the Stanley Cup final. Back in Toronto, the Leafs dominated Detroit, winning 9-3. Despite an injury to Drillon, they took the next two games and the championship. As Apps held the Cup high, he yelled out to Smythe in the stands, "Come on out Conn. Come on out and get it. You've waited long enough for this Cup. Come and get it." Indeed, it had been 10 long years. But not so long for the next one, although the Second World War would complicate matters for all NHL teams.

When war had been declared in 1939, Smythe had sent letters to all the Leafs urging them to enlist. All the players took army training and belonged to militia units while they were still with the team. Not surprisingly, Smythe, despite being well into his forties, was determined to establish his own artillery battery and take it overseas. Finally, in September 1941 he formed his 30th Battery, or Sportsmen's Battalion, as it was known. It included Don (Shanty) McKenzie, a former Argonaut who worked as superintendent of the Gardens after the war, Jim Boeckh, a prominent golfer, and a couple of sportswriters, Ted Reeve, who worked for the Toronto *Telegram* for many years, and Ralph Allen, who was a sports reporter and then sports editor at the *Globe and Mail* from 1938 to 1941.

The Sportsmen's Battalion saw action in 1944 at Caen, where in July Smythe received an injury that would handicap him for the rest of his life. During a night attack by air, he was hit in the back by debris. The wound damaged his bowels and urinary tract. There was also nerve damage to one leg. The tendons pulled and his toes turned under. He returned home in a wheelchair and for a while there was some question as to whether he had much longer than five years to live. But he was tough and he fought back, eventually walking with the aid of a cane, although he lived in pain for the rest of his life.

Early 1942 has often been referred to as the dark days of the war. Pearl Harbor had been bombed 7 December the previous year. Germany and Italy controlled most of Europe at the time as well as northern Africa, and the heavy call-ups started in Canada. After the 1942 Cup triumph, the Leafs' best players–Apps, Broda, Drillon, Taylor, and Gaye Stewart–marched off to war.

In the war years, the Leafs and most other teams had to make do with a roster of players some of whom would not have been in the league but for the shortages. The Leafs, of course, were decimated and failed to make the playoffs in 1943 or 1944.

But during this period Selke and Day picked up two players who more than any other would lead the team to an upset victory in 1945. The first was Walter (Babe) Pratt, a strapping 6-foot-3, 210-pound defenceman from the Rangers. He was a free spirit on and off the ice who hated playing under Ranger coach Frank Boucher's restrictive system. Pratt had great skills and was an offensive defenceman, but Boucher refused to let him skate with the puck past centre ice.

When Pratt was traded to Toronto, he felt as if a yoke had been lifted from him, and indeed, Day, despite his own disciplined system, recognized Pratt's abilities and let him go with the puck. In the 1943–44 season, he had an amazing 17 goals and 40 assists in 50 games, and became the first Leaf to win the Hart Trophy awarded to the league's most valuable player. Day says he never attempted to stop Pratt from rushing the puck because "it would have been like trying to tell Apps to play defensive hockey."

Day and Pratt had different personalities and attitudes, but Day liked Pratt immensely, as did the other players. Pratt was good natured, easy-going, and a team man although he ran a little wild on his own time. In the year Pratt won the Hart, Day had Pratt room with him during a trip to Montreal for a particularly important game. Later, Pratt said he owed the MVP award to Day for keeping him out of trouble. "When he was on the ice, he was a hundred per cent team man," Day says. "But when he was off the ice, you always felt a little dubious about what might be going on. To try to control any off-ice escapades, I had him registered in my room. It worked out well." It has been said that Day kept Pratt with him during the entire 1945 playoff, but Day says no. "I could only stand so much, too," he recalls with a laugh.

The other player acquired during the war would come to epitomize every fan's image of a Leaf. He was fearless, determined, hard working, and a great leader. Theodore (Teeder) Kennedy would become the heart and soul of the greatest of all the Leaf teams. Kennedy was from the village of Humberstone near Port Colborne, Ontario. Two weeks before he was born, his father was killed in a hunting accident, leaving his mother, Margaret, to raise three boys and a girl. To make ends meet, she operated the hot-dog stand in the local arena and later had her own tea room.

Kennedy grew up to be a responsible young man, a non-smoker, non-drinker, and so talented that at the age of 16 he was playing senior hockey for the Port Colborne Sailors. In those days, an NHL team could put a player on its negotiation list without telling him, which was exactly what the Canadiens did, to the dismay of Kennedy who had no interest in playing in Montreal. He had grown up listening to Hewitt, and the Leafs were his team.

It happened that Nels Stewart coached the Port Colborne team at that time. He had played for the Maroons, the Bruins, and the Americans, was from Toronto, and was a good friend of Day's. When Stewart tipped the Leafs about his young player, Day and Selke came down to have a look. They were impressed enough to approach the Canadiens about getting his rights, and eventually a trade was worked out. Kennedy did not come cheaply. Montreal asked for and received defenceman Frankie Eddolls, one of the leading prospects in Canada at that time.

When Smythe, who was stationed overseas with his battalion, heard about the deal, he was furious about not being told and also over losing Eddolls. Later, of course, all was forgiven. However, when Selke went to Montreal to manage the Canadiens he called it the worst trade he ever made, because, as Selke said, "Kennedy always beat us."

In the spring of 1945, the Leafs, still without most of their top players, finished third. That winter the Canadiens dominated the league, winning 38 games and losing only 8. Maurice (Rocket) Richard scored 50 goals in 50 games. He was on the big line with centre Elmer Lach, who was selected MVP that year, and Hector (Toe) Blake on left wing. The defence was led by 6-foot-2, 205-pound Emile (Butch) Bouchard who scored 11 goals and earned 23 assists in 50 games. And in goal was Bill Durnan, who would win the Vezina Trophy for six consecutive seasons.

They were a star-studded group, and before the semi-final series against Toronto, Irvin boasted that the Canadiens were "the greatest team of all time." These were the kind of words that would motivate any team, but the Leafs did not need motivation. The most bitter rivalry in hockey existed between Montreal and Toronto. A few words from Irvin didn't mean much one way or the other. Kennedy says, "There was an awful lot of animosity. We didn't need any more motivation. We didn't need anything like that to stimulate us."

The rivalry played out on several levels. There was Irvin coaching against his old team. There was Lach, whom Smythe disliked and felt was disloyal because he had left St. Michael's College in Toronto to play out West before joining the Canadiens. And there were the two solitudes, French and English.

The tension between the two founding peoples was heightened during the war when it was widely reported in English Canada that the Province of Quebec had the highest percentage of call-up deferments in the country, with some of the deferred recruits playing for the Canadiens. In that context, there were those who felt Richard's record of 50 goals was worthless, at best tarnished, because of the low calibre of competition during the war years. Smythe himself was certainly no paragon of tolerance and liberalism. He routinely referred to French people as "frogs" and at least once began a speech with: "Ladies and gentlemen, and Frenchmen. . . "

Although there was resentment in Ontario and the rest of English Canada over the deferments in Quebec, Kennedy says that the issue never reached the team level. "We didn't pay attention to politics," he says. "We just stuck to playing the game."

So began a memorable series between the Canadiens and the Leafs. In the years to follow it would be hailed as Day's finest hour as a coach. He knew he couldn't match Montreal's three lines, so he used two lines plus four defencemen. Up front, Gus Bodnar played between Schriner and Lorne Carr. Kennedy centred Mel (Sudden Death) Hill and Bob Davidson. Nick Metz, who had just been released from the armed forces, spelled off Kennedy and Bodnar at centre. The defensive pairings were Pratt with Elwin Morris, and Stanowski, recently discharged, with Reg Hamilton. The goaltender was 26-year-old Frank (Ulcers) McCool, who would win the rookie-of-the-year award that season and was brilliant in the playoffs.

But the star of the series was Kennedy, a 19-year-old kid whose line was sent out against the Canadiens' big line of Lach, Blake, and Richard. Davidson can remember Lach saying to Kennedy, "You come near me and I'll take your head off with my stick," and Kennedy sticking his nose in Lach's face and snarling, "You try it and I'll put you in the goddamned hospital."

Said Davidson, "Lach had been in the league quite a while and he would try to run most centremen. He was trying to give it to Teeder, but Teeder'd bring his stick up on Lach. You could not scare Teeder one iota."

Irvin's "Greatest Hab Team of All Time" lost the first game to Day's clutch and grabbers 1-0. The Leafs won the second 3-2. In Toronto, Montreal finally got a victory, 4-1. But then the Leafs took a 3-1 lead in the series with a dramatic overtime victory at the Gardens. They lost at the Montreal Forum, but back in Toronto they took the sixth game and the series. "By then," says Kennedy, "our tongues were hanging out."

When Leafs of that era are asked about memorable playoff series, this one in the spring of 1945 usually comes up first. They were undermanned and weren't supposed to win, but they didn't quit and never believed their task was insurmountable. The little guy had taken on the giant and won.

The final against Detroit was a splendid seven-game matchup, with Toronto winning the first three games, 1-0, 2-0, 1-0, but then losing the next three. In the seventh game, the teams were tied 1-1 in the third when a bouncing puck came out in front of the Detroit net. Davidson couldn't get to it. Kennedy took a swing but missed, and then suddenly, in from the blueline came Pratt. In a second, the puck was on his stick; he shot and before goalie Harry Lumley could move, the puck was behind him to make the score 2-1 Toronto. That was how the game ended.

Again the Leafs were the Cup champions and the future looked bright. The war was drawing to an end. Apps and Drillon and Broda would be back. That fall at training camp in Owen Sound, Ontario, Kennedy told a reporter that the Leafs were a cinch to repeat as Cup champions. As it turned out, Kennedy was a better hockey player than prognosticator.

Instead, the Leafs fell apart and failed to make the 1946 playoffs, finishing in fifth place with a losing record. The team was beginning to get old, and Kennedy had been hampered during the year with a groin injury. Selke, however, received a large part of the blame from Smythe and left the organization in May, 1946.

In his memoirs Smythe said he felt Selke had been disloyal and had plotted with other Gardens directors to remove him while he was away during the war. As Frank Selke, Jr., remembers it, Smythe bullied his father. The last straw, apparently, was when the elder Selke returned from lunch to see a note on his desk from Smythe berating him for leaving the building without permission. Selke's response was to send a letter to Smythe saying: "Lincoln freed the slaves. Goodbye. I quit." Selke immediately joined the Canadiens as managing director and built the great Montreal teams of the 1950s.

That summer Smythe brooded over the state of his team and finally came to the conclusion that it had to be taken apart and reassembled. This was done with considerable expediency. Schriner, Carr, and Davidson retired. Pratt, who had been suspended for allegedly betting on NHL games that season and then reinstated, was sold to Boston. Taylor went to Detroit for winger Harry Watson. Forward Vic Lynn was picked up from Montreal.

But most important, Smythe and Day rebuilt the defence. Of the six rookies who joined the team, four were rearguards who had been recruited at the age of 16 or younger during the war years by Selke. They were big and tough and they had talent. Jim Thomson, Garth Boesch, Bill Barilko, and Gus Mortson would anchor the Leaf defence for years to come. That same season, Meeker, a right winger and superb skater, played well enough to be selected the league's rookie of the year. Smythe's rebuilding job was so thorough that there were only eight holdovers from the previous season–Apps, Kennedy, Stanowski, Broda, Nick and Don Metz, Bill Ezinicki, and Gaye Stewart.

But even Smythe could not anticipate the degree of success the changes would bring. Instead of developing into a contending team, the Leafs became champions immediately. Over the next five years they would dominate the NHL, winning four Cups, three consecutively from 1947 to 1949. The Leafs also were a tougher team, largely because of their bruising young defencemen. Mortson wasn't big, but Meeker remembers him as mean. "If you went in the corner with Mortson and came out with the puck, he'd take your ankles off," Meeker says. Thomson was a good puck handler, and tough. Barilko and Boesch were hitters. Meeker says, "If Barilko got a piece of you, you hurt for a week. He just tore the man apart."

Other teams complained that the Leafs were intimidating or dirty. Richard, a vicious stick man himself, would explode during games against Toronto after sustaining punishing body checks from "Bashing Bill" Barilko or Boesch or both. At no other time did Smythe's famous quip, "If you can't beat 'em in the alley, you can't beat 'em on the ice," seem more fitting, or more successful.

The rallying call in those days came from John Arnott, a regular customer at the Gardens, who would stand up and yell, "Come o-o-o-n Teeder!" And indeed, when it came around to the playoffs, Kennedy would be there. In the Leafs' championship years of 1947, 1948, and 1949, he was the team's leading scorer in the playoffs. In

1948 he led all players in points in the postseason play, and finished second the two other years.

Still, Smythe wasn't satisfied. Although he had two of the top centres in Apps and Kennedy, he wanted a third, perhaps anticipating that Apps would soon retire. The man he had in mind was Max Bentley of Chicago, a superstar of that period who had won the scoring championship the two previous years as well as the MVP in 1946. For obvious reasons, the Blackhawks did not want to give him up, but the Chicago team needed players and was in some financial trouble. In 1945, the Blackhawks had finished second last in the league and in 1947 were at the bottom. Defensively, they were the NHL's worst club and lacked depth.

So when Smythe offered the complete forward line of Bodnar between Bud Poile and Gaye Stewart, as well as defencemen Bob Goldham and Ernie Dickens–all for Bentley–the Blackhawks couldn't refuse.

Perhaps the easiest way to explain the significance of Bentley to the Leafs is to say they now had three of the best five centres in the league, the other two being Lach and Milt Schmidt of Boston, with Sid Abel of Detroit perhaps number six.

Bentley, who was from a farm in Saskatchewan, was called a dipsy-doodler, probably first by Hewitt on the radio, because he was slight (5-foot-8, 159 pounds), elusive, and clever with the puck. People from that era often compare Wayne Gretzky to him. The Leaf fact book from Bentley's first year in Toronto reported that, "Milking chores, [Bentley] claims, developed his wrists and is the reason for the snap that goes into his drives on goal. . . . He's a chronic worrier, always imagining he has contracted some rare disease, but Max is at his best when he feels worst."

Bentley was feeling pretty mediocre in 1947-48. He was second in team scoring behind Apps and helped the Leafs to their best season in 10 years, first overall with a record of 32-15-13. In the playoffs it was no contest. They beat the Bruins in five games and then swept the Red Wings in the final. These Leafs are considered by many, including Smythe, to be the best Toronto team ever. They had an all-star cast at centre, the best four defencemen in the league, and, of course, the reliable Broda in goal.

But more changes were underway. Apps retired after the 1948 championship and accepted a job in marketing with the Simpson's department store chain. Two years later, when the Leafs failed in their attempt to make it four Cups in a row, Day decided it was time for him to step down, or more specifically, move up–to assistant general manager. Replacing him was Primeau, who had just taken the senior Marlboros to the Allan Cup championship.

In Primeau's first year, 1950–51, the Leafs, no longer a young team, but aging and battle weary, still had enough in them for one more championship. It was another Montreal-Toronto confrontation in the Cup final, and it became a classic. Every game went into overtime. In the final game, the Leafs were behind 2-1 in the last minute of regulation time, when Primeau pulled Al Rollins, who shared the goaltending with Broda, for an extra player. With the seconds disappearing, Bentley passed to Sid Smith. Smith sent it over to Todd Sloan, and suddenly, with only 32 seconds left, the puck was behind Montreal goalie Gerry McNeil, who had replaced the recently retired Durnan, and the game was tied.

The winning goal is probably the best remembered of all Toronto Cup winners. The teams were into overtime. The speedy Meeker had fired the puck into the Montreal zone and then had chased it down behind the net. He was able to work it out to Harry Watson, who moved it to the left side. It was then that Barilko charged in from the blueline. From the faceoff circle he wound up with such momentum that he fell forward as he shot.

At that instant a photographer caught the big defenceman in the air as he was about to hit the ice. Ahead of him, McNeil had already tumbled back into the goal. The puck was behind him, high over his right shoulder, in the mesh. The game was over. The championship belonged to Toronto.

That summer, Barilko embarked on a fishing trip from his hometown of Timmins, Ontario, with a friend, Henry Hudson, who was a dentist and pilot, to the James Bay area. They never returned. The disappearance of the Fairchild 24, a single-engined pontooned craft, sparked wide-spread alarm as well as a massive manhunt. But Barilko and Hudson were not found. The Leafs began training camp in the fall without their Stanley Cup hero amid all kinds of rumour and speculation. Some still held hope that Barilko was alive on a wilderness island after surviving a crash in a lake. The most exotic rumour had it that Barilko's plane had not gone down, but instead he had flown to the Soviet Union to secretly coach the national team. Barilko's parents, you see, were of Russian descent.

The famous photograph and the tragic disappearance came to signify the end of an era. Eleven years would pass before the Leafs won another championship. Ahead of them that night in Montreal amid the celebration lay a decade of frustration and disappointment, but behind them were the greatest years in the team's history. The crashed Fairchild and the bodies of the two men would eventually be found, but not until May, 1962, one month after the Leafs had won their next Stanley Cup.

4

A NEW

GENERATION

C onn Smythe gradually removed himself from the running of the team after the 1951 championship, although he retained the title of general manager. He was getting older and his health was not good. With the chill of the winter months intensifying the pain of his war wounds, he began spending more time at his West Palm Beach home.

Hap Day was in charge of the organization and kept in regular contact with Smythe by telephone. But as the years passed, the team declined. It finished third in 1952 and fifth in 1953. In 1959, the Leafs had missed the playoffs three times and had not advanced past the first round in any year since 1951. The two dominant teams of that decade were the Canadiens with five Stanley Cups and the Red Wings with four.

Joe Primeau resigned in 1953, and was replaced by King Clancy, whose three-year coaching term was the least successful of any in that period. Then, near the end of the 1956-57 season, Smythe called a news conference in New York. He'd arrived from Florida, and a private railway car supplied by the Leafs had brought in the Toronto sportswriters. Smythe told the media that the Leaf hockey operation was out of date and that Day would be asked if he was available for the following season. The message was clear. Smythe wanted Day to resign. Day's reaction was one of shock. He had had no private indication of Smythe's unhappiness, and he was hurt by the public rebuke. When he was approached by reporters in

Toronto, he said, "My legs have been cut out from under me." He added he would be "unavailable" for the following year.

So ended Day's career at the Gardens. He sold his shares in Smythe's sand and gravel company, moved to St. Thomas, Ontario, and bought Elgin Handles Ltd., a company that produces wooden handles for tools. A few months later, he received a telephone call from Smythe, lamenting the state of his team. At one point, Smythe said, "Things wouldn't be like this if you came back." Day replied, "There's no chance of that happening."

Day does not speak badly of Smythe, and they maintained a cordial relationship in the years that followed. Many years later, Day said: "My wife told me it would happen some day, that blood was thicker than water, and she was right."

The blood in this case belonged to Stafford Smythe, Conn's eldest son. He wanted Day's job and he got it. As Day's successor, he was instrumental in building the successful teams of the 1960s. Stafford had played hockey as a youth and is remembered as a tenacious competitor but was not big or talented enough to advance to a high level. He was very much like his father, or at least attempted to emulate him by being abrasive and arrogant. He had the same cocky strut and raspy voice. Those who knew him say much of this was a false front to cover an inferiority complex. He had grown up in the shadow of a famous and demanding father who had been neither warm nor very supportive.

After the war, Stafford had taken over the operation of the junior and senior Marlboros. The Marlboros (originally spelled Marlboroughs) were named in honour of the Duke of Marlborough. In the 1920s, they were operated by Selke. A few years after Selke went to work for Smythe, the Marlies were absorbed by the Leaf organization and used as farm teams. Smythe's partner in operating the Marlies had been Ballard, who had managed amateur teams in Toronto during the 1930s.

Ballard was 18 years older than Stafford and closer to Conn's generation. But he became Stafford's best friend and closest confidant. He looked after financial matters and provided comic relief. He was amusing and entertaining. His jokes and banter relaxed his intense partner.

Ballard was never involved in the hockey part of the operation. Stafford, as general manager, was the boss. The assessment of talent, the acquisition of prospects, and other key decisions were left to Stafford and his scouts. "Harold went along for the ride," said Buck

Houle, who assisted Smythe for years in minor hockey. Billy Harris, who played for the Marlies before joining the Leafs, says the only time the players saw him was when the annual team photo was taken.

In those days the Marlboro junior team fed players directly to the Leafs. There was no universal draft. NHL teams simply signed 16-year-olds to standard "C forms," put them on their protected list, and, if they were good enough, sent them to play for their junior team, which in the case of the Leafs, were the Marlies and the St. Michael's Majors, a team from a Toronto Catholic boys' school run by Basilican Fathers.

The NHL also endorsed a system of sponsorship in which an NHL club could claim a player simply by financially supporting his minor-hockey team. When the Leafs heard about Dave Keon, a 14-year-old in Noranda, Quebec, for example, they immediately sponsored (in fact, purchased) his team, thus locking him up as a Leaf property. Toronto was heavily involved in the sponsorship system and had affiliates across Canada. In the 1930s and 1940s, the system produced stars who had come from all areas of the country. But there were few from Toronto, which Stafford thought was a missed opportunity. Conn seemed to disagree, to think that Toronto kids had better things to do than strive to be hockey players. Nevertheless, he dared Stafford to find local talent.

Stafford accepted the challenge and, with the help of Houle and others, set up the Marlie minor-hockey network in the late 1940s and 1950s. It started with Shopsy's peewee team and moved upward to the Marlboros and St. Mike's. Harris can remember Stafford's watching him play for the Riverdale Mercuries who won the Toronto peewee championship in the late 1940s. The following year the Marlboros sponsored the team and it became the Marlie minor-bantams. Next on the chain was the Junior B team, the Weston Dukes. Carl Brewer, Toronto's great defenceman of the 1960s, played there as did Bob Pulford, another Leaf of the 1960s.

Houle says, "We would scout all the little-league teams. During the summer we'd try to get them to play for Shopsy's. It was a process of elimination. The ones we missed at the peewee level, we'd get at minor-midget, or minor-bantam or midget. We just sifted them out. If they were any good by the time they were 16, we'd put them on our protected list for the NHL."

Eventually the best ended up on the Marlboros or the St. Michael's club. Conn Smythe would say, "Put the dogans in the

Micks' school and put the Protestants in with the Marlboros." If it came to a choice between the Leafs and another NHL team for a 16-year-old, St. Mike's often worked to Toronto's advantage. Catholic parents would feel better about their son signing with Toronto because he would have the opportunity of attending a respected boys' school and continuing his education. That was how the Leafs convinced the parents of Frank Mahovlich to let him leave home in Timmins, Ontario. In addition to Keon and Mahovlich, other Leafs to come from St. Mike's teams included Dick Duff and Tim Horton, who was not Catholic but was from Cochrane, Ontario, and continued his education at the school while playing hockey.

The Leaf organization valued the St. Mike's team so much that in the early 1960s it set up its own league called the Metro Junior A Hockey League, which included the Marlboros. St. Mike's had threatened to discontinue its hockey program because the club's manager and coach, Father David Bauer, felt the heavy travel and long schedule of the OHA was incompatible with the education of students. But the new arrangement lasted only two years. The Marlies went back into the OHA and St. Mike's hockey program was moved to Neil McNeil High School.

The effectiveness of the recruitment job done by Smythe and his scouts in the early 1950s was evident when the Marlboros won Memorial Cups in 1955 and 1956. Some of the better-known prospects to come up through the Marlie chain included Brewer, Pulford, Harris, Bob Baun, and Bob Nevin.

Stafford's good work at the minor-hockey level made him the logical person to succeed Day in 1957. But in a surprising move, Conn also removed himself as official general manager. In his place he set up a hockey committee of which Stafford was chairman. In addition to Stafford, Ballard, and John W. Bassett, the owner of the Toronto *Telegram,* it included four affluent young Toronto business-men: William Hatch, the vice-president of McLaren's Food Products; R. J. (Jack) Amell, the vice-president of Robert Amell and Co. Ltd., a large jewellery manufacturing firm; George Mara, a former Marlboro and president of William Mara and Co., a wine importing business; and George Gardiner, the president of Gardiner, Watson Ltd., a stockbroking firm. He also owned and bred thorough-bred horses.

The committee was nicknamed the Silver Seven, after the legendary turn-of-the-century Ottawa hockey team. But the members had no real role other than to support the team and serve as boosters. Stafford was in charge. His first important decision came after a disastrous 1957-58 season, in which the Leafs finished last in the league with Billy Reay as coach. Stafford felt someone had to be hired to manage the club. He offered the GM's job to Reay, who opted instead to coach for one more year, hoping to turn the team around.

In a surprising move Smythe turned to a virtual unknown, a 40-year-old balding man of average height who had never played in the NHL. The hiring of George (Punch) Imlach as assistant general manager was not considered a significant event. To begin with, the Leafs didn't have even a general manager, so his title of assistant GM seemed somewhat meaningless. And measured beside the giants in Leaf management of the past, such as Conn Smythe and Day, Imlach didn't seem all that impressive. "He was a guy who came in, and it appeared to us he didn't have a lot going for him," Mahovlich says. "But he was cocky as hell. He had nothing to lose and everybody liked him."

Imlach would transform the team in a matter of months, putting them back on top as Stanley Cup contenders. And over the next 10 years he would become, arguably, the most popular sports figure in Toronto–and the most successful. He was colourful, outspoken, and usually controversial. When first approached by Smythe, however, Imlach had been hesitant to take the job because of the vagueness of his responsibilities. He wasn't the coach. He wasn't the general manager. His authority was limited. And he had been used to being in charge of just about everything.

Originally from Toronto, he had played for, coached, managed, and eventually owned the Quebec Aces minor-pro team. It was Imlach who had signed Jean Beliveau to a contract in 1951, denying the Canadiens their future superstar for two years. In 1957, he joined the Bruin organization as coach and manager of their AHL affiliate in Springfield. Eddie Shore owned the team, and for most of the winter he fought with Imlach over who was in charge.

That spring during the NHL's annual congress in Montreal, Imlach was approached by the Leafs, but he held out for the general manager's job. At the very least, he wanted the opportunity of being appointed general manager in the future. Given that assurance, he accepted.

His first significant trade was made before the 1958-59 season began when he acquired defenceman Allan Stanley from the New York Rangers and for Jim Morrison, who was also a defenceman and five years younger. Stanley had never lived up to his early billing in New York, and Madison Square Garden fans were merciless in their treatment of him. But in Toronto he played like a youngster and, teamed with Horton on the Leaf blueline, would have 10 more productive years.

That same season, Carl Brewer joined the team and was paired with Baun, another Marlie alumnus. Brewer was a remarkable talent and he developed quickly. He was an excellent skater and puck handler, and was one of the few defencemen of that time to rush the puck. Brewer was noted for his head fake as he moved up ice. Baun says, "Carl was probably as good as any defenceman I've seen. He had all the abilities of Orr. He was certainly more durable and stronger. The only thing he was lacking was desire and a head to go with it."

Horton and Stanley were just about as effective as Brewer and Baun, and perhaps even steadier, but they lacked the pizzaz. Brewer was a needler who infuriated players, such as Howe, and of course Baun's nickname of Boomer spoke of his strength and crashing body checks.

So, in the autumn of 1958, the Leafs started the season with a rebuilt defence. Horton and Stanley were the old guys, 28 and 32 years old, respectively. Brewer and Baun were the kids. Together the four men gave the Leafs the best blueline in the NHL and were instrumental in the team's winning four Stanley Cups.

But that was yet to come. In the early stages of the 1958-59 season things went poorly. Near the end of November, the team had won only 5 of 16 games. The fans were booing and the hockey committee wanted answers from Imlach. During a meeting, he told the committee that there wasn't much he could do without full authority. They agreed and, with the team in a prolonged losing streak, Imlach was appointed general manager, prompting Rex MacLeod of the *Globe* to write, "So meteoric has been the rise of this young hockey executive that it is conceivable he might make it to president if the Leafs lose a few more games."

With Imlach in charge, it became only a matter of time before Reay was replaced–one week, to be exact. When the team failed to win any of its four games after Imlach's promotion, he went to Conn Smythe, who had hired Reay, to say that he (Imlach) had decided to take over as coach. Smythe did not enthusiastically endorse the idea, but he didn't object either.

Imlach's first move was to speak to the players individually and ask if they would play for him as coach. They were all agreeable, including Bert Olmstead, the veteran recently acquired from Montreal who was a good friend of Reay's and had been with him in Chicago. Olmstead was important because of his leadership in the dressing room and on the ice. Stafford also addressed the players.

"When Imlach fired Reay," says Billy Harris, "he was our fourth coach in less than four years. There had been a lot of instability. On the day Imlach replaced Reay, Smythe talked to the players in the dressing room and said we had the nucleus of the best juniors in the country and that we were going to be very successful."

Stafford turned out to be correct, because over that winter, the team came together, played above .500 hockey, and moved closer to fourth place in the six-team league.

In addition to stability, Mahovlich says, Imlach brought leadership and made the players feel that they could win and be competitive. "All of a sudden there was somebody in charge. Nobody had done that before, and he did instill a lot of confidence in a lot of players."

At that point the Leaf team was divided fairly evenly between the young players who had come up from the Marlies or St. Mike's, and the veterans who included George Armstrong, the captain, Horton, Stanley, goaltender Johnny Bower, brought up from Springfield to replace Ed Chadwick, and Olmstead. Baun says Imlach was a good motivator, and effective behind the bench during games, but that the veterans, such as Red Kelly who came later, did most of the teaching during practices. "The fellows we had at that particular time—Olmstead and Kelly and others—they were the levellers. They taught all the young fellows of the early 1960s. They were really the guys who moved the club. Punch was very much the motivator, but as far as what was taught on the ice, it wasn't very much."

Kelly and Olmstead, of course, had been members of the Detroit and Montreal powerhouses of the 1950s (9 cups in 10 years). They also brought with them tactical and strategical knowledge. The only members of this squad to have had their names engraved on the Stanley Cup, they knew what it took to go all the way.

Perhaps Imlach's greatest skill was making adjustments in the heat of a game. He had excellent instincts and could tell immediately when a certain player wasn't performing up to potential, and then would make the necessary change on the line.

When Day was coaching, Conn Smythe would view the game from his seat in the Gardens greens, called Berchtesgaden by the sportswriters, a reference to Hitler's wartime retreat which was both ironical and appropriate. During a game he would send a messenger–it could have been Clancy or his son Hugh–to the bench to tell Day that a certain player was looking good and should have more ice time, or the other way around. But with Imlach, Smythe noticed something almost like telepathy. Imlach would make the necessary adjustment just as Smythe was about to dispatch one of his missives. Later Smythe would write of Imlach in his memoirs, "He was the best coach I ever saw. It was like he was a mind reader."

As well as a mind reader, it appeared the Leafs would need a magician to get into the 1959 playoffs. By 14 March, they were seven points behind the Rangers for the fourth and last playoff spot with only five games remaining.

On the eve of a weekend home and home series against the Rangers, the league had sent out to the media various playoff combinations and the dates of the games. Among the different match-ups no mention was made of the Leafs. Imlach used this to motivate the players for the two critical games against the Broadway Blueshirts, and the Leafs responded by winning both.

The two victories moved the Leafs out of last place ahead of Detroit and three points behind New York. What worried Imlach was that his team had not won more than two consecutive games all season, and to get into the playoffs, they had to keep winning, beginning with a game in Montreal against the first-place Canadiens. It was the Leafs' most important match of the season up to then, and they responded with a victory, pulling to within one point of the Rangers. But a few days later, the Rangers turned up the heat with a win over the Red Wings. That was followed by another Toronto triumph, this time over the Blackhawks.

So it came down to the final day of the season. Montreal was in New York, the Leafs in Detroit. The game at Madison Square Garden started an hour earlier than the one in Detroit, so by the end of the first period Imlach and the Leafs knew that the Canadiens had defeated the Rangers 4-2. Now all the Leafs had to do was to beat Detroit, which didn't seem likely after one period of play with the Red Wings ahead 2-0.

According to Imlach in his first book, *Hockey Is a Battle,* Stafford came along between periods, talked to Imlach in the hall, and said, "Well at least you had a good try. You have nothing to be ashamed of."

"What the hell are you talking about?" Imlach exploded. "We've come too far to lose now. Don't be stupid."

On the way out for the second period, Armstrong told Imlach, "We'll get it for you." And they did, fighting back twice to tie the game and then taking the lead in the third period. It ended 6–4 with right wing Larry Regan scoring twice as well as setting up Duff's game winner. In the semi-finals, the Leafs lost the first two games to Boston but then came back and defeated them in seven games. They fell to the Canadiens in the final in five games, but they were competitive. Every game was close.

For the players, the events in the spring of 1959 are among their fondest memories. Harris says the season-end surge was deliciously satisfying after enduring the difficult years. They were finally seeing progress and they knew it would get better. "We got slapped around pretty good for a few seasons before it happened. I travel around with Henri Richard playing old-timers hockey and I guess his first five years in the league he played on five Stanley Cup teams. I don't think it could have been as thrilling for him to come into the league and it's automatic for five years. We missed the playoffs twice and had a lot of frustrations, but after 1959, there was a feeling it was just a matter of time before we won everything."

In the following season, 1959–60, Imlach made arguably the most important trade of his 11 years in Toronto, acquiring Red Kelly who would centre the Leafs' top line for the next 8 years. In the 1950s, Kelly had been a superstar with the Red Wings. As a defenceman, he had been a first-team all-star six times and a second all-star twice. He had won the Lady Byng Trophy as the league's most gentlemanly player three times, the Norris Trophy (best defenceman) once, and had finished in the top 10 in scoring in three consecutive years, a remarkable accomplishment for a defenceman in those days.

In 1959–60, however, he was 32 years old, and the Red Wings were looking for younger players after finishing last the year before. That summer Imlach attempted to make a deal for Kelly, who at the time was having contract problems with the Red Wings. But nothing came of it and Kelly eventually signed on again with the Red Wings.

Then suddenly, in February, Detroit manager Jack Adams traded Kelly and forward Bill McNeill to the Rangers for defenceman Bill Gadsby and winger Eddie Shack. But the deal stalled when Kelly, who had played his entire NHL career in Detroit, refused to report. When Adams suspended him, the Leafs got in touch again. This time Clancy, Imlach's assistant manager and coach, made the call. He offered Marc Reaume, who had been the Leafs' fifth defenceman the previous season, the same player Imlach had offered in the summer. Adams said he would make the deal if Kelly would agree to it. At a meeting in Toronto with Imlach, Kelly accepted the club's contract offer.

Toronto had a good season in 1959–60. They finished second with a winning record of 53-26-9 and established themselves as a tough, aggressive team. They reached the final for the second straight season, but were swept by the Canadiens in four games.

The rebuilding continued. Imlach picked up Shack from the Rangers for Pat Hannigan and John Wilson, and Shack lived up to his nickname as the entertainer. He was a great skater, had loads of enthusiasm, and was entirely unpredictable. But most important, he was tough and his antics on the ice served to motivate his team.

And then there were two rookies, right winger Bob Nevin who had come up through the Marlboros and Dave Keon from St. Mike's. Nevin would give the Leafs four good years until his trade to the Rangers. At 5-foot-9, 163 pounds, Keon was small for the NHL and only 20 years old but he was a terrific skater and an inexhaustible worker–"Mr. Perpetual Motion," Hewitt would call him. In the years to come Keon, Mahovlich, and Brewer were the team's three most talented players. With these additions, the personnel was in place. Now it was a case of waiting for the players to come together and be a team.

Imlach decided to use Kelly at centre ice. Kelly made the transition quite easily and became an ideal playmaker for Mahovlich. With Nevin on the right side as a checker and 20-goal scorer, these three became the team's big line.

Of all the Leafs Mahovlich had the most natural talent. He was a big man, (6-foot-1, 194 pounds), a wonderful skater, with long powerful strides, and he had a booming slap shot. But he had only one great year in Toronto, in 1960–61, when he scored a club high of 48 goals. He was never the fan favourite he should have been. His inconsistency was a frustration not only to the fans, but also to Imlach, and over the years the relationship between player and coach deteriorated.

The second line was made up of Keon at centre between Duff on the left side and Armstrong on the right. Both usually had seasons in the 20-goal range, and Duff was known as a money player, at his best in a big game. Armstrong, the affable captain, was part Ojibwa Indian and nicknamed the Chief. Over the years he was among the steadiest of all the Leaf players.

The third line consisted of Pulford at centre with Shack and Olmstead on the wings. All three players were tough and strong defensively. Pulford could score and Olmstead was considered one of the best players in the corners.

The goaltending was handled by Johnny Bower, with Don Simmons as his backup. Bower had spent 15 years in the minors, with the exception of 1953-54 when he played a season with the Rangers, before joining the Leafs in 1958-59. A gentle and likeable man, he was intensely competitive. And in an era of legendary goaltenders—Glenn Hall in Chicago, Terry Sawchuk in Detroit, and Jacques Plante in Montreal with the Canadiens—Bower was among the very best.

In 1960-61, Bower won the Vezina Trophy as the league's best netminder, despite suffering a leg injury that kept him out of the lineup for 12 games. The Leafs were battling the Canadiens for first place at the time, and Imlach said later that Bower's injury had not only cost them the top spot, but he felt that it had left them tired for the playoffs. Indeed, the Leafs were upset in the first round, which was a bitterly disappointing way to end a good season.

Still, there was much to be enthusiastic about. Mahovlich had developed into a superstar, falling just short of Richard's 50-goal mark. Keon had won the Calder Trophy as the league's top rookie. Bower had the Vezina. Both Bower and Mahovlich were first-team all-stars, and Stanley had made the second team. At centre, on defence, and in goal, the Leafs were as good as or better than any team in the league. Now they had to learn how to win.

5

RETURN TO
GLORY

As it turned out, the 1961–62 season would change the Maple Leaf hockey club forever. It marked the beginning of the Leafs' drive to be the dominant team of the decade, but more important, an ownership change set the team in another direction. The new proprietors were not strangers to the club or to the arena, but they had different ways of doing things and the long-range effects would be significant.

In the late 1950s, Stafford Smythe, Harold Ballard, and John W. Bassett, the three leading members of the Silver Seven, formed a pact by which they would buy Conn Smythe's shares in Maple Leaf Gardens Ltd. if the shares came available. Stafford was constantly fighting with his father, often publicly, over the operation of the hockey team. Ballard viewed the Gardens as a gold mine and had always dreamed of running it. And as a sportsman and businessman, Bassett could do no better than to own the Leafs.

"Staff and Harold and I figured we'd have a crack at control of the Gardens and we started buying a lot of shares, big bunches of them," Bassett told journalist John Gault. "When Connie found out we were buying them he became very cross with Stafford. But Ballard and I kept buying."

Ballard had bought stock continuously from the day it was first issued in 1931. By 1957, he owned 3606 shares, 1556 of which belonged to his personal holding company, Harold E. Ballard Ltd.

Stafford, on the other hand, owned only 500 shares. Bassett's company, Telegram Publishing held 1000.

In November 1961, Conn Smythe finally handed over the company to his son and two partners. Conn, at 66 and in poor health, had grown tired of the business and the bitter arguments with his son. He felt it was time to get out. Later Conn said he didn't realize that Ballard, and particularly Bassett, were in on the deal. Still, without them, Stafford, who was not a wealthy man, could never have raised the $2 million in capital needed to take control. Ballard used his own assets as well as the Gardens shares, which he was about to purchase, to secure a loan from the Bank of Nova Scotia. It was basically a leverage buyout. Conn ended up selling about 45,000 of his shares for $40 a share, $6 more than the market value of the day. Combined with the shares already owned by the three partners, the total came to 87,000–about 60 per cent of the outstanding Gardens shares.

In the new regime, Stafford replaced his father as president. Ballard was executive vice-president in charge of the arena. Bassett was appointed chairman of the board, although his involvement was minimal. Other things took up his time, most notably his newspaper, which was in a circulation war with the *Star*, and the Toronto Argonauts, of which he had majority ownership.

At the team level, everything stayed the same. The Leafs were a set team. They had finished solidly in second place the year before, only 2 points behind the Canadiens and 15 points ahead of the Blackhawks. The only change for 1961-62 was less emphasis on first place and more on winning the Stanley Cup. When the playoffs came, the team was rested and healthy. In the first round, they eliminated the Rangers in six games, which set up a final against the defending champion Blackhawks.

In those days the Leafs and the Blackhawks were the league's two toughest teams. Chicago could not match the Leafs in depth, but their front-line talent was remarkable. At left wing, Bobby Hull scored 50 goals that season. Stan Mikita was probably the most skilful centre in the league, as well as the dirtiest. Kenny Wharram was among the best right wingers. On defence Pierre Pilote was an all-star, as was Hall, one of the top goaltenders.

But before the series started most of the talk was about which team was going to intimidate the other. Tommy Ivan, the Blackhawks' general manager, said, "No Leaf is going to push us around." Imlach was quoted as saying: "The Hawks should know by now they can't run us out of any rink." It did turn into a rough series, but the Leafs more than held their own. After the fifth game, with the Leafs leading the series 3-2, Reggie Fleming, a muscular Chicago winger and noted hothead, sounded more like an effete observer than his team's toughest player when he said, "They're crude, just crude. You know who they are. They're always waving their sticks in somebody's direction."

The Leafs finished off the Hawks in six games, and of course the city of Toronto went wild. At the airport, hundreds of fans were there to welcome home their heroes. They carried players on their shoulders, they chanted, "Go Leafs Go." There was a parade down University Avenue and a reception at City Hall. After 11 long years the Cup was back in Toronto.

The next season, 1962-63, turned out to be the high point of the Imlach era. The team finished in first place–something it hadn't done since 1947-48. The Leafs eliminated the Canadiens in the first round of the playoffs in five games, and then used five more to knock off Detroit.

In ranking the top Leaf team of all time, authorities on hockey place this team close or equal to the 1947-48 squad. There were many similarities. Both were strong at centre, the best of their particular era. Both had great defences and were quite content to sit on a one-goal lead. The Leafs of the 1960s probably had a better defence, but the centres on the 1947-48 team are considered superior. Both teams had veteran goalies who played their best under pressure.

One significant difference was that Day's team won three Cups in a row without a great deal of difficulty and would have won five consecutively except for an upset in the first round in 1950 by Detroit.

Imlach's team, on the other hand, struggled to win three straight and would not have been able to do it without a key trade which was made in February of the 1963-64 season. The Leafs did not look anything like defending champions that winter. It was clear that Mahovlich could no longer play for Imlach. Duff wasn't scoring, nor was Nevin. In one game, the Leafs were humiliated 11-0 by the lowly Bruins.

For most of the season, Imlach tried to make a deal for Andy Bathgate, a slick playmaking right winger who could also score goals. In 1958, Bathgate had won the league MVP with the Rangers, but by 1964 he was 31 and a step or two slower.

Finally it was agreed the Leafs would send the Rangers a package of veterans and younger players for Bathgate and Don McKenney, a centre and a left winger. The Rangers received Duff and Nevin, minor-league right winger Bill Collins, and two young defencemen in the Leaf organization, Arnie Brown and Rod Seiling.

McKenney took Duff's spot on the line with Keon and Armstrong, and Bathgate played with Kelly and Mahovlich. The addition of Bathgate, who had three goals and 15 assists in his 15 regular-season games with Toronto, brought the big line back to life. The team was playing well going into the postseason play.

One of the debates during the 1964 playoffs was about the effectiveness of Imlach's long and tough practices. Mahovlich always felt that Imlach, who was often described as a "martinet" in those days, worked the players too hard. "I think he over-practised us," Mahovlich says. "I think he worked us into the ground, really. We left a lot of our games at practice. It was like a horse running three days before the big race and having nothing left."

In the final against Detroit, the two teams took quite different approaches to working out. Like the Leafs, the Red Wings were a veteran team with older players such as Howe, Alex Delvecchio, and Bill Gadsby. Their coach, Sid Abel, went easy on them. On off days, they didn't practise. Instead they would go to the track or lie by the hotel pool. Imlach, on the other hand, felt that hard workouts improved endurance, and he whipped his players, even during the final. This seemed to upset the Red Wings who were quite critical. Gadsby said, "That Imlach must be nuts. Those older guys like Kelly, Stanley, and Armstrong can't take it. The business of working out every day, it's killing them."

Events seemed to prove the Red Wings correct when the Leafs fell behind 2-1 in the series and then 3-2. But in the sixth game in Detroit, Bower was magnificent, holding his team close in the first two periods until Harris tied it near the end of the second. After a scoreless third, the Leafs went into overtime facing elimination. A goal by the Wings would win the Cup and end Toronto's string at two.

The hero that evening would be Baun, who left the game with a suspected fracture of his lower leg. He refused to have the injury X-rayed, and when overtime started he was on the bench. After the first line change, out he came. When the puck was sent into the Detroit zone, Baun skated in to take his place on the right side of the blueline. Pulford was able to control the puck in the Detroit zone and get it back to Baun. It wasn't a hard shot, but he fired quickly. Sawchuk seemed to be in position to stop it, but Gadsby was in front of him. Suddenly it hit Gadsby's foot, changed direction, and fell in behind Sawchuk. The Leafs jumped to their feet and mobbed Baun. The series was tied, and back in Toronto, it was a decisive 4-0 triumph for the Leafs, with Bathgate scoring the winner.

It was an immensely satisfying win for Imlach. Bathgate had made a significant difference in the playoffs. Imlach's theory of working his players hard in practices proved right, at least in this case. And one of Imlach's greatest critics, Gadsby, turned out to be the so-called goat of the series.

At this point, Imlach was at the peak of his popularity in Toronto. Despite his unimpressive appearance, there was a charisma about him, a self-confidence and a sense of invincibility that drew followers, not only from the sports public, but also from the media. Some of the best sportswriters of the day grew almost to worship him. One writer titled his notes at the end of his reports, "Punch Lines." Red Burnett, the beat writer at the *Star,* was an old friend and almost a father figure going back to the 1930s when he coached a minor hockey team that included Imlach. George Gross of the *Telegram* was a great supporter, as was Scott Young who worked as a columnist at the *Globe* and later the *Telegram.*

Imlach was flamboyant and outspoken and could be very charming. Fans took vicarious pleasure in seeing him succeed. He was every man's dream of the little guy who made it to the top because he was a fighter and wouldn't back down. But as his popularity grew, so too did his ego. Some of the more cynical reporters called him the "Big I" because when the team won it was "I" and when it lost it was "them." When he underwent a gall bladder operation, Rex MacLeod wrote, "They removed the bladder, but left the gall."

One criticism of Imlach was that he was never able to get along with his two most talented players, Brewer and Mahovlich. This might be unfair, because, arguably, Keon was of that calibre and he had a good relationship with Imlach.

Brewer was intense and very much his own man. Kelly describes him as "panicky." He was high-strung and easily frustrated. During the season, he would lose a large amount of his hair from the stress of competition. Often Brewer's conflict with Imlach was over money. As general manager, Imlach negotiated the contracts, and he wasn't generous. Mahovlich can remember haggling over $500 after he had scored his 48 goals.

In the early 1960s Brewer decided to enlist the help of a friend when he needed to negotiate. Brewer had grown up in the west end of Toronto with Pulford, and one of their pals had been Alan Eagleson, a good lacrosse player who had opted for law. Eagleson was interested in the representation of athletes and agreed to act for Brewer. This was something that had rarely been done in the past, and Imlach and the Leafs were violently opposed to it.

When Brewer was chosen as a first-team all-star in 1963, he felt his accomplishment warranted more money than Imlach was willing to pay. When nothing was done, Eagleson advised Brewer to retire and go to university, which he did at McMaster in Hamilton. When he was photographed in a McMaster football uniform, the Leafs started to worry. Before long, Clancy arrived on campus to tell Brewer his contract demand had been accepted.

A year later, Brewer broke his arm in the playoffs. He felt he should have been compensated for not being able to work that summer, and when the Leafs refused, it was back to school. Not long after, Clancy showed up again and a settlement was reached. This, of course, infuriated Imlach. Later, in 1967, Brewer, Baun, and Pulford assisted Eagleson in establishing the NHL Players Association, which was about as much as Imlach could take. Eagleson would say, "There are two names Imlach can't stand. Mine and Brewer's."

Imlach had a policy of treating everyone on the team the same, and, as Kelly recalls, the laziest, most ineffective players usually determined the tone of his practices. "He tended to take his worst players, ones not in top condition, and drive everyone from that standpoint." It worked for most of the players, particularly the veterans who were mature enough to accept what Imlach was doing.

But it didn't work for Brewer or Mahovlich. Baun says, "Punch sort of psyched Carl out. He did much the same thing with Frank Mahovlich. Imlach could be very difficult with the needle and he sort of put everyone in one category. He had the big hammer and he used it in the motivating end. It wasn't really motivation. It was play or else. And that didn't work for a guy like Carl, who was very headstrong."

For Mahovlich it became a torturous experience. Imlach would attempt to motivate him through intimidation but it didn't work. Instead Mahovlich became withdrawn. He didn't play well and his ice time was decreased. The fans booed him. The stress resulted in his taking two leaves of absence from the team. Finally he was traded.

"They put me in the hospital for a rest," Mahovlich says. "There were a couple of times it happened. I was just exhausted. And I think the main problem was that I wasn't getting along with Imlach. The outcome of that was they had to get rid of me. I wasn't going to perform up to my ability there. There was the pressure to perform from the fans, and here's some guy whipping you. It was tough."

In 1968 he went to Detroit and in 1971 to Montreal. He had outstanding seasons with both clubs. In his final two years in Toronto he scored 18 and 19 goals respectively. But with the Red Wings and Canadiens the enthusiasm returned. He had 49 goals one year in Detroit and 43 in Montreal a few years later. Mahovlich says, "As soon as I left, my production went sky high. It was as if a piano had been lifted off my back."

The Leafs went into eclipse after the 1964 championship. They failed to get past the first round in either 1965 or 1966. Brewer retired in 1965 at the age of 27. New players came in. There were wingers Jim Pappin, Ron Ellis, and Brit Selby, centre Peter Stemkowski, and defenceman Kent Douglas. Dickie Moore, the former Canadiens star, attempted a comeback with the Leafs.

By the spring of 1967, nobody expected Toronto to be a factor in the playoffs. In a 10-game stretch during the season, they had gone winless and had slipped as far down as fifth. Imlach had been admitted to hospital suffering from exhaustion. But as the season drew to a close, the Leafs played better and finished up in third place. Still, they were a very old team. Armstrong was 36, Kelly 39, Horton 37, Stanley 41, and Bower 42. Newspapers called them the Over-the-Hill Gang, or the Old Folks A.C.

There was one other old-timer–Sawchuk. He had been left unprotected by the Red Wings in the 1964 draft and was claimed by Imlach. The 37-year-old Sawchuk had accomplished amazing things in the NHL. Today, in fact, he would be the choice of many as the greatest goaltender of all time. He was rookie of the year in 1951, won four Vezina Trophies, and helped lead the Red Wings to three Stanley Cups in the 1950s. His most remarkable record is his 103 shutouts over a 20-year career. That is unlikely ever to be surpassed. He also leads in career wins (435).

But in 1967 Sawchuk was considered well past his prime. He had been discarded by the Red Wings–and Bower was five years

Sawchuk's senior. Still, together they would work a miracle for the Leafs and provide them with one more Cup. In the final, they faced the Canadiens, a good team led by such veterans as Henri Richard and Jean Beliveau as well as a younger group that included John Ferguson and Yvan Cournoyer. Another was Rogatien Vachon, a 21-year-old goalie whom Imlach dismissed as a "Junior B goaltender." That remark was a headline grabber in Montreal, but as the series progressed, Imlach revised his assessment to "the best Junior B goaltender in Canada" to, finally, a "Junior A goaltender."

The Canadiens handled the Leafs easily in the first game, winning 6-2. Sawchuk left the game in the third period with an injured ankle and was replaced by Bower, who started the second game and was brilliant in a 3-0 shutout. Imlach came back with Bower for the third game, and again he stopped the Canadiens, this time 3-2.

In the warmup for the fourth game, however, Bower pulled a groin muscle and had to be replaced by Sawchuk. As in the first game, he was shaky. He let in two in the first period, three more in the second, and another in the third. The Leafs were trounced 6-2 and the series was tied.

It was at this point that Sawchuk received a telegram from a fan in Newfoundland. The same fan had sent a congratulatory telegram when Sawchuk had earned his hundredth shutout. Earlier in the playoffs when he had starred in the series against Chicago, winning three games, he had received another telegram from the fan, wishing him well. This third telegram simply asked: How much did you get? Sawchuk was shocked and deeply hurt. "How can people say those things?" he said later, "I tried just as hard."

Despite Sawchuk's poor performance, Imlach had no choice but to come back with him for the fifth game at the Forum because of Bower's injury. But this time, the clock turned back 20 years and Sawchuk played one of the greatest games of his career. Time after time, he stopped the Canadiens. They came at him in waves. Beliveau–Bobby Rousseau–Richard. One went past him, in the seventh minute of the first period, but no more. The Leafs beat the Canadiens 4-1 and now were a game away from their fourth Cup in the 1960s.

Back in Toronto for the sixth game, the Leafs continued to check the Canadiens. Keon, who was his team's best player in the series aside from the goaltenders, spear-headed the attack. Sawchuk was brilliant. He stopped the Canadiens in the first period, and then the Leafs scored two of their own in the second. The Canadiens netted one early in the third and then pulled their goalie in the final minute.

For the faceoff in the Toronto zone, Imlach chose to send out the men who had been with him from the beginning. In those days, the Leaf defence took faceoffs in their own zone, which meant that Stanley would be up against Beliveau. Horton was the other defenceman. The forwards were Armstrong, Kelly, and Pulford.

When the puck was dropped, Stanley beat Beliveau cleanly, and directed it to Kelly. Quickly Kelly moved it up to Pulford. Then Pulford hit Armstrong with a perfect pass that sent him toward centre ice by himself. Calmly and deliberately Armstrong measured the target and fired from 90 feet away. As the puck slid in, the Gardens exploded in joy. Almost to a man, the Leafs said later that that championship was special. No one had expected them to win. No one had expected them to be in the final. But backstopped by the two aging goaltenders and led by Keon, they had prevailed for one last upset.

The following season, 1967-68, the personality and style of the team started to change. Baun was picked up in the expansion draft by Oakland, one of the new teams. Stanley retired. More new players were moved in. Finally, in April 1969, following a four-game sweep by the Bruins in the playoffs, Imlach was fired by Stafford Smythe.

Imlach returned to the dressing room and shook hands with his players as he always did when the season ended. But this time it was goodbye, not just thanks. Some picked up on it, others did not. Later he would toast the Imlach era with champagne among his closest friends. It had been a controversial and sometimes turbulent 11 years. But above all–and overall–it had been successful. He had continued the tradition.

6

DEATH
AND TAXES

To find the first crack in the Maple Leaf empire one usually looks back to 1967 and 1968 when the two minor-pro farm teams, the Rochester Americans and the Victoria Cougars, were sold, leaving the organization without an adequate supply of players. But the decline really started before then and was a result of a new attitude at the Gardens, a new perception of what the team was and what it represented.

In Conn Smythe's days winning was paramount. His pride would accept nothing less than a successful team, and he would go to great lengths to achieve that goal, even if it meant buying players. He had purchased Clancy for $35,000 and in the 1940s had offered the Canadiens $25,000 for Rocket Richard.

In the beginning Stafford was like his father. His ego demanded a winner, and the Leafs won. But as profits took off at "$8 million an hour," as his partner Ballard said, priorities gradually changed.

More than anyone, Ballard was responsible for the new, huge amount of revenue earned at the Gardens. During Smythe's era, the arena made its money basically from hockey games and the occasional ice show or other sporting event. Most nights of the year it was empty. But Ballard threw down the welcome mat and actively solicited business. There were conventions, circuses, boxing cards, and leading entertainers such as Bob Hope and Frank Sinatra. Later, he brought in the rock bands. One of his first moves was to tear down a large portrait of Queen Elizabeth II to make room for more seats, which outraged the monarchists, of whom Conn Smythe was one. Ballard's response was, "If people want to see a picture of the Queen, they can go to an art gallery. What the hell, she doesn't pay me. I pay her."

On the east side of the Gardens, Ballard put in a licensed restaurant called the Hot Stove Lounge, which became a favourite watering hole for businessmen and a home away from home for Ballard. He sold advertising anywhere he could. Shick razor ads were placed on escalator risers. Ads were slapped on the underside of the seats, which showed when they were folded up. To increase the seating capacity, the old seats were torn out and replaced with smaller but higher priced ones. Conn Smythe's much-repeated line was, "They're too high priced for the thin and too small for the fat folks who can afford them."

Ballard would do almost anything to make a buck. One of the more outrageous stories of that era was about his promotion of the Beatles concerts in 1965. Ballard had signed the Beatles to play one concert, but he sold tickets for two shows. When the Beatles arrived in New York, Ballard was there to meet them and to tell their manager, Brian Epstein, about the second show. Epstein was upset and remained so even after the group arrived in Toronto. When he threatened to pull out after one show, Ballard told him that the fans would tear down the building with the Fab Four inside.

Ballard got his two shows and the Beatles were paid for two performances. But the Gardens also made a killing on the concessions. On one of the hottest days of the summer, he postponed the first show by 90 minutes and the second by 75 minutes. He also instructed the maintenance men to shut off the water lines to the fountains and turn on the heat. The concessions operators were told to put away their small cups. An estimated 300 fans fainted and had to be carried out.

Ballard showed himself to be unscrupulously resourceful and somewhat brazen in operating the arena. Many agreed with Conn Smythe that crass had replaced class at the Gardens. But nobody could argue about what Ballard was doing for the company. In 1961, before the three partners bought out Smythe, Gardens stock was trading at $26.50 a share. Four years later, shares were worth $114.75 each, before they split five for one. In 1960, the total of dividends paid was $176,539. Seven years later it had multiplied more than 10 times to $2.28 million.

The first sign that the Leaf owners might consider placing a financial windfall ahead of the team came in the fall of 1962 when Jim Norris, the Blackhawks' owner, attempted to buy Mahovlich for $1 million. Ballard wanted to make the deal and told Norris it could be worked out. Stafford, however, decided against it after consulting with his father.

As time went on, success bred a certain arrogance. The club won Stanley Cups almost every year and the revenue continued to increase. There grew a feeling of invincibility, a sense that the team would continue to win, no matter what.

The profits earned from the Gardens seemed to feed rather than sate an atmosphere of greed. Unsatisfied with the large dividends earned from their shares, Ballard and Smythe started in 1964 to steal money from the Marlboros, which had annual expenditures of $250,000. They set up a bank account in the name of S. H. Marlie (S. for Stafford, H. for Harold) and used it as a depository for money syphoned from the junior club, which they withdrew at their pleasure.

This impulse for more money had no damaging effect on the Leafs until 1967 and 1968, when Smythe and Ballard sold the club's two minor-league affiliates. In 1967 the Victoria Cougars were sold to a group in Phoenix for $500,000, and the Rochester Americans went to Vancouver buyers for $400,000. The sale of the Victoria team was botched in the sense that the terms of the deal were not explicit. A lawsuit resulted, and it is questionable whether the Leafs ended up with much of anything when the dispute was finally resolved.

The sale of the two clubs was the first tangible evidence of a crumbling empire. The Leafs had won their fourth Cup of the decade a year earlier, but decay had already set in. Through the sale, the organization lost 45 players, some of them NHL calibre. In the 1960s it was sometimes said that Rochester was so strong that it could have competed in the NHL and finished ahead of Boston and New York.

Among those sold or lost in the 1967 expansion draft were defenceman Al Arbour who went on to play in St. Louis with the Blues, right winger Gerry Ehman who had some years with Oakland of the NHL, defenceman Larry Hillman who joined Minnesota, and centre Bryan Hextall who went to Pittsburgh. So, the Leafs entered the NHL's new 12-team era with no depth and very few good young players. The result was last place in their division in 1968. And for the first time in 10 years they missed the playoffs.

In contrast, the Canadiens kept their farm teams, and then traded off excess players and veterans for high draft choices that were used to stock the great Canadien teams of the 1970s. Players obtained with these picks included Guy Lafleur, Steve Shutt, Bob Gainey, and Larry Robinson. Under different circumstances Smythe might have finally come to the realization that the Leafs had to do the same thing. But beginning in 1968, his life, and that of Ballard, changed forever. The status of the Leafs would be the least of their worries. In the summer of 1968 the Royal Canadian Mounted Police entered Maple Leaf Gardens with search warrants and seized company documents. On the same day, the Gardens' accountants, Price, Waterhouse and Company, sent out letters informing the directors that a provincial court judge in Ottawa had authorized federal authorities to search the arena and the homes of Stafford Smythe and Harold Ballard. This was totally unexpected, and the directors were shocked.

In the beginning, the Gardens and the Department of National Revenue argued over the status of $2.16 million received in NHL expansion money, the disagreement being whether it was capital gain or earned revenue. A few months later, the Gardens' annual report informed shareholders of more complications: "The Department of National Revenue is making a special review of the company's income tax returns for the past several years. The only known adjustment at the time is in respect to the claim for 1966 and 1967." In another report, the shareholders were told, "Incorrect invoices submitted by a construction company resulted in the inclusion in property additions for the years ended Aug. 31, 1966 and 1967 of amounts aggregating $212,800."

Those close to Smythe and Ballard during this period think the tax problems could have been settled but for bad feelings between Smythe and the governing federal Liberal party. Stafford, a Progressive Conservative, had feuded with high-ranking Liberals for some time. When the government organized Hockey Canada in 1970, for example, Stafford dismissed it as "a goofy move by a bunch of dumbos." At the time of the tax problems, a prominent cabinet minister told a friend of Ballard's: "It's not Ballard we're after. It's the other guy."

Because the irregularities in the Gardens books were pinned directly to Ballard and Smythe, the directors felt they had no choice but to remove them from positions of influence, at least for a while, to protect the company's integrity. This unsavoury task fell to their partner and pal, John Bassett, as chairman of the board.

When the meeting was held in June 1969, only 15 of the 23 directors showed up. Nobody relished turning against old friends who had made all of them a great deal of money over the years. George Mara, a close friend of Smythe and Ballard, advised them to resign, but their lawyers told them otherwise, arguing that resignations would be interpreted as admissions of guilt.

After arguments and accusations, there was a secret vote, the result of which stunned Mara and others who now felt it imperative that Smythe and Ballard be removed. It was a tie, 7-7. Had it been a public show of hands, Mara thinks the two would have been rejected by a large margin. But with the advantage of a secret ballot, old loyalties were not threatened by public scrutiny. As a result seven stood with Conn's son and his partner who had enhanced their investment. It fell to Bassett to break the tie. He voted against his two friends—and in doing so acquired two life-long enemies. In the years to come, the Ballard-Bassett feud would reach epic and sometimes comic proportions.

Smythe and Ballard now plotted to punish the Gardens directors who voted against them. They intended to throw them out, and reinstate themselves as president and vice-president. And they fought with Bassett for control of the company.

The directors were removed early in December 1970 at a shareholders' meeting. Ballard and Smythe called in old favours and most of the 50 shareholders who met that day lined up beside them. This was not a revelation to the 20 incumbents. Sixteen decided not to run again. The remaining four were Ballard, Smythe, Paul McNamara, who at the time was president of Northgate Hotel Ltd. and is still on the board of Maple Leaf Gardens Ltd., and T. D. Jeffries, who was president of Viceroy Manufacturing Company Ltd. Bassett had resigned, Mara too. In fact, all the other original members of the Silver Seven had left.

The war between Ballard and Smythe and Bassett continued into 1971, with each side attempting to secure more shares and support from shareholders. Finally, Bassett capitulated. With his newspaper rife with union trouble and on the brink of collapse, he was quoted in the *Telegram* as saying, "I've been trying for five months to gain control of the Gardens. Finally, I realized that this operation is so much a part of Mr. Ballard and Mr. Smythe there is simply no way. So I told them to take me out. I should emphasize that any shareholder can only have the deepest gratitude for the management of Ballard and Smythe. When we bought the stock from Conn

Smythe we paid $40 for shares listed at $27. Yesterday, even after a five-way split, the price was $30."

Two problems had been solved. Ballard and Smythe were back in their positions of power at the Gardens, and Bassett was no longer waging war for control. Still, these were small matters compared to what was to come.

In 1970 and 1971, the Attorney General's office under the direction of special prosecutor Clayton Powell investigated the business activities of Ballard and Smythe; 180 people were interviewed in the course of the investigation, which discovered that cheques from the Marlboro hockey club between 1964 and 1969 had been deposited in the S. H. Marlie account. In addition, major construction work done to the homes–as well as the cottages–of Ballard and Smythe had been charged to Maple Leaf Gardens.

The investigation lasted one year. Then, in July of 1971, police walked into Smythe's office at the Gardens and arrested him on charges of defrauding the Gardens of $249,000. Ballard's fraud charges amounted to about $82,000. Ballard and Smythe were charged jointly with theft of $146,000 in cash and securities.

Of the two, Ballard held up better. Stafford Smythe suffered through the summer. Always a heavy drinker, he drank even more. His health failed. In October, three weeks before he was scheduled to go to trial, he was admitted to hospital with a bleeding ulcer. After surgery he started to bleed in the stomach vein and the esophagus. The doctors were forced to operate again, this time removing a large part of the stomach. Near the end, with his father by his side, he said, "See Dad, I told you they wouldn't put me in prison."

Mara said later, "The fact is, he couldn't stand the pressure. However deserved or undeserved, it was harassment, and there were a whole lot of people who enjoyed his discomfort. He felt very much persecuted and he couldn't stand it. Unlike Harold–Harold is Harold–he lived a very tough time."

Smythe's death had a devastating affect on Ballard. Two years earlier, his wife Dorothy had died of cancer, and now he had lost his best friend. Still, he was on the verge of realizing a dream by taking complete control of the Gardens. Critical to Ballard's accomplishing this was a clause in the 1961 pact struck among Ballard, Smythe, and Bassett. It stated that if one of the partners wanted to sell his shares, or if he died, the shares must be offered first to his partners.

After the death of Stafford, Ballard was immediately appointed president of the club. At that point, the Smythe family noticed a change in Ballard. He refused to speak to Stafford's widow, Dorothea, even though the families had been close. When Stafford's 25-year-old son, Tom, went to Ballard to determine his future in the company, Ballard sent him away. He made disparaging remarks in the newspapers about the family.

A few years ago, Hugh Smythe, the head of the rheumatology division at Wellesley Hospital and Stafford's younger brother, said, "I don't think [Ballard] changed. I think he was the same guy. We were just seeing his other side. My father never liked Harold. They never really got along at all. . . . Most of the ones my father didn't like, he got rid of. But when the Marlies fell under the direction of my brother, he protected Harold and Harold survived."

The Smythes made a half-hearted bid for Ballard's shares. Then early in February 1972, Ballard made his move. As an executor of Stafford's will, he simply sold Smythe's shares to himself at market price. Permission was not required from Smythe's family. Tom Smythe heard about the sale on his car radio.

With the purchase, Ballard's private holding company, Harold E. Ballard Ltd., owned 71 per cent of Maple Leaf Gardens Ltd. A few weeks later, Hugh Smythe sold his own 1200 shares to Ballard who asked Smythe also to relinquish his season's tickets, which he did. Hugh Smythe did not return to the Gardens until November 1980, when his father, Conn Smythe, died, and only then to pick up his father's belongings.

7

PYRAMID POWER
AND CAPTAIN VIDEO

By 1972 the NHL had experienced an enormous transformation over a period of five years. It doubled in size in 1967 and then added two more clubs in 1970. This was followed by an additional two in 1972. No longer was it a small house league consisting of six teams. Now there were 16, all with equal access to the marketplace of amateur and junior players.

One of the biggest changes occurred in 1969 when the old system of acquiring prospects was replaced by the amateur draft. Under the procedure of placing players on protected lists, the Leafs had enjoyed some built-in advantages, particularly in Ontario. When Stafford and Conn ran the club, the team had a network of part-time scouts in all areas of the province, as well as across Canada.

Because of the Leafs' popularity a teenager would usually choose Toronto ahead of another club, if he was given a choice. Bob Davidson, Toronto's top scout in the 1950s and 1960s, can remember being nonplussed when a teenager said he didn't want to sign with Toronto because his favourite team was Chicago.

But with the advent of the amateur draft, later to be called the NHL entry draft, these advantages no longer existed. All professional teams had to acquire their players through a draft in which the team with the worst record picked first, the one with the second poorest record selected second, and so on. Not only had the rules changed, but now there were more teams searching for players. Competition had increased significantly. The Canadiens' managing director, Sam Pollock, responded by adding more scouts. The Leafs did not.

Many hockey executives had trouble adjusting to the NHL's new era. In Toronto, it was a time when the team needed a shrewd and knowledgeable hockey man. Ballard, with no experience in running an NHL hockey team, was neither. Davidson remembers Smythe as a very hands-on type of president. He went out and scouted players, and checked over the reports submitted by his scouts. Ballard never did this. "Smythe read all the reports and signed them," Davidson said. "He would say 'I don't think this boy's a pro prospect.' He wouldn't say it as if he was upset. It would just be an observation. I don't think Ballard ever reads scouting reports. The main difference is that the Smythes ran the company for the hockey not the dollars."

Ballard's involvement in hockey went back decades but was limited to managing the finances of amateur teams or helping out the coach or manager in some minor way. He did attempt coaching once, and was a spectacular flop.

His first job as an assistant manager came in 1928 when he accompanied the Varsity Grads to the Winter Olympics in St. Moritz. Conn Smythe originally had agreed to coach and manage the team, but after buying the St. Pats he had to decline. Instead, the job went to W. A. Hewitt. The 24-year-old Ballard, as Hewitt's assistant, was a favourite of the hockey players. When Canada's Olympic contingent arrived in St. Moritz, it was decided that Ballard would carry the Canadian banner in the parade of athletes, even though he wasn't a competitor.

Goaltender Joe Sullivan said before his death in 1987 that Ballard was chosen because the Grads liked him. And besides, his father had been generous enough to supply the Ballard Rockered Tube Skate, which he manufactured in those days. "We were wearing his skates and he was part of the team," said Sullivan. "He had a very likeable and amiable personality. Everybody liked him. We didn't overrule the Canadian Olympic Association. We told them what we wanted done. It wasn't the first time we did that either." The Grads easily won the gold medal, defeating Sweden 11-0, Great Britain 14-0, and Switzerland 13-0.

Ballard's next opportunity to manage came in 1930 when the National Yacht Club, of which he was a member, sponsored a senior team in the Ontario Hockey Association. It was named the National Sea Fleas, after the outboard motor boats that raced on Lake

Ontario. In its first year, Ballard worked as the team's business manager. The following season he took over as manager. Then in the fall of 1932, he found himself behind the bench when the coach suddenly quit. The previous spring the Sea Fleas had won the Allan Cup, as the best senior team in Canada, and they were favoured to win it again.

Depending on how you look at it, the season was either pathetic or comic. Following a slow start, several of the team's best players quit, refusing to play for Ballard. This occurred after he criticized them in the newspapers as lazy and uncommitted, promising an "iron hand." By midseason he had a full-scale mutiny on his hands.

After missing the playoffs, Ballard hoped to salvage the season by organizing a two-month European tour with stops in London, Paris, Berlin, Zurich, and finally Prague for the International Ice Hockey Federation world championship. If the OHL senior season was disappointing, the European experience would turn into a fiasco.

European teams were no match for Ballard's gang, who had more talent but less couth. As the Canadians routinely gooned the opposing teams, the fans retaliated by throwing beer mugs and bottles. Several brawls resulted. In a game in Zurich, one of Ballard's players beat up a referee. Off the ice the Canadians were viewed as rowdies. Hap Day says Ballard told him later that he spent most of his time getting his men out of jail.

The most publicized incident occurred in Paris when Ballard was clubbed over the head by a gendarme following a champagne party that ended up in a brawl in a hotel. Ballard was hauled away to jail for the night and wasn't released until a representative from the Canadian embassy came to get him out. This, of course, created headlines back home, and when the tour ended the Canadian Amateur Hockey Association censured the team and investigated its behaviour.

The biggest embarrassment, however, was the performance at the world championship when the favoured Canadians lost the final 2–1 in overtime to an American team from Boston. It was an omen perhaps, that Ballard would have the humiliating distinction of coaching the first Canadian team to suffer defeat at the world hockey championship. As it turned out, this was Ballard's one and only attempt at coaching. It was a brief experience, but it gives us an early look at the personality, attitude, and judgment of Ballard that would be sadly evident when he owned the Leafs.

In the 1930s, Ballard not only coveted the Gardens, but deeply admired Smythe, the tough, self-made businessman who had become in a short period of time the dominant figure in Canadian hockey. Ballard wanted badly to be part of these exciting years, but Smythe was consistently cool to his overtures. He was suspicious of Ballard's motives, didn't trust him, and, although cordial, kept him at arm's length. In his memoirs, Smythe wrote, "I've known him [Ballard] most of my life as a good giver, a good friend, but I would not give him a job at 10 cents a week. His way of doing things is not mine."

Ballard did not give up easily, and through Day, he gradually worked his way into the Leaf organization. Day and Ballard had been close friends for years. Their wives socialized and they both lived in the west end of Toronto. In the 1930s when Day was still playing for the Leafs, they operated amateur hockey teams together, Day as coach and manager, Ballard as business manager. Years later, Day, then coach of the Leafs, recommended to Selke that Ballard run the Toronto Marlboro junior and senior teams, both of which were owned by the Leafs. That gave Ballard a foot in the door.

Ballard owed a great deal to Day. But loyalty and even friendship was forgotten when it came to a power struggle years later between Day and Stafford. When Day was forced to resign in 1957, his friendship with Ballard ended. To those around the Leafs, it was obvious that Ballard had rejected Hap because his old friend was no longer of any value. Howie Meeker, who coached the Leafs in 1956-57, said, "When Harold made that choice, it hurt Hap deeply. He was fighting for his hockey life and he was closest with two people, Connie and Harold."

Many years later Day would say, "Harold had to make up his mind, either to stay close to me or stay close to Stafford. And judging by where he is now, I'd say he made the right decision." Ballard might have disagreed with that observation in 1972 when he finally stood trial on 49 counts of fraud and theft of money, goods, and services worth a total of $205,000. Ballard was convicted of 47 of the 49 charges; he was acquitted on two counts of fraud, one for $11.95 and one for $184.80. In October 1972 he was sentenced to three years in prison.

When he was released the following summer, he was 70 years old. It would have seemed logical to leave the running of the team to his general manager, Jim Gregory, and perhaps spend time in Florida during the winters. Gregory had worked in the Leaf organization for

14 years and had managed the Marlboros before replacing Imlach in 1969. He had experience and seemed reasonably competent.

But Ballard insisted on following in the footsteps of Conn and Stafford. He was eager to have a high profile. He wanted to be the undisputed boss, the all-powerful president and owner, the tough and outspoken hockey man. For decades, he had lived in the shadow of the Smythes, Bassett, and even Imlach. Given his huge ego, his extroverted personality, his immense appetite for public attention, he was not about to pass up the opportunity of becoming a major figure in Canadian sports.

During this period the Leafs had some good young players, the kind clubs hope will someday help them win a championship. Among them were Paul Henderson, Canada's hero in the 1972 series against the Soviet Union; Bernie Parent, a brilliant goaltender; and two young defencemen, Rick Ley and Brad Selwood.

But the Leafs would lose these players and more in the years to come to a rival professional league, the World Hockey Association, which began operation in the fall of 1972. The inept handling of the WHA's threat turned out to be the most devastating blow to the Leafs since the sale of their farm teams in 1967 and 1968.

The Leafs learned in 1971 that Parent was being wooed by the WHA. His contract, which paid him $25,000 a year, expired at the end of the season, and a team called the Miami Screaming Eagles was offering him close to $150,000 annually over five years. When Parent's agent, Howard Casper, a lawyer in Philadelphia, told the Leafs of the proposal, they refused to believe a club would pay a hockey player that kind of money.

Smugly, the Leafs chose to ignore the WHA, feeling that it would never become a reality. When Casper sent a telegram to Ballard asking for a meeting, Ballard ceremoniously tore it up in front of reporters. Casper responded by calling the organization archaic.

The next shoe fell early in 1972 when Parent flew to Miami on a Sunday for a news conference to announce he was signing for the following season. Amazingly, even at that point, the Leafs felt they could stop Parent from leaving. This was mainly because of an NHL rule called the reserve clause, which essentially made a player the property of his team unless he was traded or given his freedom. It was illegal and in the future would be struck down in a court of law. But in 1972 the rule carried weight.

Finally, on the advice of Gregory, Ballard agreed to meet Casper, who flew to Toronto. But Casper says Ballard refused to look at him.

When he outlined the offer put forth by Miami, Ballard laughed at him and said, "Tell him to go and get it. Let him go. I don't want to hold him back." Ballard then repeated the remarks to reporters. At that point, Casper believed Parent was a free man. He said to Robert Sedgewick, Ballard's lawyer, "Bob you've got a dead loser on your hands."

"What do you mean?" asked Sedgewick.

"There's no way in the world you can hold us to the reserve clause. Ballard just said he wouldn't hold him back. He gave Parent his freedom. You guys are dead ducks."

And they were. The Eagles never did get off the ground, but instead a WHA team, with Parent, was established in Philadelphia as the Blazers. Parent, after signing a five-year-deal for $600,000, lasted only one season before returning to the NHL. But he refused to go back to Toronto and forced the Leafs to trade his rights to the Philadelphia Flyers for goaltender Doug Favell and a first round draft choice that was used to take defenceman Bob Neely.

In Parent, the Flyers acquired a man who would lead them to two Stanley Cups, winning the Conn Smythe Trophy both times as the most valuable player in the playoffs. He would win two Vezina Trophies and come to be regarded as one of the finest goaltenders in the history of the league.

Commenting years later on the dispute with the Leafs, Casper said Gregory was not to blame for the failure to sign Parent. "I really had no trouble with Gregory because in my opinion, Gregory was a gentleman. I think Gregory understood the modern world of athletes and the realities. But Ballard didn't want to recognize them. In my opinion, Ballard was going to rule his fiefdom the way he was going to rule his fiefdom and was not going to pay attention to outside agencies, and I think history shows that he was wrong."

Parent was not the only player the Leafs lost. Jim Harrison, a young centre, went to the Alberta Oilers while Ley and Selwood joined the New England Whalers.

The Leafs salvaged something by re-signing captain Dave Keon to a huge contract, worth something well in excess of $100,000 annually. But Keon was 32 and past his prime. Three years later, he would jump to the WHA's Minnesota Fighting Saints. A smart management would have used the money to keep Parent.

Over the years, WHA teams would continue to raid Toronto. Henderson eventually signed with the Toronto Toros. Darryl Sittler, a fine young centre, had actually reached a verbal agreement with

Toros owner John F. Bassett, son of John W., before backing out at the last minute. By the time the WHA merged with the NHL in 1979, the Leaf organization, counting its Central Hockey League affiliate and its junior team, the Marlboros, had lost 18 players.

Despite the setbacks, the Leafs continued with a rebuilding program. In the winter of 1972-73, Gerry McNamara, who recently had been hired as a scout by Gregory, went to Europe to check out Swedish players. He returned with two recommendations, defenceman Borje Salming and forward Inge Hammarstrom. When Red Kelly was fired as coach of the Pittsburgh Penguins, Ballard decided to bring him in as coach of the Leafs for the following year.

In June of 1973 Toronto did well in the draft, picking up right winger Lanny Mcdonald in the first round as well as Neely and Ian Turnbull, a defenceman with good offensive skills. Sittler was showing signs of becoming a star and team leader. For the first time in more than 10 years, there was a nucleus of good young players.

Over the next five years the team steadily improved. But modest gains were achieved within the restrictions of a sometimes circus atmosphere created by Ballard, who showed himself to be a loud and mouthy owner and almost continuously disrupted the team. If the Leafs were playing poorly he would ridicule or denounce a player. It was usually one of the better players, often the captain, or even the coach. Over a period of 15 years, he would force three captains to leave the team, one way or another.

Dan Maloney, who played for the Leafs and later coached the team, once told Allen Abel, a *Globe* columnist, "He's always around. He's in the dressing room, he's on the bus, he's at the hotel." Ballard lived in the arena in a small studio apartment he had built just off his office on the second level. He watched every game from a box, popularly referred to as the bunker, at the north end of the area. And he made every road trip. The team and Gardens employees became his surrogate family. He was the Great Patriarch figure and was treated with great deference by anyone who wished to get ahead in the organization or even keep a job.

The first sign of Ballard's peculiar skill for attracting media attention by way of attacks on the team occurred in November 1974, when he told Lawrence Martin of the *Globe and Mail* that Keon was a weak captain, Kelly was a poor coach, and generally the players were lazy, out of condition, and not committed. He called their playing a "stinking exhibition" and threatened to make a "major trade" for a "team leader." He also ridiculed Hammarstrom, calling him a cowardly player who "could go into the corner with six eggs in his pocket and not break any of them."

In the years to come, Ballard's diatribes became something of a tradition. They usually happened in November when it became apparent things weren't working out as well as had been anticipated. These outbursts had a debilitating effect on team morale. Hammarstrom was hurt and humiliated by Ballard's comments. In the case of Keon, he made up his mind he could no longer work for Ballard and joined the Minnesota Fighting Saints the following year. Kelly's position as coach was undermined.

In the two playoff series in 1976 and 1977 when Toronto was pitted against Philadelphia, Ballard's meddling was at its worst. The Leafs were a young and relatively inexperienced team–and decidedly the underdogs. Still, that didn't inhibit Ballard who told sportswriters that the Leafs were a far better team than the Flyers–the defending Stanley Cup champions in 1976–and were going to "knock 'em off in five games."

It was the kind of pressure the players didn't need. In an attempt to get them thinking about something other than Ballard and his wild boasts, Kelly tried what might be called amateur psychology. In 1976, it was "pyramid power," a theory that purported pyramids sent off waves of energy. The players sat under a huge pyramid hanging from the ceiling of the dressing room, while the hockey sticks were placed under a smaller model. When Sittler had a five-goal game, the story grew to large proportions, but the team still lost the series.

The next year, Ballard continued to issue threats to the Flyers and to predict their early demise. This time, Kelly turned to negative ions, another kind of energizing force, supposedly. It worked for the first two games, both Leaf victories. But then the Leafs went quietly, losing four in a row.

It had become apparent to those around Ballard that he couldn't stand to be left out when the attention shifted to the team. It seemed that he was jealous of the attention given his own team. When things went badly, which was most of the time, there was an obvious absence of tact.

Roger Neilson, who coached the team from 1977 to 1979, remembers Ballard knocking the players in the dressing room. For example, he said to Neilson in front of defenceman Brian Glennie, "Why do you keep that fucking Glennie around? He can't even skate!" Neilson would try to make light of the situation by saying with a laugh, "Hey, he's got the same kind of hair as me."

Ballard might have been envious of Neilson's popularity, as well. When he was hired, Neilson was considered one of the brightest young coaches in the business. He had been a high-school teacher and had coached the Peterborough Petes of the Ontario Hockey Association for 10 years. The Petes had been consistently respectable during this time, never slipping below third in their division.

Neilson taught during practices and believed in preparation, which meant the use of videotapes and statistical information for instructional purposes as well as for scouting. He also placed more emphasis on physical conditioning. Ballard even acceded to Neilson's request for an assistant, Ron Smith.

As it turned out, it was the first and last time Ballard would look outside the organization for someone other than an old friend. His experience with Neilson was something he didn't enjoy. Neilson seemed more interested in building a winning team than spending time with Ballard, flattering him, listening to stories, or laughing at his jokes. This didn't sit well with Ballard. Nor did it go over well when Neilson began receiving a lot of media attention. The newspapers called him Captain Video because of his use of video-tapes. The players raved about their innovative new coach. For the first time, they had a modern man behind the bench.

Ballard, of course, was resourceful enough to hold his own in any battle for media exposure. In February, with the team on its way to a very good season, he called some of his players "garbage" and said that he–not general manager Jim Gregory–was attempting to unload this garbage. The untouchables, he said, were Sittler, McDonald, Salming, and Turnbull.

Ballard also began to impose himself more on the operational aspects of the club. In those days a committee met periodically to decide strategies, which included trades. The committee during Neilson's time was made up of Gregory, McLellan, scouts Johnny Bower and Gerry McNamara, the coach, Ballard, and his most recent best friend, Clancy, who was the vice-president of Maple Leaf Gardens Ltd.

During a postseason meeting, Neilson argued strongly that Turnbull be traded. In the 1978 playoffs against the Islanders, with Salming hurt, Turnbull had been outstanding, playing probably the best hockey of his career. His value would never be higher, and

Neilson felt that was the time to move him. Despite his strong offensive skills, Turnbull was unpredictable on the ice and weak defensively. As it turned out, Neilson's hunch was correct because Turnbull never played well again.

But Ballard happened to like Turnbull. The logic in moving him and the problems with him as a player were not important considerations. Finally, as Neilson pressed, Ballard said, "Let's get something straight–I wouldn't trade Ian Turnbull for God."

With Ballard's declaration, Al Dunford, a young man who assisted Neilson with travel arrangements and game preparation, leaned around the corner from his cubicle and said to no one in particular, "How about God and a fourth-round draft choice?" The committee members snickered. Ballard seethed.

Ballard had only grudgingly agreed to hire Dunford. In Neilson's first season he had looked after travel arrangements, videotapes, and statistical information himself. It had become too much of a burden, and Dunford, who had played for Neilson in Peterborough, and worked as his assistant, seemed ideal for the job. Finally Ballard agreed to bring him in, at $400 a week.

But Dunford's wisecrack got him off on the wrong foot. Another mistake was in failing to defer to Ballard. The others did, in various degrees, but Dunford pretty much ignored him, and went about his job. He was a quiet man who was well liked by everyone except Ballard, who started bullying him.

Ballard called him the "fucking cruise director." When a flight was delayed because of bad weather, Ballard said in a loud voice, "Will the fucking cruise director please tell us how long it's going to continue snowing. And how the hell we're going to get to Denver?" On another occasion, within earshot of Dunford at an airport, Ballard said "What do we need this guy for? Why are we paying $1000 to have him around on the trip?"

Dunford didn't know how to respond. Ballard was his boss, and, out of loyalty to Neilson, Dunford didn't want to resign. But the putdowns were undeserved and they hurt. Dunford quickly learned to dislike Ballard. Once, after a loss, Ballard yelled at Dunford, who was boarding the team bus with a video cassette recorder and pages of statistical information, saying, "The game's over for Christ's sake. What are you going to learn from those goddam things now?"

This time Dunford did react, with a brief explanation of his duties. But that wasn't enough for Ballard, who replied, "You're just about the dumbest son of a bitch I've ever run into."

"I guess you're right," Dunford said. "I'd have to be pretty dumb to take your bullshit."

Ballard then went to Gregory and told him to fire Dunford when the team returned to Toronto. An appeal by Neilson stayed Dunford's execution, but a few weeks later both lost their jobs—temporarily.

With the Leafs hovering around the .500 mark in February, Ballard told his two best media friends, Milt Dunnell and George Gross, that Neilson would be fired if the team lost in Montreal the following night. That morning, Gross led off with, "Goodbye Roger. . . ." Ballard told the *Globe* the next day, "Roger placed too much emphasis on videotapes and statistics. He's a school teacher, a nice fellow who handled kids all his life. But the novelty of schoolboy hockey has worn off."

The Leafs did lose in Montreal, and, true to his word, Ballard told journalist Dick Beddoes, who at that time was working on the Leaf television broadcasts, that Neilson was finished. This was done on the air, right after the game. But Ballard had failed to solve the second part of the equation. He did not have a replacement. The Blackhawks refused to release Eddie Johnston, the coach of the AHL team in Moncton shared by Toronto and Chicago. When McNamara, who had coached the Leafs' Central Hockey League affiliate a few years earlier, was asked to go behind the bench, he declined. Then later, the players, led by their captain, Darryl Sittler, met Ballard and told him they wanted Neilson back.

Ballard really had no other option but to reinstate Neilson. What he hoped to do was make the whole thing appear as if it had been a hoax, contrived right from the start. With everybody unaware of who would be the coach for the next game, Neilson would go behind the bench with a bag over his head. Before the drop of the puck, he would pull it off. Minutes before game time, Gregory tried to talk Neilson into going along with the charade.

"Look, he's got you back in," Gregory said. "Why don't you do it for the reporters. They'll have their story and that'll be it."

Tired and under pressure for several days, Neilson was ready to do it, until Dunford took him aside and said, "Look, you can't. Right now, you're coming out of this thing looking pretty good. But if you do that, you'll just be part of the circus."

When he refused, Gregory said, "Okay, but you've got to tell Ballard."

Neilson did, and nothing was said. The single most aggravating element of Neilson's return for Ballard was accepting Dunford as well. Fifteen minutes before the start of the game, Ballard said, "I suppose I'll have to take back the fucking cruise director."

There was one final humiliation for Dunford. Ballard kicked him out of the hockey office, took away his telephone, and made him work out of a room in the basement of the arena. This would last for only a few months. When the season ended, the whole gang was fired–Neilson, Gregory, Smith, and of course Dunford. Not that they deserved it. The real problem was the owner, whose attitudes and reputation were continuing to pull the team down.

When McNamara made his Swedish scouting trip in the winter of 1972-73, he was on the cutting edge of the NHL's involvement in the European market. His major find, Salming, became one of the two best Europeans to play in the NHL, the other being Jari Kurri of the Edmonton Oilers.

But after McNamara's trip to Sweden, the Leafs pulled out, opting not to establish a scouting base in Europe. This was a missed opportunity that became most obvious in the 1980s when winning organizations such as the Islanders, the Oilers, and the Canadiens spent large amounts of money scouting Europe. Each of these teams had two or three key European players on rosters that won Stanley Cups. Other than Salming the Leafs had no quality Europeans.

Gregory says that there was no official decree from Ballard stipulating that Europeans were not welcome. But Gregory doesn't deny there was an implicit understanding that the owner didn't want to spend money scouting Europe; 1974, after all, was the last time the Leafs drafted a Swede until 1988. In 1974, Per Alexandersson received a large amount of publicity prior to training camp. But he turned out to be a bust and never played a game in the NHL.

This gave Ballard additional ammunition for shots at Swedish players. He continuously put down Hammarstrom as a coward, even after he was traded. He often said publicly he figured Swedes were chickens who were afraid to fight and play the game like real men.

There was an eventual irony to this, because the success of the Leafs in the 1978-79 season hinged on the acquisition of two Swedish free agents from the Winnipeg Jets of the WHA. Anders Hedberg, a right winger, and Ulf Nilsson, a centre, were two world-class forwards who had played four years in Winnipeg. With Hull on the left side, their line had become one of the most exciting and talented in hockey.

When the contracts of Hedberg and Nilsson expired at the end of the 1977-78 season, they made a decision to jump into the NHL, sensing that a merger between the two leagues was imminent. As free agents, they were in a position to sign with any team in the league for the highest price.

The Leafs had just completed their most successful season during Ballard's ownership, with 41 wins, 29 losses, and 10 ties. In the playoffs they had upset the Islanders before losing in the semi-finals to the Canadiens. This was the farthest the team, with Ballard as owner, had advanced in the playoffs.

The Leafs, with Neilson in his first year behind the bench, were a tough, defensively oriented team. They had a good goaltender in Mike Palmateer. The defence was strong, the key players being Salming, Turnbull, Randy Carlyle, and Trevor Johansen. Up front, Sittler had completed an outstanding season with 117 points (45 goals and 72 assists). McDonald, after a slow start to his career, had developed into a goal scorer. He had 47 that year. In addition to his strong defensive work, the veteran Ron Ellis scored 26 goals.

Complementing this core was an amalgam of grinders, checkers, and fighters, such as Dave (Tiger) Williams, Pat Boutette, Jimmy Jones, Stan Weir, and Dan Maloney. These were role players who worked hard and played effectively within Neilson's disciplined system.

But what the Leafs needed to put them over the top, to seriously contend for a Stanley Cup, were more skilled players, particularly at the forward positions. Nilsson and Hedberg would have fit in perfectly. The club expressed interest in the two Swedes, and their wives visited Toronto. But contrasted with the promotional strategy of the New York Rangers, the Leaf effort lacked both sophistication and preparation.

Bill Jennings, then the president of the Rangers, enlisted the help of a prominent Swedish businessman, Bengt Fasth, who was the vice-president of the Swedish-American Chamber of Commerce. Fasth showed Hedberg and Nilsson everything New York had to offer—the best residential areas, such as Scarsdale, where Nilsson still lives; the neighbourhoods that included affluent Swedish-Americans; and the best schools. They saw the parks and the exclusive shopping areas of Manhattan. The wives' concerns about crime in the city were allayed. The promotional and business opportunities were outlined comprehensively by Fasth.

Ballard did not feel it necessary to promote his team or the city.

And despite the prosperity of Maple Leaf Gardens Ltd. Ballard refused to offer anything close to what the Rangers put on the table, which was a $1 million (U.S.) contract over three years for each player. As well, some gaping tax loop-holes were made available by the Rangers' parent company, Gulf and Western. When the contracts expired, each player had paid out only five per cent in taxes.

What should be remembered, however, is that Hedberg and Nilsson wanted to play in Toronto. They liked the city and viewed the Leafs as a team very close to being a Stanley Cup contender. Asked about the possibility of the Leafs signing them, Nilsson says now, "They should have done it. We were very interested."

But in addition to all the other considerations, the Swedes weren't impressed with Ballard. They had heard and read his denouncements of Swedes. They were well aware of the circumstances that led to countryman Hammarstrom's fall from grace and his trade. They had been around Ballard in the past, and what they saw they didn't like. He told racist jokes. He called blacks "niggers," Jews "sheenies," and Poles "polacks."

"He was a little bit like George Steinbrenner," Nilsson said, in reference to the New York Yankees owner. "I don't know if that kind of personality should have been running a professional sports team. It's really sad. A hockey town like Toronto deserves a better owner and better person running the hockey club."

It's impossible to tell what the Leafs would have accomplished with Hedberg and Nilsson in the lineup. Without them they had a very average season in 1978-79. In the quarter-finals of the playoffs they were swept in four games by the Canadiens.

In New York, Hedberg and Nilsson played well, although Nilsson broke his ankle in the second half of the season and missed 23 games. Hedberg had 33 goals and 45 assists in 80 games, Nilsson 27 and 33 in 57. In the playoffs the Rangers went all the way to the Stanley Cup final before losing to the Canadiens.

The Rangers at that point were an interesting team that included the veteran Phil Esposito along with excellent young players such as Don Murdoch, Ron Duguay, Dave Maloney, and Don Maloney. For the first time in years, the team started selling out in Madison Square Garden. Hedberg and Nilsson were two of the reasons that this happened. In Toronto, of course, filling the Gardens to capacity was never a problem nor a consideration when it came to recruiting players.

In addition to a reluctance to spend money on free agents, there was a gradual reduction of personnel in the Leaf hockey office during the latter part of the 1970s. In 1978, Davidson, at the age of 66, was forced to resign as senior scout when Ballard cut his salary by two-thirds. He wasn't replaced. When Gregory's assistant general manager, John McLellan, died in 1979 of a heart attack, he wasn't replaced. This diminished an already small staff of scouts and hockey executives.

In assessing Gregory's 10 years as Leaf general manager, it is unfair to hold him accountable for these things, just as it is unfair to lay all the blame for the team's failure in the 1980s on McNamara. Gregory was able to build the team up to a certain level–a much higher level than was reached during McNamara's term. Gregory and his staff acquired some excellent players–Sittler, McDonald, Salming, and Palmateer were some of them. He had brought in a young man with progressive ideas to coach the team. It was the right thing to do, but more than anything else, it is probably what caused his dismissal.

Where Gregory can be faulted is in the trades he made. He sent Randy Carlyle and centre George Ferguson to Pittsburgh for defenceman Dave Burrows–a terrible trade. While in Toronto, Carlyle was young, single, kept late hours, and enjoyed bachelor life. He also had a few mishaps with his automobile. Gregory once told a friend he simply got sick of receiving late-night distress calls from Carlyle. But Carlyle was talented, and with the Penguins matured to become an all-star. In 1981, he won the Norris Trophy as the league's best defenceman. Gregory thought he was getting a tough, defensively strong player in Burrows. But Burrows was neither tough nor effective defensively in Toronto.

Then there was the Dan Maloney trade, made in March 1978 with Detroit. For several years, Errol Thompson had been the team's best left winger. In fact for one season, 1975-76, the Leafs might have had the best forward line in the league with Sittler between Thompson and McDonald. Thompson had 43 goals, Sittler 41, and McDonald 37. Thompson was an outstanding skater and had an excellent shot. But he was weak defensively and had trouble playing Neilson's defensive system. Neilson felt he should be moved if the right deal could be made.

Maloney was considered to be among the toughest players and best fighters in the league. Many times Ballard had said Maloney was just the kind of guy the Leafs needed. But when he came available he was almost 28. His best years were behind him and he could no longer fight with any effectiveness because of damaged hands.

In addition to Thompson, the Leafs sent to the Red Wings two first-round draft choices, neither of which the Red Wings put to good use. They took Brent Peterson with one and Mike Blaisdell with the other. There was also a swap of second-rounders. Still, the Leafs grossly overrated Maloney and paid too high a price.

Perhaps the most puzzling trade by Gregory was with Montreal. In 1975, Gregory sent centre Doug Jarvis to the Canadiens for defenceman Greg Hubick immediately after taking Jarvis in the second round of the entry draft. Hubick turned out to be a minor-leaguer who played one below-average season in Toronto. Jarvis, on the other hand, was a fine player who went on to become an important member of the Canadiens' four Stanley Cup teams as a defensive specialist.

8

PUNCH IMLACH'S
BACK IN TOWN

I t can be said now that the idea was a good one. First you hire the best general manager available. Then you bring in a coach with equally impressive qualifications. To Ballard's credit that seemed to be his plan in the spring of 1979, after he had fired Gregory and Neilson. For the post of general manager, he wanted Scotty Bowman. After a coaching career, first with the Blues and then the Canadiens where his teams won six Stanley Cups, Bowman decided to seek a general managing position. He was a brilliant hockey man and few doubted his ability to be a first-rate executive.

Bowman had been told that Ballard might find a replacement for Gregory at the end of the season. But he had heard a much more intriguing rumour, one that made him feel that the Leafs would be the perfect team to manage and Toronto the ideal city in which to live. The rumour suggested that Ballard was about to sell the club to the Eatons, the wealthy Toronto family of department store fame.

If Bowman had known Ballard better he would have realized this would never happen, because of the Eatons' close relationship with John W. Bassett. John David Eaton had bankrolled Bassett when he had bought the *Telegram* years earlier, and the two families had been close ever since. As far as Ballard was concerned any friend of Bassett was an enemy of his. Shortly after he took control of the Gardens, he broke up a block of tickets owned by the two families and dispersed them to different areas of the arena. The Bassetts and the Eatons sold their tickets and never returned.

With a stable ownership, Bowman would have accepted the Leaf managing job. But with Ballard still there he quietly scratched Toronto off his list, although he didn't stop using Ballard as a bargaining chip in negotiations with the Buffalo Sabres. Ballard continued to pursue Bowman, who listened, but ultimately signed with the Sabres. Bowman's first move in Buffalo was to hire Neilson as associate coach. Ballard was furious, feeling he had been used by Bowman and then embarrassed by Bowman's hiring a coach Ballard had dismissed for incompetence. "I've never been jacked around so much in my life," Ballard said.

For coach, Ballard wanted Don Cherry. During five years in Boston, Cherry had taken the Bruins to two Stanley Cup finals. He was colourful and outspoken, but he didn't get along with Harry Sinden, which is why he was fired at the end of 1978-79. But Ballard was too late. Cherry, considered one of the best coaches in the league, already had agreed to join the Colorado Rockies.

Ballard could have continued his search. With the help of others, he could have prepared a list of the best candidates for general manager. He could have interviewed them, listened to their ideas, and then made his decision. But instead he turned to an old friend, someone he knew and felt comfortable with–Punch Imlach.

After being dismissed by the Leafs, Imlach had been hired in 1970 to manage the Buffalo Sabres, which were an expansion franchise. He did an outstanding job, quickly building the team into a Stanley Cup contender that advanced to the final in 1975.

But after the trip to the final, the team gradually declined, and Imlach's relationship with the Sabre owners, Seymour and Northrup Knox, as well as with the players and the Buffalo media, deteriorated. In his final season with the Sabres, Imlach antagonized the Knoxes by refusing to allow the Sabres to play an exhibition game against a team from the Soviet Union. He interfered in the coaching of the team by visiting the dressing room between periods to criticize players. And he carried on a feud with a reporter who covered the team for the Buffalo *Courier-Express*.

Just before Imlach's dismissal, a delegation of players including Craig Ramsay and Danny Gare went to Seymour Knox and told him they would no longer play for Imlach. That seemed to be the deciding factor. Imlach was fired in December along with his coach, Marcel Pronovost.

Imlach was one of the true giants of the game. But in his role as a hockey executive, he was neither a compromiser nor a diplomat, whether it was with owners or players. This factor and his abrasiveness had earlier soured his relationship with Stafford Smythe, who had much the same personality, as it did now with the Knoxes. In the handling of players, Imlach came from the Conn Smythe school which taught coaches that players did what they were told and were not to ask questions. Imlach was tough, unyielding, and often insensitive. Just the man for Ballard.

When Ballard decided to bring back Imlach he was hoping for a return to the wonderful 1960s. Instead, he got a man who was in poor health and out of touch with the realities of hockey in the 1980s. Imlach lasted only two years, but in that time he tore apart what had been a reasonably good team.

Some people would say later that the Leafs were on the verge of being a Cup contender before Imlach dismantled them. But that is unrealistic. They were a .500 team with four or five good players, most of whom were starting to get old. Still, there was cohesiveness, leadership, and pride–three elements many teams lacked. They were things worth keeping and building upon. Instead, Imlach destroyed these things. He belittled the team in the news conference announcing his appointment. He said the players lacked talent and that there was a country-club atmosphere. Then he alienated the captain, Sittler, and Palmateer before the season started by refusing to allow their participation in a between-periods television program called "Showdown."

This was a skill-testing exercise that had been endorsed by the NHLPA, headed by Eagleson and the NHL owners. Imlach said he was worried about players getting injured, but others felt it was another example of the on-going feud with Eagleson. Whatever the motivation, Imlach persisted, and even applied for a court injunction to stop the two players from participating. Sittler and Palmateer did compete, but by then the sides were drawn up and the stage set for a rancorous 1979-80 season.

Imlach decided he would hold the dual positions of general manager and coach, although he was coach in title only. Doing the actual work was Floyd Smith, who had played and later coached for Imlach in Buffalo, as well as Joe Crozier, an old friend and former coach in Buffalo, and Dick Duff, who had had a brief coaching career in junior hockey. They were all Imlach men and loyal.

The next bit of trouble occurred at training camp, when Imlach did things that seemed to accomplish little except to increase the tension between management and players. He removed the ping-pong table from the dressing room. (The Oilers have had one in their room for years and it hasn't hurt their performance.) He disallowed beer in the dressing room or on the bus. Players couldn't use the telephone in the dressing room, but had to go through the Gardens switchboard. When the team started off poorly, he put the two stars–Sittler and McDonald–on recallable waivers, which was widely reported.

The animosity steadily grew and then reached a peak in early November, when Imlach said on a radio show that Sittler had lost a step and was "tradeable for any member of the all-star team." Indeed, Sittler, at 29, had slowed down, and a trade for an all-star might have been a good move. But it was a stupid and insensitive comment to make about the captain of the team, and it prompted Sittler, for the first time, to speak out publicly against Imlach.

Bitterly, he said there was no communication between players and management. He said most of his teammates had never spoken to Imlach, and that the dressing-room rules were examples of Imlach's lack of regard for the players. Ballard had been relegated mostly to second billing during the Imlach-Sittler problems. But a few days after Sittler's remarks, he was back across the top of the sports pages, lashing back at Sittler, saying Imlach wasn't about to "hold his hand or give him a sucker to play." He said Imlach had been right in establishing new dressing-room rules. "It's time we got rid of these childish innovations and buckled down to win some games," he said.

Despite Ballard's best efforts, however, a large part of the fight that season did not directly involve him or his players. Instead, it was an opportunity for two old enemies–Imlach and Eagleson–to resume hostilities. It's probably fair to say that Eagleson represented most things in hockey that Imlach disliked, the two most important being players' rights and the growth of player representation.

By the late 1970s, Eagleson, in addition to his position as head of the NHLPA, was Canada's top negotiator for international hockey. He was also the leading agent in the hockey business. In Toronto he represented seven Leaf players, the big three being Sittler, Palmateer, and McDonald. He was considered the most powerful man in the hockey business.

After "Showdown," the next dispute involving Eagleson occurred in December, when Ballard took it upon himself to organize an exhibition game in February between the Leafs and the Canadian Olympic team, the revenue from which would go to a charity. It meant that the Leafs would play four games in five nights, and for those in the all-star game, five in six nights. Although agreement was needed from the players, Ballard had gone ahead without them.

When the players were told of the proposal on the morning of the news conference, they called Eagleson. They weren't enthusiastic about playing another hockey game in an already long season, but they knew they would be criticized if they didn't. Instead, they hoped to work out a compromise. In return for participation, the Leafs and Eagleson wanted Ballard to agree to an exhibition game the following season with a team from the Soviet Union.

Ballard had been opposed to playing the Soviet Union for some time, although back in 1972 he had taken great interest in the first series, donating the use of the Gardens for Team Canada's training, and travelling to the Soviet Union for the final four games. But in the intervening years, he had grown to hate the Soviet Union, referring to their hockey people as "parasites who steal our money." Still, some players on the Leafs, who were not good enough to play for Canada in international events, had always wanted the opportunity of competing against a Soviet team. Tiger Williams was one.

When the news conference started, Sittler stood up and asked Eagleson to read a statement, which outlined the players' demands and was signed by Sittler, Salming, and Palmateer. As well as the Soviet game, the Leafs wanted the exhibition game with the Soviets to be arranged in such a manner that the teams exchanged defensive pairings and goaltenders.

Ballard was stunned by the ultimatum. Never had a Leaf owner been confronted by players in such an aggressive way. When he finally stood up, he reiterated his opposition to playing the Soviet game, saying, "But if this is the situation, I'll have to swallow my pride and accept it." A few minutes later, however, he changed his mind and said he would never allow it to happen. The Olympic game was scratched as well.

The consequences of this were considerable. It heightened Ballard's anti-Soviet and anti-Eagleson sentiments, but the more immediate result was an intense dislike for Sittler. There had been a time when Ballard had viewed his captain as another son. He called himself Sittler's biggest fan. A large portrait of his hero hung in his office. But now Sittler was a man who had betrayed him–publicly no less–before the media.

A few days later, Imlach made his move, which was to start breaking up the team. Pat Boutette, a hard-working winger who had supported Sittler, perhaps too vocally, especially in front of Smith, was traded to Hartford for a player by the name of Bob Stephenson who played 14 games and was never seen or heard from again in the NHL.

Then, two weeks later, the blockbuster came. McDonald and defenceman Joel Quenneville went to the Colorado Rockies for wingers Pat Hickey and Wilf Paiement. Imlach made some bad deals during his second term in Toronto, but this was by far the worst. It was done not so much out of an urgency to improve the team, but more to hurt Sittler, to take away his support, to leave him vulnerable. Imlach would have traded Sittler as quickly as possible, but he couldn't because of a no-trade clause in his contract. From Imlach's perspective, the alternative was to move Sittler's best friend.

The trade outraged the Leaf fans in Toronto, and when Sittler was told, he wept. In the dressing room before the next game, he cut the C off his sweater and had a statement released to the media renouncing his captaincy. In the statement, he said the club had attempted to sue him over the "Showdown" incident, a reference to the court injunction; that he had been barred from "Hockey Night in Canada" by Imlach; and that he had been the brunt of criticisms from Imlach.

If anything, this reinforced Imlach's conviction that more changes were needed. The next player to be moved out was Dave Hutchison, who, not surprisingly, was another friend of Sittler's. On the day of that trade, some of the Leafs met at a bar near the Gardens, tore a picture of Imlach out of a newspaper, pinned it to a dart board, and started firing away. Jim Kernaghan, a hockey reporter for the *Star,* happened to come along and was invited in on the provision he not publish the names of the players in attendance.

The story in the *Star,* in which the players attacked Imlach mercilessly, evoked enormous response. Media friends of Imlach's from the 1960s felt it had been wrong to report the players' remarks without giving their names. To others it was an indication of just how badly team morale had deteriorated. One player said Imlach "was responsible for the destruction of a franchise. We don't quite know what he's doing except he's proving one thing. He is the boss. There is only one way this team can go under the circumstances. Down."

In February, Imlach made his first good trade, although at the time the team lost two of its hardest workers in Jerry Butler and Williams, who also was a leader. They went to the Vancouver Canucks for two young players, Rick Vaive and Bill Derlago. Derlago, a centre, would have some fairly good years in Toronto. Vaive, a right winger, matured to become one of the best goal-scorers in the NHL and the first Leaf to score 50 in a season.

But despite the trades and the accusations hurled back and forth, probably the most distasteful element of the 1979-80 war were the attacks by Ballard on Sittler. When Sittler resigned as captain, Ballard saw it as another slap at him from an ungrateful employee, and he made Sittler pay for it. He started denouncing Sittler as a "cancer"–a sort of malignant tumour that had to be removed from the team. He said it repeatedly and the public attacks took their toll, on Sittler as well as his wife and his children, who were school age and had to endure schoolyard confrontations over their father, the disgraced Leaf.

Obviously unhappy, Sittler appeared to withdraw. At the Gardens he rarely talked and seemed emotionally exhausted. At a charity function during the winter he broke down and wept as he sat in the audience listening to a handicapped girl describe her life. Photographs were taken and the picture was displayed prominently in the *Star,* along with a story. At one point, Imlach called him into his office and suggested he remove himself from the team and perhaps spend some time in Florida. Sittler refused, feeling it was a ploy to get him away from the Leafs. He also suspected that media people close to Imlach would be told that he had suffered a breakdown, although there was no evidence that this was Imlach's intent, and many felt that Sittler was, indeed, in a state of depression.

Before the season ended, Floyd Smith suffered a breakdown of his own, but it was definitely physical. His car went out of control outside St. Catharines, causing the two deaths and his conviction of impaired driving. While Smith was in hospital, Dick Duff went behind the bench, and then Crozier. The players didn't like either one, and said so.

By season's end, the team was a shambles even though its win-loss-tie record of 35-40-5 did not reflect a sharp decline from the previous year. There had been a drop of only six points. Still, the slide was on its way. And the incline was getting steeper. There are those who feel Imlach deliberately destroyed the team out of some feeling of revenge for his dismissal in 1969. But given Imlach's ego, that doesn't make sense. What he really wanted to do was to come in and make the Leafs a winner and then take the credit. But it had to be done by his people and his players.

Sittler, McDonald, and the others were products of the Gregory years, and it was widely known that Imlach held Gregory in contempt. He felt he had been undermined by Gregory in the late 1960s and had not considered him a worthy successor. With Gregory gone and Imlach back in charge, the Leafs had to be Imlach's creation and could not be tainted by the mediocrity of the past.

But Imlach never did get his chance to rebuild. That summer his power slipped away. After Imlach failed to sign Salming to a new contract in Sweden, Ballard negotiated the deal himself, agreeing to pay him $300,000 a year. In August, Imlach suffered his second heart attack, which was caused, he felt, by stress from reading information leaked by Ballard to the newspapers about trade negotiations between the Leafs and the Calgary Flames regarding Sittler.

While Imlach was in hospital, Ballard called a news conference to announce he had made peace with Sittler. Imlach was stunned when he read this, given the events that had occurred over the winter. A few weeks later, Ballard returned the captaincy to Sittler. Then comments from Ballard to the effect that Imlach was no longer in charge began to appear in the newspapers. Ballard was quoted in the *Sun* as saying: "The job's his, depending on what the doctors say. Sure I want him back, but I don't want to be the one to put him in a box. I'm going to be the one in control of things and if the players want to argue instead of playing hockey they'll get an earful from me."

This was a key period in the Ballard years because it signalled a change in how the front office operated. During Gregory's watch, Ballard interfered, meddled, held the purse strings, and made a lot of noise. But Gregory still ran the hockey operation, as it were. He signed the players and made the trades.

But with Imlach in the hospital and perhaps unable to continue, Ballard essentially took over as general manager, and he was very visible in exercising his mandate. There was the Salming signing and the peace with Sittler. It was obvious, too, that Ballard had turned against Imlach, which didn't seem to make sense, given Ballard's strong support during the winter.

In the case of Imlach, Ballard might have looked back to the previous season and the turmoil, and decided he didn't want any more of it, unless of course he was the one causing the turmoil. Imlach had traded away some of Ballard's favourite players, particularly McDonald and Williams. Williams had always sat with Ballard on the team bus and chartered flights. He would tell Ballard dirty jokes and they would laugh uproariously. It's probably true, as well, that Ballard didn't like the idea of his general manager having total control. Unlike Gregory, Imlach did exactly what he wanted and then informed Ballard.

When Imlach did return to work, he had no real power. Joe Crozier started the season behind the bench and the team got off to a quick start—something that would become almost a characteristic of Leaf teams in the years to come—with six victories in their first eight games. But then they fell apart. By mid-December, Crozier, a tough and aggressive coach, was telling the media that all he wanted for Christmas was a team leader. This was an obvious shot at Sittler, who wasn't playing well. The man in trouble, however, was Crozier.

In early January, with the team in terrible shape, Ballard decided Crozier had to go. Imlach had no say in the matter, nor was he able to select a replacement. He favoured Doug Carpenter, a successful junior coach who was then coaching the Leafs' minor-league team in Moncton. But Ballard said no. He wanted to bring in a friend, someone he'd feel comfortable with. He chose Mike Nykoluk—who had no experience as a head coach.

Nykoluk and Ballard went back to the mid-1950s when Nykoluk had been captain of the 1955 Marlboro team that had won the Memorial Cup. As president of the Marlies, Ballard once had to get Mike's brother Danny, later a lineman with the Toronto Argonauts of the Canadian Football League, out of a Guelph jail after a fight in the stands during a playoff game. Nykoluk played 32 games with the Leafs in 1956-57 but the remainder of his career was in the minors. It was in Winnipeg of the old Western Hockey League that he met and befriended Fred Shero, a minor-league defenceman. Years later, when Shero took over as coach of the Flyers, he remembered Nykoluk and brought him in as his assistant.

After six years and two championships in Philadelphia, Shero jumped to the Rangers as coach and general manager. Again Nykoluk followed him as his assistant. Nykoluk claimed later he had been promised the coaching job after a period of a year or two, at which time Shero would limit his involvement to managing. But things didn't work out in New York. The team struggled and it was decided Shero would stay behind the bench. Feeling that he had been misled, Nykoluk quit and returned to his hometown of Toronto to take a job as colour commentator on the Leaf radio broadcasts.

Ballard and Nykoluk had been friends for years and they became closer during the 1980-81 season. When the team travelled, Nykoluk would pick up Ballard and drive him to the airport. Nykoluk was always hanging around the Gardens. He would watch the Leaf practices and say, "You know, Joe says he has a system. But I don't see it."

Nykoluk wanted Crozier's job, but when he got it, there were real questions about his own ability. In his final year in Philadelphia, Keith Allen, the general manager, had removed him as Shero's assistant and appointed him co-ordinator of player development. The implication at the time was that Nykoluk was not performing adequately as an assistant. In New York, of course, the hierarchy was against his taking over from Shero.

Nykoluk was a big, friendly, easy-going man. He had a soft voice and a soft personality. In stressful situations, such as facing an unwanted question from a reporter, his voice would rise and take on a whiney tone. He appeared to lack sharpness and decisiveness. When he talked, there were a lot of likes and you knows–"Like, you know, we gotta get the kids playing more." Needless to say, he was a sharp contrast to Crozier, a high-strung disciplinarian.

He didn't seem to have any real answers to the Leaf problems, except that "the kids" had to play. The young players he was referring to included Laurie Boschman, a young centre drafted high (ninth over all) in 1979; John Anderson, a winger and high draft in 1977; Rocky Saganiuk, another winger and second rounder in 1977; and Vaive and Derlago.

Nykoluk did set up an advisory committee of players. Maloney was appointed his playing assistant, and Turnbull, Salming, and Ellis were made alternative captains. There was some improvement, but not much. Sittler had a good year, as did Paiement, Vaive, and Derlago. But the team was weak defensively. This, in fact, was the beginning of the team's inept defensive work, both on the blueline and in goal.

With Nykoluk behind the bench, the Leafs had a record of 15-15-10, compared to Crozier's mark of 13-22-5. For the season, they finished in last place in the Adams Division, sixth from the bottom of the league. And for the first time in the team's history, it had won fewer than 30 games in an 80-game schedule. Morale was low, and there was no confidence in the management or coaching.

In fact, many players sensed it was going to get worse. Among them was Sittler, who made a decision during the summer that, finally, he would leave Toronto, but on his own terms. He had won the war with Imlach, and now before his career ended, he wanted to play for a good team with the hope of winning a Stanley Cup.

In September, during the rookie training camp in St. Catharines, Imlach suffered his second heart attack in a little more than a year. He was taken to hospital and then he underwent triple-bypass surgery. There was no visit from Ballard, no get-well card, no communication at all. Imlach was told later that Ballard ordered employees not to visit him. One morning, during his recovery, he was handed a copy of the Toronto *Sun*, which said he was finished as Leaf general manager. Ballard was quoted as saying: "I'm not going to have Punch back as my general manager." Later it was reported that Imlach's name had been removed from his parking spot outside the Gardens.

When Imlach was released he visited Ballard, when he felt well enough, to determine where he stood. During the meeting, Ballard suggested to Imlach he should retire. When that was rejected, Ballard offered him a position as an adviser, which he also refused. And so, with uncharacteristic quietness, the second Imlach era came to an end. It had been a crisis-ridden period, but the years ahead would be worse.

9

Ballard
and His Broads

Those who knew Ballard's wife, Dorothy, describe her as attractive, refined, warm and without pretensions. She was, in many ways, an unlikely partner for Harold, the rough, unsophisticated sportsman, who had little education, drank, and often made a fool of himself.

Still, Ballard had come from a wealthy family. His father, Sidney, was a Toronto industrialist who invented and manufactured the Ballard Straight-Knife Cloth-Cutting Machine for the garment trade, in addition to manufacturing ice skates. Before the First World War, he owned a small factory in the heart of the city. By the 1930s he was a millionaire.

As a young man, Harold drove around town in a Pierce Arrow roadster and was a regular at dancehalls such as the Palais Royale on Sunnyside Beach and the Silver Slipper on the Humber River. In the summer, he raced motor boats on Lake Ontario and in the winter he did some speed skating. This was before his involvement in hockey. Good-looking and with a certain charm, he was one of the city's more eligible bachelors.

At a dance in 1924, Ballard met Dorothy Higgs. Dorothy, a 17-year-old nurse in training in Wellesley Hospital, was escorted by a young man who later became a prominent politician, but after being introduced to Ballard she spent the remainder of the evening dancing only with him. Harold reminded Dorothy of her father, who was big, outgoing, and cheerful. The Reverend William Higgs was a

Methodist minister who served communities in the Belleville, Ontario, area. There were four children in the family–a boy and three girls–and there wasn't much money. Dorothy had hoped to attend university and study English literature, but because of financial considerations she took nursing at Wellesley.

Her courtship with Ballard lasted 17 years. She nursed at Wellesley, and Ballard, when he wasn't tied up in hockey matters, worked in his father's business. After the death of Sidney in 1936, Ballard ran the company on a smaller scale on Maude Street between Adelaide Street and Richmond Street, selling and repairing sewing machines for Spadina's garment district.

Suddenly, in the fall of 1941, Dorothy got a telephone call from Harold. At the age of 38 he had decided to get married. So, in November there was a wedding, held at the Avondale United Church in Tillsonburg in southwestern Ontario, where one of Dorothy's sisters lived. The reception was held in her home.

After a brief honeymoon in Niagara Falls, they moved to a new home on Montgomery Road in Etobicoke. Ballard had purchased property there and built a large, comfortable house. In 1942 Mary Elizabeth was born. She was followed by Bill in 1946 and Harold Junior a year later. By appearances at least, the Ballards were a normal, happy upper-middle-class family. The children were bright, good-looking, and well educated.

But in the mid-1960s, any pretext of an idyllic family life ended forever when Dorothy discovered she had cancer. When she died in 1969, Mary Elizabeth says Ballard grieved for weeks, often weeping. There are those who say Ballard loved Dorothy considerably more posthumously. During their marriage, he was often away from home with Stafford and the team, and indulged in a lot of partying with Smythe. Still, after her death, he felt he could no longer live at the Montgomery Road home, with its memories, and chose instead to move to the Gardens where he had a studio apartment built on the second floor, behind his office.

It took him years, apparently, to get over his wife's death. In the summer, when he had trouble sleeping at night, he would drive out to her grave at Park Lawn Cemetery and sit there in a lawn chair for most of the night. When nearby residents reported a large figure roaming the area, it turned out to be Ballard.

When he got out of prison he dated several women, including Sylvia Train, a gossip columnist at the Toronto *Sun,* and Ruth Sullivan, who struck up a relationship with him by writing him letters while he was in prison and then went to see him after he got out.

When Ballard wanted to be alone with a woman he would sometimes use his close friend Joey Faraco's apartment, which was next door to the Gardens. This was in the early 1970s when Faraco was still manager of the Hot Stove lounge, a bar and restaurant at the Gardens.

Part of Faraco's job in the 1960s was to maintain a penthouse apartment for the Silver Seven, which they used for parties and was situated in the same building as Faraco's apartment. Faraco remembers arriving home late one night from work to find his chesterfield missing. The next day, Ballard told him he had broken it and had it taken to the Gardens workshop for repairs.

In the early 1980s, Ballard was involved with a woman from New York. She was in her fifties and some would say unattractive. She had thin dark hair pulled tightly back, didn't wear makeup, and dressed poorly. In NHL circles she was known as "the league's oldest groupie." A friend of Ballard's is even less flattering. "She looked like a bag lady," he said. Sometimes she would fly to Toronto for the weekend to see Ballard. But she paid her own way and stayed at the YWCA across the street from the arena.

At the time of the NHL's annual draft and meetings in Montreal in 1983, Ballard's relationship with Yolanda MacMillan was well underway. But the woman from New York wasn't aware of this, and made the trip to Montreal to see him. What followed was something you might imagine happening to a teenager who has just dropped his girlfriend but doesn't have the courage to tell her. Ballard hid in his room. He left the hotel from a back exit. And when his phone rang he wouldn't speak until the party at the other end said something, for fear it might be *her*.

Not that Ballard was pursued by many women. One who went out with him said she found him boring. His range of interests was narrow and almost nonexistent outside his hockey team and football team. He would rail against enemies in the media and any one of his children who was temporarily in his disfavour.

For public consumption, however, he was a ladies' man with a "broad" in every NHL city. Two years before meeting Yolanda, he told journalist Earl McRae, "The one in New York is a real beaut. When I'm really horny I fly down for a quickie. Then there's this one in L.A. I was at the hotel and couldn't sleep, so I got up to go for a swim. It's about three in the morning. I'm approaching the pool when I hear splashing and here's this redhead swimming all alone. Gorgeous broad. About 26, 27 and bare naked. I said, 'Hi honey, I see you're a real redhead, eh?' She laughed and asked me to join her. I took off my trunks and did. Had a great time. See her whenever I'm out there."

There is a theory that Ballard doesn't really like women at all. That is the opinion of Pat Surphlis, a former secretary who found him ill-mannered, intimidating, and moody. McRae can remember Ballard embarrassing a woman in front of sportswriters in a hotel lobby in Winnipeg. In a loud voice, he said, "Look at the tits on her." The woman turned red and kept walking, as somebody in Ballard's group said, "Harold, bite your tongue," to which he replied, "I would, but I'd rather bite something else, ha, ha, ha."

Many times Ballard has stated his belief that women belong only in the kitchen and the bedroom. He is openly disdainful of women who attempt to achieve equality with men and refuses to allow female reporters in the Leaf dressing room, although that rule was challenged by reporters a few years ago.

Ballard's best-known confrontation with a woman occurred in 1979 when he was on CBC Radio's "As It Happens" with Barbara Frum, who is now host of CBC Television's "The Journal." This was a few days after he had fired his hockey coach, Roger Neilson, only to reinstate him because he couldn't find anybody willing to take his place. Also on the show was Dick Beddoes, the show's resident hockey expert. Frum was friendly and cheerful during the telephone interview, but Ballard was rude and eventually hung up. Frum started by saying hello in a pleasant voice. Ballard, who was obviously still embarrassed by the incident with Neilson, said cooly, "How are you?"

"How are you?" said Frum.
"Well, I'm all right," replied Ballard.
"You won a hockey game," said Frum.
"Well I won two hockey games," said Ballard. "What's the matter with your addition?"

BEDDOES: That's right, Harold, you won two—

BALLARD: I don't know what damn females—

FRUM (still friendly and pleasant): Listen, I just go for the hearts and flowers. So I'm there Saturday night—

BALLARD: They shouldn't let females on the radio anyway. They're a joke.

BEDDOES: They're a joke are they Harold?

BALLARD (in almost a growl): Yeah.

BEDDOES: Well Harold–

BALLARD: You know where they're good–

BEDDOES: That's what people are saying–

BALLARD: You know where they're good don't yah?

BEDDOES: Well I do know where women are best. I do–

FRUM: Do you mind that millions of people are going to hear you say that?

BALLARD (louder): You know where they're best, don't yah?

BEDDOES: Yes, and I like it that way.

BALLARD: So do I, and that's where they should stay. I let them out once in a while. I give them their shoes once in a while–

BEDDOES: But talking about jokes, Harold, that's what some people are saying you pulled in respect to the rehiring after the firing of Mr. Neilson.

BALLARD: Oh?

BEDDOES: Is it a joke? Is it a hoax?

BALLARD: Well, ah, no, not necessarily a hoax or a joke or anything else. I got what I wanted. I got the team winning so you can't call it a joke.

BEDDOES: Well, I'd hope to say I didn't think it was a joke when you and I talked at the Montreal Forum last Thursday night.

BALLARD: That's right.

BEDDOES: You said then–and certainly you were serious–that he was gone as your coach.

BALLARD: Yeah.

BEDDOES: And you were going to have somebody else as soon as you could find somebody else.

BALLARD: Mmm-hmmm.

BEDDOES: And your problem probably was, Harold, you didn't have anybody you could grab immediately. If you could have grabbed Eddie Johnston from Moncton, I suspect you might have.

BALLARD: Well, I don't know. I'd have to give it a little more consideration. I mean to say, when you caught me coming out of the Montreal Forum, I mean to say, it was a very tense moment as far as I was concerned.

BEDDOES: Yeah.

BALLARD: When I came back, I called Roger and we sat down in the lounge and had a little meeting and rehashed the whole thing. And it's quite simple, the reason Roger was axed, if you want to call it that, was the fact the players let him down, and they admitted that to me, and I went to talk to them and they took full responsibility.

FRUM: Dick, would you describe the drama of his return on Saturday night? It was genuinely moving and as Mr. Ballard so politely just said, I am something of a weak hockey fan.

BEDDOES: Well indeed Barbara it was one rare—rare ovation at Maple Leaf Gardens when the people—17,000 of them—saw who was behind the Maple Leaf bench.

FRUM: Well it was a definite two-hanky scene, wouldn't you say?

BEDDOES: Well the people were saying, "Hey! Something's happened. Hard-hearted Ballard has given in. And here we got back the guy we think should be coaching the hockey club and we're going to stand up and show how—"

BALLARD: Just a minute—

FRUM: And there's the godfather up in the window looking down benignly—

BALLARD: I'll tell you something! The night before, the *Daily Star* had an article saying the worst-coached team we've ever seen—

BEDDOES: Harold, there's no question the Atlanta game—

BALLARD: And everybody–all you media guys, the whole bunch of you–"you should get rid of Roger Neilson" and the calls, and–

BEDDOES: I beg your pardon Harold. The news media did not say that.

BALLARD (loudly): They certainly did! I'll show you clippings out of the paper!

BEDDOES: No, very few of the media–

BALLARD: Now I'll start on you–there was a lot–

BEDDOES: There was very few that I read–

BALLARD: Of course I shouldn't pay any attention to you fellows, because you don't know the difference between a puck and a ball–a baseball.

FRUM (still friendly): Well lookit Mr. Ballard, you *did* fire him–

BALLARD (very upset, and loud): I'm talking to Dick and you don't know the difference between them, and why I should allow myself to be taken in by a few dummies that don't know hockey–they don't write, they're critics!

FRUM: Hang on there Mr. Ballard–

BALLARD: Would you keep quiet?

FRUM: No. This is still my show.

BALLARD: Well it isn't–

FRUM: *I* have another question for you.

BALLARD: I'm not talking to you. I'm talking to Dick. So when you learn to mind your own business and let me talk to Dick, it'll be fine. Goodbye.

With that, the line went dead. It was one of the few times a guest had hung up on Frum. They attempted to get him back, but a Gardens secretary said he was no longer in.

Frum took it in stride. Her reaction to Ballard's blackguardly behaviour was one of amusement. The next night, she read a poem over the air, part of which said, "Many [listeners] wanted to do naughty things to you. Our more generous listeners thought you should be stoned in the public square." She concluded by referring to herself as Ballard's favourite *broad*caster.

A few days later a group of women celebrated International Women's Day by marching on the Gardens, angrily chanting obscene slogans at Ballard. Ballard attempted to make the best of what had been a petulant performance by joking about it. He would later tell McRae, "You should have heard those feminist broads calling me after the Barbara Frum thing. I had all the calls put through to me. I'd say, 'Hi honey, what's the matter? Can't get a man today? You after my body? You wanna get laid?' Boy they went nuts. Loved it. *Loved* it. Can't stand those feminist broads. Bunch of frustrated old maids."

A few years later, Ballard would meet a woman who was anything but a feminist. She could be just as loud and foul-mouthed as Ballard, which was no doubt part of the attraction. As Ballard would say, Yolanda was a good-lookin' broad–blonde, bold, and brassy.

10

YOLANDA

In the late spring of 1982, after serving four months of a two-year prison sentence, Yolanda MacMillan was released from the Prison for Women at Kingston, Ontario. A middle-aged divorcee, she returned home to Toronto where in a matter of weeks she arranged to meet Ballard.

She left the joint in style, an inmate remembers, wearing expensive jewellery and a mink coat. A limousine picked her up and took her to the 45th-floor luxury condominium at the Palace Pier overlooking Lake Ontario where she lived with Robert Irwin.

Yolanda was 49 when she met Ballard, although her driver's licence gave her age as four years younger. She was about five feet tall, with blonde hair, a round face, and a beauty mark on her cheek. As a young woman she had been attractive, but by the time she met Ballard, hard living had taken its toll. Still, she struck those around Ballard as friendly and extroverted. She was once described as a "remarkable woman of determination and ambition." She swore a lot, but then so did Ballard. And like Harold, she could be very charming.

Yolanda had been in prison for conspiracy to commit fraud and perjury relating to a forged signature on a phony will to an estate worth $3 million. Harold had served his time 10 years earlier. This is what they had in common, Yolanda thought, and this is what they should talk about.

Thus Yolanda entered the Ballards' lives. Over the next six years, she would come to be disliked by Ballard's three children and by many of his friends and employees who saw her as a manipulative woman living off an old man. But others saw her as the victim of attacks from Ballard's jealous children. Still, nobody disputed Ballard's need for a companion. Except for some casual relationships, he had been alone since the death of Dorothy.

One of the early stories about Yolanda had to do with her eviction from the Palace Pier. After her condominium fees had been in arrears for some time, two bailiffs from the Toronto Sheriff's office were brought in to eject her. Yolanda, however, locked herself inside and ignored the bailiffs' demands that she let them in. As well as the main lock, there were three dead-bolts on the door. They couldn't be moved, so the bailiffs brought back tools and proceeded to cut a hole in the door.

When they finally entered, Yolanda fled to another room. The bailiffs, of course, followed and found Yolanda standing in front of the bathroom. What followed was a scene that even veteran bailiff Ross Moore, just a few years away from retirement, hadn't witnessed during his many eviction experiences. Yolanda, says Moore, took off her clothes in front of the two officers.

"She proceeded to do a strip-tease act," Moore recalls. "She took off all her clothes and stood there with nothing on. Then she said, 'Throw me out now, if you dare.'"

Moore says his response was, "Lady, that's exactly what I'm going to do if you don't come with us." Yolanda yelled and fled to the bathroom. "If you don't come out, we're going to knock down that door and carry you out in a bedsheet," Moore shouted.

Yolanda finally concluded that she was leaving one way or the other, so she came out and got dressed. On her way out, she said, "I can't leave without my mink coat." But the bailiff said no, and, indeed, the coat was confiscated along with everything else in the residence.

Moore was surprised one more time before the day was over. When they got downtown and the necessary paperwork was completed, Yolanda went over to him and gave him a kiss. She said, "I want to thank you for being a gentleman. You're the politest policeman I've ever met. You didn't manhandle me or anything."

In the future, Yolanda would call Moore at the sheriff's office more than once to check on her belongings. The officers would joke that his "girlfriend" was on the line. It is worth noting that Yolanda got her possessions back. Ballard paid the bill and the furniture was taken to the Gardens where it was stored in the office at the southeast corner of the building that had once belonged to Conn Smythe.

Yolanda was born in Fort William, Ontario, now part of Thunder Bay, during the Depression, on 3 January 1933. Back then, she was Yolanka Babic, the child of middle-class Canadians of Eastern European descent. The Babics were not rich, but better off than most, owning and operating the Kimberley Hotel in Port Arthur. In addition to attending a local public school, Yolanda also was enrolled in a boarding school in Duluth, Minnesota. At the age of 20, she struck out on her own, determined to find wealth and status above that of the Lakehead in the early 1950s.

Toronto was her destination and it was there that she found work as a Bell Telephone operator. As an attractive young woman with a certain *joie de vivre* she dated many men until William MacMillan, a recently graduated lawyer from Windsor, Ontario, came along. Soon they were married.

When MacMillan started his legal practice in Toronto, Yolanda helped by acting as his secretary. Then, in 1957, they moved to Windsor, where MacMillan's father, Angus MacMillan, was a prominent citizen. He was a magistrate and had been an alderman on Windsor city council. In 1958 the MacMillans had their first child, William Jr., and in 1963 a daughter, Anastasia.

By the mid-1960s, however, the marriage was on the rocks, and in 1967 there was an acrimonious divorce which attracted a great deal of publicity in Windsor. Yolanda accused her husband of "fooling around" with other women but attempted a reconciliation. "I chased him half-way around the world," she once said.

Following the divorce, she lived in Chatham, northeast of Windsor, and sent her two children to private schools, William to St. Andrews in Aurora, outside Toronto, and Ana to Bishop Strachan School in Toronto.

During Yolanda's years in Windsor she was viewed by some as a social climber who had tried to ingratiate herself with the city gentry. In a probation report, William MacMillan described his ex-wife as being overly concerned with receiving recognition from the "high society" of Windsor. She would entertain lavishly, hoping to obtain acceptance into Windsor society and achieve the status she desired. She would be extremely generous and give flowers and gifts to friends and acquaintances, MacMillan said, but also could be mean, sometimes cheating local tradespeople out of small sums of money.

Another route to social acceptance and personal wealth was real-estate deals. In 1961, she purchased a 20-room mansion and coach house from a religious order of Maltese priests in the upper-class residential area of old Walkerville in Windsor. She borrowed the down payment from her parents. It didn't take long for Yolanda to make enemies of her neighbours, however, when she attempted to tear down the mansion and coach house, and subdivide the property. Local ratepayers dogged her all the way to the Ontario Municipal Board.

As the dispute continued into the 1970s, the old building deteriorated until it was no longer usable. "Vagrants started living in it," said Windsor *Star* columnist Jim Cornett, a long-time resident of the area. "Thieves used it to stash stolen goods. Then they were tearing out the panelling. Windows were smashed, the rain got in. It was a god-awful mess." A few years later, it was torn down and replaced with another large home.

Her other spectacular failure involved the purchase of the bankrupt Baldoon Golf and Country Club near Chatham in April 1978. Her business partner and lover, by this time, was Robert Irwin, a lawyer with the law firm of Burgess and Irwin in Wallaceburg, north of Chatham. Some people in the area say Irwin was considered a "pillar of the community." He was a Queen's Counsel, had served on the local school board, and had been a member of the town council.

In an article in the Windsor *Star,* Yolanda claimed she had purchased the 54-acre property "sight unseen." Upon arrival, what she did see was a club that had been closed for five years and was in a state of disrepair. "I almost cried the first time I saw it," Yolanda was quoted as saying. "It was a real wreck." At the time, she refused to reveal Irwin as her partner, saying only: "I'm really glad I trusted his judgment. Otherwise I would never have bought the place. It's just as well I didn't see it until the deal went through."

Yolanda and Irwin renamed the property the St. Clair Golf and Country Club. They redecorated the clubhouse dining-room, fixed up the pool area, and added "Le Club Disco" which featured special lighting and a fog machine. Said Yolanda: "We poured a fortune into this place. And we're planning to do a lot more–like adding a new wing for conferences. This area really needs a place that can provide recreation, accommodation and good food at almost any hour of the day or night."

A package deal offered dinner for two, admission to the disco, a night at the motel next to the club, and breakfast. The cost was $59.99, but it wasn't low enough to attract customers. The club went under in 1980. Yolanda then attempted to convert the property into a health club to be called the Country Club Total Health Retreat, to provide accommodation and treatment for a maximum of 30 clients. She figured it could break even with 12 clients. That didn't work either.

People who frequented the golf course during Yolanda's ownership remember her as quick-tempered and sometimes abusive. Said a journalist who covered occasional meetings there: "She was known for having a pretty wild temper. I know that on more than a few occasions she would fly into rages. Once I heard her wail into some waiter. Somebody dropped a tray of drinks or something, and she just stood there and completely lambasted the poor guy. He was maybe 18 or 19, just barely old enough to be working out there. I'm sure it would make a drill sergeant blush, the kind of language she was using, in front of a crowd of people."

When the club failed, Yolanda lived for a while in a limousine parked outside the main building. During the day she attempted to collect green's fees from people using the course, even though it was closed. At night, she slept in the back seat of the car, which also contained food, such as cases of Coke and bananas, that she had salvaged from the restaurant.

By then she was in serious trouble over a scandal involving an old Chatham family. Soon after the MacMillans moved to Windsor, Yolanda became acquainted with Donald Lloyd, a wealthy businessman. In addition to being a manufacturer and owner of the Lloyd Bag Corporation in Chatham, he had another company, Donald Lloyd Enterprises, which owned property that included houses and apartments.

Yolanda was invited by Lloyd to act as his agent in renting and managing the properties, and she accepted. Over the years she became a close friend of Lloyd and his second wife, Marion. Irwin, too, was part of the social circle and did legal work for Lloyd.

In 1971, Lloyd had Irwin draw up a will to his estate. It contained provisions for his first wife, his second wife, Marion, and his son by his first wife, Dr. Gary Lloyd, a plastic surgeon in Oakville, Ontario. Both of Lloyd's wives were to receive $20,000 a year for life. If

Marion remarried her amount was to be halved. She also was to have full use of the matrimonial home situated in Chatham. If she no longer wished to live there, it would be sold with her receiving half the proceeds. She would also inherit Lloyd's personal belongings, including automobiles. Except for $60 a week to Lloyd's brother, the remainder of the $3 million estate would go to his only child, Gary, thus making him the principal beneficiary. Gary was also named executor of the estate. This will was signed by Lloyd and kept in a safe at the offices of the Lloyd Bag Company.

In February 1978, with the 71-year-old Lloyd gravely ill, the existence of a second will, executed in 1977, became an issue when Irwin and Marion met with the bag company's accountant and asked if he knew where it was. The accountant didn't know what they were talking about.

Less than a month later, Lloyd died of a heart attack. On the evening of the funeral in March, Irvin met Robert Savage, who was Gary Lloyd's lawyer, at the Sutton Place Hotel in Toronto. Irwin requested the meeting because he said Marion was dissatisfied with her bequest. They were joined at dinner by Yolanda who was introduced as Irwin's client and Lloyd's property manager. At one point, Yolanda left the table, during which time Irwin offered not to contest the 1971 will if Marion were given $900,000 or Lloyd's Windsor properties valued at that amount. When Irwin's offer was refused, he attempted to stall the reading of the will, arguing that there had not been a proper search for the so-called second will.

There was no legitimate second will, of course, but Irwin was determined to create one, and was assisted by Yolanda. Their next move was to enlist the help of Louis Puskas, a Windsor real-estate agent and friend. Puskas was told he would be paid $50,000 (U.S.) and promised the real-estate listings of all of Lloyd's properties and the commission from the sales, estimated at $100,000. One evening a few days later, Puskas met Irwin in his office where he signed as a witness the phony will dated 8 October 1977. The forged signature of Donald Lloyd was already on it. Yolanda was also there, and she too affixed her signature as a witness to the phony will.

Then, Irwin and Yolanda told Puskas how he should act and what he should say about the circumstances surrounding the signing of the new will. He was instructed to say he was present when the will was executed in a Las Vegas hotel room. The final step was to stage the discovery of the will. This occurred in July 1978, when Marion arranged for a handyman to clean out Lloyd's bedroom. She made sure he picked up a Bible from Lloyd's bedside table. When he did out fell the will.

Marion called Irwin, who came over immediately and together with the handyman they drove to Toronto for the purpose of authenticating the will. The next day, Puskas and Yolanda also went to Toronto and swore affidavits under oath indicating they had witnessed the signing of the 1977 will.

Not surprisingly, the 1977 will was much more generous toward Marion. This time she was to receive everything except $500,000, which was to be divided equally among Gary Lloyd, his mother, and his children.

But then the conspiracy started to fall apart. Gary Lloyd and his mother were deeply suspicious. So was the judiciary. When the will was filed for probate in Surrogate Court, the court ordered the will to be sent to the Centre for Forensic Sciences in Toronto. There it was examined and found to be a forgery. Irwin asked for a second opinion, so an examiner from the United States was called in, and he too found it to be a forgery. Irwin attempted to get a Toronto law office to file the will. Again, the conspirators testified in an attempt to prove the validity of the will, thus perjuring themselves.

At this point, the Chatham Police Department, and then the Ontario Provincial Police rackets branch began investigating. In November of 1979, police with search warrants seized documents in Irwin's desk as well as a piece of tracing paper that bore a simulated signature of Donald Lloyd. In January 1980, all four were arrested and charged by the rackets branch of the Ontario Provincial Police.

Following the convictions of Puskas and Marion for conspiracy to commit fraud, Yolanda and Irwin were also convicted in 1981 of conspiracy to commit fraud and perjury. Irwin pleaded innocent, but not Yolanda. She said she was guilty of one count of fraud and one count of perjury. Irwin was sentenced to four years; Yolanda was given three, which was later reduced to two on appeal. After sentencing, she was taken to the Prison for Women at Kingston Penitentiary in February 1982, where she spent four months.

One of the inmates at the prison was Gail Bradley, who was serving a six-month sentence for a drug-related conviction. On Yolanda's first day, Bradley recalls being in the cafeteria when another inmate brought in the new prisoner for lunch. Bradley remembers that Yolanda stuck out like a sore thumb.

"I kind of watched her and thought, 'Holy shit, what is this woman doing here?' She didn't look like the jail type. Of course I didn't think I did either," Bradley says. "She had makeup on and was wearing this gold and diamond bracelet. I said to her, 'If I were you, I'd go and have that locked up. There might be several people around here who probably think it looks better on them than on you.' She was very naive, or pretended to be. She said in a sort of little girl's voice, 'What do you mean. You mean somebody would hurt me to get my bracelet? Why would they do that? I never did anything to them.',"

Bradley says Yolanda's story was that she had been framed and she was really a developer and "builder" in the Sarnia, Ontario, area. Because she was in for only four months, she did not participate in a prison program. Bradley thinks she might have worked a little in the beauty salon. She was often seen running, wrapped in plastic garbage bags, to lose weight. Bradley describes Yolanda as "very mouthy, very verbose, flamboyant, flowery, dresses weird. She's narcissistic and histrionic."

A 1981 pre-sentence report by probation and parole officer M. J. Suttaby gives a devastating personality profile:

The offender was described by her former husband as being a compulsive liar, who was adept at deception. She would use exaggeration, promises and evasions to achieve her objective. He described her as being very persuasive with manipulative skills, enabling her to convince all kinds of people.

In the conclusion of the report, Suttaby wrote:

The offender is a remarkable woman of determination and ambition. She is both manipulative and persistent and able to employ an assortment of tactics including domination and flattery as the situation dictates.

She will not hesitate, according to several sources, to lie if necessary to achieve her objective. More frequently she has used the strategy of selective memory in not having available figures, facts and dates that are necessary.

She admits to having been described as "theatrical" in her behaviour, where she calculated it might prove profitable. She proudly asserts that she is an emotional person and is prone to weep when describing a touching or a sad scene or event.

When she wishes, she can be charming, generous and considerate. She can and does extend hospitality, though comments suggest that it is done for effect and for her own glorification and gratification. . . .

As a woman of strong personality and manipulative skills, she has found that she is able to avoid or delay a confrontation by evading the facts, giving misleading information or by giving information that is false.

She is adept at this and sometimes lies when the other party is aware of the true situation. She is not embarrassed at the situation she finds herself in and does not consider telling falsehoods a breach of business ethics. . . .

She admits freely to her guilt [conspiracy to commit fraud] but claims that she was led astray, insisting that she didn't read the document, that she lied to help another person and that she was taken for a "true blue sucker." She accepts no feeling of guilt or remorse for the part she played in the offence but asserts that she was naive, and in her offer to help she was taken advantage of.

Regardless of what other disposition is considered by the Court, it is felt by the undersigned [Suttaby] that because of the offender's personality and attitude toward the offence, community supervision would be of little, if any, benefit.

A gentler voice in the report came from F. J. Newhouse, a management consultant who said he had met Yolanda in 1978 and had become her "father confessor." He listened to her problems, he said, and became her adviser and friend. Newhouse said that Yolanda had freely admitted her guilt to him. He viewed her essentially as a warm-hearted person and a good mother. Yolanda's lawyer challenged some of the opinions expressed in the report, particularly the observations of her ex-husband, whose views were obviously subjective. In sentencing Yolanda, the judge said her husband's remarks had no bearing on his decision.

By the summer of 1982, Yolanda had been released from prison. One weekend, Gail Bradley was given a pass from a Wellesley Street halfway house, where she had been transferred to serve out her sentence. With her fiancée, Ron Bradley (they weren't yet married), she drove to her family cottage at Thunder Beach near Midland, Ontario, a comfortable summer vacation area on Georgian Bay, 110 km north of Toronto, with old cottages owned by people with old money.

Bradley's summer place was just down the road from the Ballards' and she had known the children most of her life. She liked them, and also their father, who she says is "really a nice old guy." On the beach, Ron and Gail bumped into Harold Jr., and they spent the day together.

"Harold was going on and on all day about his dad's friend," Bradley recalls. "He was saying how happy he was that his dad had finally found someone who wasn't after his money. She was this big developer, she was this, she was that, she was wonderful.,.,.,.."

Bradley hadn't paid much attention, but late in the afternoon, she said, "What's the woman's name, anyway?"

"Yolanda MacMillan," said Harold.

Bradley was speechless. "My mouth could not have fallen further to the floor if you'd shot me in the head," she says. "I couldn't talk, my mouth went dry. I just stared at Ron and Harold."

Finally, Bradley asked if the woman was "short, fat, blonde, with a mole on her face."

"Yes."

"Well, Harold, I'll tell you something. She isn't a developer. She just got out of jail a couple of months ago. I just did time with her. She was in for forgery of a will."

Now Harold was shocked. He suggested that Bradley accompany him to the cottage to see for herself. Ron said he was coming too. "I want to be there to see the look on her face," he said.

When they arrived, Bradley remembers Yolanda's reaction changing from pleasure to perplexity to anxiety. Bradley recalls, "She said, 'Oh hi. How are you?' Then all of a sudden she stared at me and the expression on her face went from 'I'm really glad to see you,' to 'Why am I glad to see you?' to 'Oh my God, oh shit.',"

After a few seconds, Yolanda said, "What are you doing here?"

"Yolanda, I own a cottage here," said Bradley. "The question is, what are you doing here?"

"Oh, Harold and I are going out," she said.

"Oh really," said Bradley.

At that point Bradley says Yolanda hauled her into the living-room.

"You didn't say anything to Harold [Jr.] did you?"

"Absolutely," said Bradley. "What do I look like? New?"

"Well, Harold knows everything about it anyway," Yolanda said. "But I don't want you causing me any trouble."

Bradley said: "You can rest assured about one thing: I'm not going to rain on anybody's parade. As long as you're on the uppity up and everything's fine, I'll definitely not get in your way. But if you step out of line and cause any problems for my friends, I'm going to be all over you. You're going to be just like a bear with a sore ass."

Problems did arise, of course, and with them the gradual and painful break-up of the Ballard family. In the years to come, their antics provided comic relief in the press, but behind this lay the pathos of the children trying to hang on to their father as he slipped further and further away.

11

BIG MAC
TAKES CHARGE

By the fall of 1981, the Leafs had been under the leadership of Ballard for nine years. Except for one season, Neilson's first behind the bench, the team had been either mediocre or bad. But the potential existed for it to get much worse. Indeed, the winter of 1981–82 would be an indication of just how lamentable things could get.

For the first two months there was no general manager. Imlach was in the hospital, and according to the news reports would be out of a job as soon as he attempted to come back to work. The team got off to a poor start, and by November, Ballard started to look for somebody to blame. In the past, he had attacked his captains and his coaches, but this time he decided it would be a young hockey player who was a born-again Christian.

Laurie Boschman had been a high draft choice in 1979 (ninth overall) and the Leafs had hoped they were getting somebody to follow Sittler as the team's offensive leader. However, his development had been slower than hoped, and the previous season he had come down with mononucleosis. But Ballard figured that Boschman's problem was his religion. In the press box one night, he told Dick Beddoes that Boschman's Christianity was hurting his play, and he was going to demote him. Boschman suddenly became a new victim, thrown into the Gardens zoo that included scrums of reporters and illogical tirades from Ballard.

A few days later, when it became public knowledge that Sittler had asked for a trade, Eagleson said on television that one of the reasons Sittler wanted to leave was because of Ballard's remarks about Boschman. Sittler, too, was a devout Christian. Again Boschman was in the middle of the controversy. It seemed so unfair. He was a quiet kid from a farm in western Canada who wanted no part of the fighting at the Gardens.

The news of Sittler's trade demand eventually removed much of the attention from Boschman. For more than a month the Sittler situation was the on-going hockey story in Toronto. For McNamara, the acting general manager, the Sittler trade came to be called his baptism by fire. Although Ballard would not appoint McNamara general manager until the end of the season, he took over the responsibilities in December when it was certain that Imlach would not be back.

That winter McNamara made three significant trades, none of which were terribly beneficial for the Leafs, although he was at a disadvantage in attempting to move Sittler, who had left the team, and later Turnbull. Sittler stipulated that he would accept a trade to only two clubs, Minnesota and Philadelphia, seriously limiting McNamara's ability to make a good deal. In Turnbull's case, he broke curfew on the road and was told to stay at home until a trade could be worked out.

Sittler was still quite highly rated around the league, but McNamara didn't get much when an agreement was finally reached with the Flyers. The Leafs got centre Rich Costello, a second-round draft choice of Philadelphia in 1981 from an American high school. Costello went on to have an undistinguished minor-league career, in addition to two games played for the Leafs. Toronto also received a second-round draft choice that had belonged to Hartford. With that, they took Peter Ihnacak, a Czechoslovak centre who was a second and third liner for six seasons before being assigned to Newmarket in 1988–89.

Turnbull was traded to the Los Angeles Kings for winger Billy Harris and defenceman John Gibson. Both were fringe players by that time, and neither played well in Toronto.

Then there was the Boschman deal. Toronto was under no pressure to trade him and probably should have kept him. He went to the Oilers for Walt Poddubny and was eventually traded to the Winnipeg Jets where he has had some very good years. Poddubny, on the other hand, was a disappointment in Toronto. Nykoluk was unable to motivate him. He was used as a checker even though his skills were offensive. And he played the wing when he was most effective at centre. After a trade to New York in 1986, he led the Rangers in scoring for two consecutive seasons.

The problem with the Leafs that season was largely on the blueline. In the two previous drafts, Imlach had selected defencemen, well aware that that was the team's weakest area. In 1980, they had used their first three picks to take Craig Muni, Bob McGill, and Fred Boimistruck. The following year, Jim Benning was selected high, sixth overall from the Portland Winter Hawks.

In keeping with Nykoluk's plan of going with the kids, Benning, McGill, and Boimistruck were thrown into the lineup. Another rookie, Vincent Tremblay, played 40 games in goal. But none of them were ready for the NHL. They played poorly, their confidence was badly shaken, and they were heavily criticized in the media. Only two went on to have modest success in the NHL–McGill as a role player in Toronto and Chicago, and Benning as an average defenceman in Vancouver.

Not surprisingly, the Leafs finished out of the playoffs with a record of 20 wins, 44 losses, and 16 ties, which happened to be the worst performance by a Toronto team in the NHL since 1918-19, when the Arenas won 5 of 18 games. Still, Ballard seemed satisfied. He defended Nykoluk at the end of the season, saying, "Mike can't score goals for them and he can't play in goal." McNamara was rewarded with a four-year contract.

It was at this point, arguably, that Ballard gave up any serious attempt at winning a Stanley Cup. When he had fired Gregory he had at least tried to get an adequate replacement, turning first to Bowman and then to Imlach. Imlach had been a disaster, although at the time it didn't seem like a bad idea. Imlach's track record, after all, was pretty good.

But the 47-year-old McNamara didn't even want the job. He was quite content in his position as chief scout, where there was no pressure and where he didn't have to deal with the media. Financially he was in fairly good shape. His home in Toronto was paid for. His oldest child, David, was already on his own, teaching school in Toronto. Two were in university and two more in high school.

As well, McNamara was about to get a considerable settlement from an automobile accident in which he had sustained a head injury. He claimed he had suffered brain damage, one of the results of which was difficulty speaking in stressful situations. When he received $125,000, a headline in a Toronto newspaper read, "McNamara Proves He's Brain Damaged."

People in the business found the whole thing quite a joke. Not only were the Leafs, once a great organization and now one of the worst, owned by a bona fide eccentric, but his general manager, the man responsible for making the team a winner, had gone to court to prove he was brain damaged. The players nicknamed McNamara "B.D." Some also called him Fish, because he looked a little like the Abe Vigoda character in the television sitcom "Barney Miller."

McNamara was born in Sturgeon Falls in northern Ontario and as a teenager had attended St. Michael's College. A goaltender, he was never quite good enough for the NHL, although he played briefly for the Leafs in 1960-61 and 1969-70. For the remainder of his career he was a minor-leaguer and then later a member of the Ontario senior team, the Orillia Terriers. Away from the game, he worked at different jobs, including selling life insurance. When the insurance company that employed him went out of business, Gregory hired him to scout for the Leafs.

He was a tall, imposing sort of man. He had a quick temper and seemed to enjoy lecturing people. He could also be a bully, especially to the media. When he was a scout, he once chased a reporter out of the Toronto press box after objecting to something the reporter had said. When he was general manager, he started an incident in the press box at the Chicago stadium. A radio reporter had said something unflattering about the Leafs that was overheard by McNamara, who told him to shut up. A brief exchange followed.

Many times a reporter new to the hockey beat would introduce himself to McNamara and then listen to a lecture about how dishonest and unethical a certain co-worker was. When a *Globe and Mail* reporter stuck out his hand and said hello, McNamara said, "I want to tell you one thing about your newspaper. It's dishonest. You guys write lies." He called one reporter a "snake," another a "jerk," and a third an "armpit."

McNamara made a point of not swearing, but the words he used instead seemed every bit as obscene. Sometimes he would choose to snub a reporter who tried to introduce himself. Journalist Bob Kravitz, then with *Sports Illustrated,* was one of many who went up to McNamara, told him who he was, and watched him walk away without even speaking. A reporter who asked McNamara a question about the team would very often be told, "The Maple Leaf club pays me to give information to them, not you."

In the 1977-78 season he had coached the Leafs' Central Hockey League team in Dallas, but didn't like it and returned to Toronto to resume scouting. Once in Dallas he was penalized for allegedly swearing at a referee during a game. When he was fined $300 for the infraction, he refused to pay. The CHL insisted and it dragged on until Gregory stepped in and quietly paid the fine.

McNamara would become offended if anyone suggested he swore. There was a somewhat comical exchange in 1984 between McNamara and Trent Frayne who was a columnist for the *Globe*. A year earlier Frayne had written a column supportive of McNamara in which he had been asked if Ballard interfered. McNamara was quoted as saying, "Not a damn bit."

When they ended up standing beside each other in the press box, Frayne looked over and said, "Hello Gerry." There was no answer. McNamara looked straight ahead. Frayne tried again. "Hello Gerry." Still no answer. Finally, Frayne reached around, looked McNamara in the face, and said in a loud voice, "Hello Gerry!" McNamara's response was to turn away. Frayne said, "What's the matter with you?" For some time there had been tension and animosity between the *Globe* and the Leaf management.

"I don't want to have anything to do with you people," McNamara said.

"Do you mean me, newspaper people in general, or the *Globe?*"

"Your lying newspaper," he said. "You just make a lot of lies, you people."

"Well you've got one of the worst records in the league," said Frayne. "Your goals-against is terrible. What do you want us to do, pat you on the head?" Frayne also reminded McNamara of the positive article he had written a year earlier.

"You misquoted me," said McNamara. "You had me uttering an oath."

"It couldn't have been too awful or it wouldn't have been in the paper. It might have been a hell or a damn. . . ."

"I don't use that kind of language," snapped McNamara. "We don't use that kind of language in the organization."

Frayne could barely suppress a laugh considering Ballard was one of the most foul-mouthed people he knew. To the reporters who covered the team, McNamara came across as sanctimonious and self-righteous. He was proud of his Christianity, but seemed unforgiving and vindictive. Early in his career as general manager, when he was still talking to most of the media, he spent part of one morning during the Leaf practice talking very excitedly about a particular murder and how Canada should return to capital punishment.

"I'll be the hangman," he said loudly. "I'll be the hangman." Indeed, at the gardens he was something like an executioner, especially with the media.

In 1982, McNamara's priority should have been to upgrade the Toronto hockey operation in all areas. Nobody who knew the business expected the Leafs to rise to the top of their division immediately. They were a weak team and rebuilding would take time. But an adequate support group should have been brought in as soon as possible. The Leafs would be picking high in the draft for the next few years, so it made sense to hire more permanent scouts. The Leafs had only three full-time scouts, Smith, Duff, and Bower. Some teams had as many as 10. Nykoluk should have been given qualified assistant coaches who could have helped in teaching the young players and assisted in the preparation of games. And McNamara should have signed as free agents role players who could have helped keep the team somewhat competitive during the lean periods.

But none of these things, all of which cost money, were done. From 1982 to 1987, the Leafs participated only once in the annual waiver draft in which teams can pick, for a price, players left unprotected. The other low-level teams made use of the waiver draft every year, taking players who could fill needs, whether it was checking, toughness on the wings, or help on defence. But McNamara didn't bother.

When Nykoluk was fired after the 1983–84 season, he was sharply critical of McNamara and his failure to bring in veteran players through trades and free agent acquisitions. When the Quebec Nordiques offered winger Marian Stastny in 1982 for a low draft choice, McNamara turned them down because of his contract. Stastny was a good offensive player at that time. In 1981–82, he had 35 goals and 54 assists. The following season, he had 36 goals and 43 assists.

Nykoluk says McNamara could have traded defenceman Gaston Gingras to the Rangers for Ed Hospodar. Instead, Hospodar, a tough player, went to Philadelphia. Gingras did not play well in Toronto and eventually was sent to Montreal for Larry Landon who never played for the Leafs. Another missed opportunity, Nykoluk says, was in not taking defenceman Marty McSorley from Pittsburgh when he was offered for Saganiuk. Instead McNamara opted for two minor leaguers. McSorley went to Edmonton and then Los Angeles, where he filled an important role as a "character player" and fighter.

During this time, the Leafs were an extremely passive team that needed size and aggressiveness. McNamara often complained that his scouts were unjustly maligned in the media. But it is fair to say the Leaf scouting department was understaffed in the late 1970s and grossly undermanned during McNamara's term. For several years, the Leafs didn't even send a scout to the world junior or senior hockey championships where the best Europeans are assessed. Other clubs in the league attended, sometimes sending two scouts. A man who worked for the NHL's Central Scouting Bureau, which is a co-operative scouting service funded by the league's 21 clubs, once said that no NHL team relied as heavily on Central Scouting as the Leafs.

Another element of a winning franchise is a strong farm team with competent, professional-style coaching. The head coach should be someone who can teach and prepare young players for the NHL, and be good enough to perhaps coach there himself someday. When McNamara took over the Leafs they had Doug Carpenter in St. Catharines with their AHL affiliate.

Carpenter, a former school teacher, had been a successful junior coach in Cornwall, taking the Royals to the Memorial Cup championship in 1980. Imlach had hired him to coach the Leaf AHL team in Moncton and Carpenter was his choice to replace Crozier. He stayed in the organization and from appearances did a good job. In 1983-84, the farm team, now based in St. Catharines and called the Saints, had their best season with a record of 43-31-6 for third place in the Southern Division.

Carpenter had been assured he would be staying on with a new two-year contract. But then suddenly the decision was reversed and his contract was not renewed. No reason was given, but there was speculation that Ballard wanted him out because he was an Imlach man. Imlach's second book, *Heaven and Hell in the NHL*, had come out a year earlier, and in it he had said Carpenter was a far better coach than Nykoluk, and should have been given the Leaf job ahead of him. Then, in a column that Imlach wrote for the *Sun*, he said

Carpenter would never go very far in the organization because he, Imlach, had hired him.

But when it was announced that Carpenter's replacement in St. Catharines was Claire Alexander, there appeared a more obvious reason. Alexander, who had no experience as a head coach, was an old acquaintance of McNamara's and had just returned from playing in Europe.

In Orillia, the two had played for the Terriers. Big Mac had been the team's belligerent goalie, a sort of industrial-league Ron Hextall, and Claire had been the offensive defenceman with a big shot. Alexander had some talent and played part of the 1974–75 season with the Leafs. He was called the Orillia Milkman, because that was his job when he wasn't playing hockey.

Unhappily for Alexander, his year and a half as head coach in St. Catharines was a disaster. There were serious shortages when the parent club failed to sign an adequate number of players. To save money, McNamara opted not to sign the team's two leading scorers, Bruce Boudreau and Mike Kaszycki.

In some games, the Saints dressed only 11 or 12 players. They had to bus everywhere, even to the East Coast, which meant a nine-hour trip, because Alexander had a fear of flying. Partly because of this, many of the players disliked Alexander. They openly criticized him and said he didn't know what he was doing. Their record reflected the discontent. They won 24 games, lost 50, and tied 6, finishing with the worst record in the league.

Near the end of the season, the St. Catharines *Standard* conducted a fan poll on what was wrong with the Saints and most readers blamed McNamara. About that time, Greg Britz, a forward on the team, said, "McNamara seems more worried about people stabbing him in the back or being second-guessed than building a winner."

It didn't improve the following year. After 12 games Alexander's team had lost 8 when John Brophy, who was Leaf coach Dan Maloney's assistant at that point, asked to switch jobs with Alexander. In hiring Alexander, McNamara arguably had done a disservice to the players in the minor-league system and had been unfair to Alexander as well. Alexander soon realized he wasn't prepared for the job. And he didn't want the promotion to assistant coach in Toronto. When he was let go in June 1986, his departure was bitter.

During McNamara's first couple of years, and indeed for most of his term as general manager, scouting and player development seemed less important than settling scores with enemies, most of whom were in the media.

In this, he was supported by Nykoluk, who was beginning to have trouble dealing with the pressure of coaching in Toronto. Nykoluk had worked on other teams before, but had never been as closely watched now that he was a head coach of one of the worst teams in the league. He was a sensitive man, who became personally offended and upset when he was criticized. Most coaches learned not to let it bother them. Some had their own methods of dealing with attacks from the media. Crozier, for example, would become extraordinarly friendly with someone who had just pilloried him. This, in some ways, was more disconcerting than a blast.

So in the 1982-83 season McNamara and especially Nykoluk spent a lot of their energy raging against Imlach and the contents of his new book. It all seemed so ridiculous. Here was a team that rarely won two consecutive games, yet the attention of the coach and many of the players was on a memoir about events of two years earlier. Nykoluk's face would redden and he would chomp down on his cigar as he denounced the former general manager as a no good so and so. Salming, who was usually pretty placid, would yell, "That fucking Imlach destroyed a hockey team! He's to blame for what's wrong here!"

The next crisis for Nykoluk was an article written by Al Strachan of the *Globe and Mail* in November. For two years, there had been a strong suspicion among many in the media that Nykoluk didn't really know what he was doing. Meeker, an analyst on "Hockey Night in Canada" during that time, felt he should have been fired after his first full season. There was no discernible teaching by Nykoluk during practices. There was little or no preparation for games. Some thought he was lazy.

Once, early in a season, a reporter asked him before a game at home against the Washington Capitals if he had seen the Capitals play. "No," he said, as he stretched back in his chair and removed the cigar from his mouth. "We know them pretty good. We got the tapes from last year if we need them." What Nykoluk may or may not have known was that the Capitals had made more changes than any team in the league. There were 11 new faces in the lineup, new line combinations and new systems. The Leafs lost the game.

There was also some doubt about his ability behind the bench during games. He seemed to have trouble changing and matching lines. Sometimes after a game, he would complain about not getting desired match-ups on the ice. And this was at home, where he had the last change. At times he seemed genuinely confused during games. When, in his last season, he gave Maloney, his assistant, the responsibility of changing the forward lines, people couldn't believe it. Nobody could remember another head coach not changing his forwards.

In Strachan's article, he portrayed Nykoluk as an easy-going fellow who did not view his job as the most important thing in his life. He wrote:

> The opinion of professional hockey people is that Nykoluk doesn't get too excited about winning or losing, and therefore his players don't. The pre-game talks, usually delivered to a team by its coach, are usually delivered by the assistant coach in the Leafs' case. While this is going on, Nykoluk has been known to sit in his office doing a crossword puzzle.

Strachan also wrote that Nykoluk often spent his time at the race track on game days. The story incensed Nykoluk, and he talked about it for weeks. He threatened to sue Strachan and then changed his mind. But he swore revenge and would eventually get the satisfaction of throwing him out of the dressing room.

The trouble with Strachan was the beginning of an on-going dispute with the *Globe*. The next story that enraged the Leaf hierarchy was by Nora McCabe about a young player by the name of Paul Higgins. The 20-year-old Higgins had no discernible skills as a hockey player, but was muscular and tough, and performed in the role of a goon.

He also had some serious behavioural problems. When he was 16, he had instigated a fight with a young man in a shopping plaza by kicking his car. When the man got out, Higgins smashed a beer bottle across his face. When the victim went for friends, another scuffle broke out. This time Higgins hit him over the head with an axe handle, fracturing his skull and putting him in the hospital for three days.

The next reported assault by Higgins occurred in early 1981 when he punched a man in a doughnut shop below the eye, smashing his cheekbone. Plastic surgery was needed to repair the damage. Following his conviction, he was sentenced to 90 days in Mimico Correctional Centre under the temporary absence program. That

September, during his first Leaf training camp, McNamara drove him back and forth between the centre and the Gardens.

Higgins was a former teammate of McNamara's son, Robert, and McNamara took a personal interest in him. Although McNamara's intentions were probably good, many found it odd that he was reinforcing the type of behaviour that got Higgins into trouble. The Leafs, after all, were encouraging him, implicitly at least, to intimidate and sometimes beat up people.

By the time McCabe's article came out in December, Higgins had broken the nose of Darryl Sutter of the Chicago Blackhawks with his stick, and had been denounced by Sutter's teammate, Denis Savard, as a "brutal player." He had no goals, no assists, and 65 penalty minutes in seven games.

The Leafs, of course, were enraged by the story. First there had been Strachan's critique, and now this. McNamara's initial reaction was to bar all *Globe* reporters from the Gardens. That position was softened somewhat when it was decided Leaf management and coaching simply would not to talk to *Globe* reporters.

An uneasy relationship between the Leafs and the media continued until the next crisis in April. If anything, Higgins' behaviour on the ice had worsened after McCabe's story. He had taken a shift in January in which he fouled three players, giving one of them a black eye and receiving a double minor. In the third-last game of the season, against the Red Wings, Higgins started a fight and then sucker-punched Colin Campbell in the eye while he was being held by another Leaf.

As one of the Leaf beat writers at the *Globe,* I called up the Red Wing coach, Nick Polano, the next day for a comment on Higgins. Polano was critical and said, "Higgins can't play. I mean he's a cement head. He'a a goon, strictly a goon. . . . It's been a long time since I've seen something similar to what Higgins did to Campbell. . . . He really could have hurt this man very badly. We're fortunate that Colin got a glimpse of him at the last minute, and just turned a bit and missed getting hit directly."

Although it was a news story with the opinions of others expressed, McNamara decided to bar me from the dressing room. He felt that I had harassed Higgins. Others had criticized him, but I was the reporter with the least seniority on a newspaper that already was hated by Ballard. Perhaps McNamara felt it was easier to punish me than, for example, a senior writer at the *Star.*

The *Globe* tried to settle the matter as soon as possible, but Ballard would not return telephone calls. When Paul Palango, the sports editor of the *Globe,* asked his counterpart at the *Star,* Paul Warnick, for help, Warnick told him if one of the *Globe*'s reporters wasn't allowed in the dressing room it was all the better for his newspaper.

A little later Wayne Parrish, a reporter for the *Star,* wrote a sympathetic feature about Nykoluk, discussing the attacks from the media he had endured, specifically from Strachan and myself. At one point in the article he quoted Danny Nykoluk as threatening to get even with us. A few times, Danny Nykoluk had come over to me outside the dresing room. Sometimes he said, "What are you going to write about tonight, fucker?"

It's fair to say that any professional sports league, other than the NHL would have stepped in quickly and settled the problem. But the NHL did nothing. Its president, John Ziegler, who is often perceived as a weak man with his own media problems, had been challenged and denounced by Ballard in the past. Perhaps he was intimidated by Ballard, who had called the 5-foot-7 Ziegler "an office clerk" and a "know-nothing shrimp" among other things.

At the beginning of the next season, I thought the bad feelings would be forgotten and I would be allowed back in. But McNamara was unforgiving. When I walked into the dressing room, the trainer was ordered to escort me out. By January, it was obvious to the *Globe* that we were on our own and nobody was going to help. We felt we had to force the matter.

We decided that Strachan would attempt to enter the dressing room after the next game. He hadn't been around since his story on Nykoluk, and more recently had infuriated the Leaf management even more by reporting information from confidential league documents that showed the Leafs to be "a mediocre draw in other NHL cities" with support "eroding" at home.

When McNamara read the story, he called the NHL's head office and bitterly complained about confidential reports being leaked. McNamara seemed to keep quite active in scrutinizing the media. Lou Nanne, the former general manager of the North Stars, once told Strachan that if anything critical of him was written in the *Globe,* McNamara would call Nanne and tell him. Given the state of the team, many felt McNamara had better things to do.

Accompanying Strachan that night was a photographer who was ready to take a picture if Strachan was physically ejected. And that's what happened. Nykoluk saw him, and said, "Don't you start running me down you son of a bitch. I don't want you in here. Now get the fuck out 'cause you're no goddam sportswriter." Then he shoved him out the door.

This time all three Toronto newspapers ran stories. The wire services picked it up, and Strachan was on several television and radio shows discussing the *Globe*'s problem with the Leafs. A few people in the media disagreed with what the *Globe* had done. Dunnell, for example, thought it was a "set-up" and unfair to Nykoluk. Dunnell, of course, had expressed no opinion in his column on what Ballard and McNamara had been doing.

The "set-up" was successful in motivating the league to do something. After some pressure, Ballard opened up the dressing room to everyone. But he wasn't finished fighting. At the same time, he barred the *Globe* from the press box. As a result, we had to buy seats to watch the games, but had nowhere to work after the games. Sometimes the reporter covering the game would work out of a room rented at the hotel next to the Gardens.

With Strachan and I allowed into the dressing room, it meant we could be part of the group that interviewed Nykoluk after games. But Nykoluk literally ran to get away from us. He refused to talk to us or answer questions in our presence. "Sorry fellas," he said to the others, "there's a bad smell in here." Other times he would say, "Sorry, the dirty, stinking. . . ," and he would walk away.

When the team was on the road, McNamara attempted to keep me away from the area that included him and the other reporters. Once when Frayne walked over to Nykoluk and Maloney and started a conversation, Maloney chatted, but Nykoluk walked about 30 feet away and stood by himself smoking his cigar. Frayne had not been part of the dispute, but his working for the *Globe* was enough for Nykoluk. His team was on its way to its second-worst season ever, but he seemed obsessed by a newspaper. When his team lost 7–0 in Philadelphia in February, he told the reporters, "I can guarantee you that the *Globe and Mail* is happy we got beat today."

Earlier, he told Gary Ronberg of the Philadelphia *Inquirer*, "The stuff they've written about me you wouldn't believe. They have called me stupid and all kinds of things, but I don't care, just so long as they stick to me as a coach. It's when they go into my personal life that I really get upset."

But there had been no references in the *Globe* to Nykoluk's "personal life," unless he meant Strachan's brief mention of his interest in attending the race track. That wasn't exactly a secret. Other newspapers had reported it. His reaction to what had been written seemed extreme, given the attacks other coaches had endured in the past and would in the future.

Nykoluk's record certainly wasn't something to praise, although he wasn't solely to blame for the state of the team. In his three full seasons behind the bench, the Leafs had failed to win more than 28 of 80 games in any season. They had finished out of the playoffs once and had qualified the other two times only because they were in the league's worst division with the league's worst team, Detroit. To nobody's surprise, when the Leafs stumbled to the end of the 1983-84 season with a 26-45-9 record and out of the playoffs, Nykoluk was fired.

12

Inside
Maple Leaf Gardens

The circumstances of the first meeting between Ballard and Yolanda have become one of the Gardens' better-known stories. One day in the summer of 1982 a limousine pulled up in front of the arena. Yolanda, wearing her mink coat, got out and made her way to Ballard's office. At first, Ballard had no interest in her. He attempted to ignore her, hoping she would go away. But she kept coming back. "She was very persistent," said a former employee from the Gardens offices. "She was determined to get what she wanted."

The employee remembers Yolanda sometimes waiting as long as four hours outside Ballard's office to see him. Eventually she would give up, but before leaving she would write a note on a piece of paper and slip it under his door. When she learned of Ballard's penchant for sweets, she would bake him pastries and take them to him. She would wait, and wait . . . and wait.

Then she came up with another idea. She staked out his car in the basement, knowing that he would eventually come down to get it. Nearby was a pay-phone, which she used in an attempt to get through to him in his office. Then, suddenly, they were together. "One day she was up in Mr. Ballard's office, and that was it," said a former employee.

Some people assumed Yolanda had arranged to be introduced to Ballard through his public relations director, Stan Obodiac. Obodiac had a daughter about the same age as Yolanda's daughter, Ana, and both attended Bishop Strachan School. But Stan's widow, Emma Obodiac, say's that's not true. The Obodiac's didn't know Yolanda prior to her relationship with Harold, and they didn't like her much afterwards.

What surprised Emma and Stan Obodiac, and others, was that Yolanda continued a close relationship with Irwin. He drove her limousine and was in effect her chauffeur. After leaving the Palace Pier, Irwin, as well as his daughter, Candice, and Yolanda's daughter, Ana, lived on Wellesley Street and then Dundonald Street. It's not clear if Yolanda lived with them or at the Gardens apartment all the time. "When she started going with Ballard she was still with this guy Irwin," Emma Obodiac says. "That's what I couldn't figure out. I thought that was strange."

By December 1982, the two were almost inseparable. Yolanda started travelling with Ballard to the hockey team's out-of-town games, although she wasn't allowed on the chartered flights. Instead she would take a commercial flight and then meet Ballard at the hotel.

She used the same hairdresser as Ballard, who had his hair tinted regularly. Together they would make a visit once a month. Yolanda usually took her dog, T.C. Puck, a Bouvier, which sat beside her while her hair was being done.

She made a big fuss over Harold. A friend can remember her fawning over him after he had dressed in a tuxedo for some hockey function. With affection, she would tell him how handsome he looked. She would pinch his cheek or give him a kiss. Because Ballard was a diabetic, she watched his diet closely. When they were on the road she often carried a large bag of fruit which substituted for Ballard's usual snacks of chocolates and ice cream.

Ballard enjoyed the attention and, in turn, helped her out financially. He gave her a job in the Gardens at $25,000 a year, although nobody knows what she does. When she needed money, he agreed to buy a limousine that belonged to her. When two of Ballard's Gardens employees were given the job of driving her around, she tried to get them to wear chauffeur's caps, but they refused.

At first, the Gardens employees were mildly entertained by Yolanda, but she soon became a nuisance, and finally she was disliked. Said a long-time Gardens worker, "I'd say that she generally isn't very well thought of." From the viewpoint of the hockey office, she was an irritation. Constantly on the phone, she would sometimes tie up the switchboard for long periods of time. She would ask Gardens secretaries to do personal work for her, such as typing out résumés for her son. This particular demand came the day after the death of King Clancy.

Emma Obodiac remembers her calling Stan to tell him he should write a rebuttal to a disparaging press report about the Gardens. Obodiac was a noted defender of Ballard and often fired off letters to the three Toronto newspapers when the Gardens or his boss came under attack.

"When Stan got off the phone, he was livid," Emma says. "I found it kind of strange that she had to remind him what he had to do with his 'most famous building in Canada.' I thought she had a nerve. She stepped on a lot of employees' toes."

The people at the arena soon saw both sides of Yolanda. There was the sweet, charming woman, who talked softly and wept over the smallest misfortune. And there was the hard woman who would strike out at an employee. "She is the kind of woman," said a Gardens employee, "who can talk down a truck driver in the morning and dine with royalty at night."

For years, the employees had suffered low wages and many indignities while working for Ballard. He was cheap, paid poor wages, and was a bully. After a while, they realized that the arrival of Yolanda did nothing more than increase the number of tyrants to two.

Near the end of the summer in 1988, Yolanda and Harold had been driven to the Gardens from the summer cottage by Ron Jones, a long-time arena employee who drove Ballard's car and the team van. Ballard had a great deal of trouble walking, because of circulation problems in his feet. The procedure was to enter the arena from the north entrance and then drive up a ramp to the main level. The limousine would then turn right and move slowly down the east-side hall to the escalators on the southeast corner.

By this time, Ballard was using a wheelchair, but this day he decided to walk. Jones got out of the car and went over to turn off the escalator, so Ballard could step on. But he fell attempting to get out of the car. As Jones ran to assist him, he heard Yolanda scream. Then she struck out with her finger nails, raking the side of his face, and drawing blood. Jones was shocked but knew he couldn't do anything for fear of losing his job.

The news of Yolanda's assault on Jones spread like wildfire through the arena, and only increased the employees' dislike of her.

Yolanda's hatred of Jones went back at least one year to the previous summer when she had been denied transportation to a Tiger-Cat game in Hamilton. Ballard went himself but left word that she wasn't to come. Late in the afternoon, however, she made up her mind she wanted to go. When she asked Jones to drive her, he refused, saying Ballard didn't want her attending. Later, she complained to Ballard, and despite Jones' adhering to Ballard's request, he found himself in the doghouse.

As well as Yolanda, T.C. Puck became a fixture at the arena, and also was disliked–not for what it was but for what it represented to the Gardens employees. In the fall of 1986, the dog almost cost a worker his job. On 27 September Yolanda searched the arena without luck for someone to drive her and the dog in Ballard's limo to a downtown destination. Finally, she walked toward the ice surface at the north end where a group of workers, including Peter Thomson, an 11-year employee and lead hand on the maintenance staff, was removing a piece of plastic from behind the goal. She went to Sam DeAngelis, a long-time employee, and asked him to drive her. Turning to the other workers, Thomson said, "Why can't she walk the fucking dog herself?"

Yolanda overheard the remark, walked over to Thomson, and told him she would report the incident to Ballard. Later that day, Thomson was suspended for five days. At the end of the five days, Ballard refused to allow him to return, insisting he be transferred to Davis Printing, which is a subsidiary of Maple Leaf Gardens Limited, in Mississauga. Thomson wanted to remain at the arena, so the Teamster's Union grieved, sending the case to arbitration. It dragged on for almost four months during which Thomson sat at home, although he collected his paycheque.

Ballard hired Toronto lawyer Larry Bertuzzi, an NHL negotiator for management, to state the Gardens case. Bertuzzi argued:

1.) The fact that Yolanda was not a supervisor did not matter. The attitude of the griever was not provoked and was offensive.
2.) Strangers at Maple Leaf Gardens have a right to be treated with respect.
3.) The griever was engaged in improper conduct and the employer "has the right to expect his employees to act like human beings."

The Union, in its submission, stated:

1.) The action of the griever does not constitute a disciplinary offence as such.
2.) The griever did not intend to offend Yolanda and there is no evidence of a strong discussion with shouting and swearing.
3.) The language used by the griever is profane but his remark was not aimed directly at Yolanda.

During testimonies by witnesses, there was one obvious contradiction. All the Gardens employees stated that Thomson had uttered his remark, with the profanity, to them. Yolanda, however, told the arbitrator, in tears, that she had endured a prolonged harangue, laced with filthy words, from Thomson. The union argued that the arbitrator, when deciding upon his ruling, should take into consideration the contradictory elements of the statements and statements which tended to discredit the witnesses.

In December 1986, the arbitrator ruled in favour of Thomson. The penalty of a five-day suspension was reduced to a written warning, and Thomson was compensated by almost $10,000 because of the missed opportunity for overtime pay while away from work.

Conditions for labourers, of course, had been bad for a long time–probably for as long as the Gardens has existed. In 1984, for example, it was intolerable. Among the 21 arenas around the NHL, the Gardens was at the bottom in terms of wages. And that was with the cost of living skyrocketing in the city. An annual salary for a maintenance worker was $13,294, which was an increase of $190 from the previous year. The hourly rate was $6.85 at a time when a City of Toronto study showed that a person had to earn $10 an hour to stay above the poverty line. Some employees who had been there only six or seven years were earning more than 30-year employees, even though they were doing the same job equally well.

Finally, the discontent reached a peak when the workers were offered only a 30-cent-an-hour raise. Within days, they organized and joined the Teamsters Union. What followed were threats from management of dismissals, layoffs, and even closing the building.

During 1984, Ballard earned about $941,000 in dividends alone from his 80 per cent of Gardens shares. This was noted when a shop steward, Brent Wynne, sent a letter to the directors on the Gardens board outlining the problems the employees were having in negotiating a new contract. In part, it read as follows:

The major problem to emerge during contract talks, to no one's surprise, were the wages being paid by the company. The wages at Maple Leaf Gardens Ltd., border on being archaic and have lagged behind wages in industry and virtually every arena in the NHL. This has created a situation where many of the people employed by the company live from paycheque to paycheque, with little or no hope of achieving some degree of financial security for themselves or their families. This further results in bitterness and, at best, a lackadaisical attitude. . .

This callous and insensitive attitude only breeds anger and contempt between management and employees, which is a disturbing and disheartening commentary for Maple Leaf Gardens Ltd.

If the Gardens maintenance workers had wished, they could have mentioned their summer job at Ballard's cottage. Every summer a crew of three Gardens workers drive daily up to Ballard's cottage to work on landscaping projects and other maintenance jobs. They put in a full day's work and return home to Toronto at night. The next day, they're back at the cottage. These workers do not take a leave of absence or use holidays to do this. They get paid through the Gardens, which is a public company, with cheques in the Gardens insignia.

In 1986 Ballard had a major project for them. He wanted to build a bridge that would connect his property to a township road. This was a long-term project that took longer than one summer. When it was finished Ballard had a steel-girdered bridge that had cost him more than $100,000. "It's a monstrosity," said one of the employees who worked on it. "It can hold a six-ton truck easily."

One of maintenance people who worked several summers at the cottage says he was told by Crump that, although they are paid by the Gardens to work at the cottage, Ballard "reimburses the company."

Among the employees, many agree the most pathetic story was about Stan Obodiac. In the 1950s, Obodiac began working for the Gardens in the publicity department. He had come from Yorkton, Saskatchewan, where he had been a good hockey player–good enough in fact to play for Canada at the 1951 world hockey championship in Paris.

In a thumb-nail profile in the annual Leaf media guide, he described himself as "a world champion hockey player [who] . . .

wrote a book about it. Obodiac has been a World War Two pilot, politician, writer, publisher, radio broadcaster, publicist, student, world traveller and a champion of seven different sports."

Hyperbole was something in which Obodiac indulged liberally, whether he was profiling Ballard or describing his own achievements. However, he wasn't a snobbish or arrogant man, and he had, indeed, written several books about the Leafs and hockey, and one about Pope John Paul II, called *The Polish Pope*. Obodiac, of course, was of Polish descent.

But mostly he was Ballard's personal PR man. Rex MacLeod, when he was a writer with the Toronto *Star,* once described Obodiac as "A Boswell for Pope John Paul and Ballard–and not necessarily in that order." Obodiac idolized Ballard, and viewed the Gardens as hockey's shrine. It was "Canada's most famous building" and "the world's most famous arena." Ballard was the "supreme commander" who had "an explosion of ideas in his mind."

Reporters laughed at this hero worshipping, considering the subject and considering Ballard's attitude toward Obodiac. A joke at the Gardens used to be that Scrooge treated Bob Cratchit better than Ballard treated Obodiac. Ballard would ridicule Obodiac. On one occasion a few years ago, when journalist Charles Davies met Ballard in his office for an interview, Obodiac brought some papers in for Ballard to sign.

"Hello Stanley," said Ballard cheerfully. "What have you fucked up today?"

Obodiac smiled weakly and told him the day wasn't over yet.

Ballard replied, "We'll give you a few more hours to see what you can do."

Through all of this Obodiac's loyalty never diminished. He worked long hours, evenings, and weekends. "I can remember many times when Stan would get a call at dinner from Mr. Ballard," Emma says. "He would ask him to drive down to the Gardens to get an autograph from a player for a friend of his. Stan would get up right away and leave his dinner."

But it wasn't until after his death in November 1984, at the age of 62, that the public discovered how badly Obodiac had been treated. Up until then, Ballard had been viewed as a little eccentric, but not really miserly or cruel. Then it came out, in the *Globe and Mail,* that Obodiac was getting paid only $23,000 a year at the time of his death. An NHL publicity director with his years of service (26) should have been earning $65,000 or more. The year prior to his death, he made $20,000. He had trouble paying his bills and had to ask Ballard for an advance. When Obodiac died after a quarter century of service, the pension his family received was a pittance–$277 a month. This shocked Emma.

For three years before his death, Obodiac fought cancer of the liver. Already thin, he started to lose weight. Near the end, he looked almost skeletal. In the spring of 1984, with Obodiac's condition worsening, Ballard came through with a grand gesture by offering him a paid two-week vacation in Hawaii. But Obodiac didn't want to go alone, and asked if he could take his wife. Ballard, however, refused to pay Emma's way. So Stan, unable to afford the cost of two, went by himself. "He didn't really enjoy it," Emma says. "He was lonely."

On the day before her husband died, Emma recalls that Stan called Ballard and thanked him for everything he had done. "I remember Stan telling him what a fine man he thought he was, and thanking him for the way he had been treated," Emma says. "He really liked Mr. Ballard and had such a loyalty to the organization, regardless of how they treated him."

At the funeral, Bill Ballard and Harold Jr. came over to Emma and her two daughters and offered their sympathy, as did Tom Smythe and Stafford's widow, Dorothea. Ballard, however, ignored them. They received neither a note nor a sympathy card from Ballard, and on the morning after the funeral, at 8:30, Emma was awakened by a knock on the door. It was a Gardens employee who had been sent to pick up Obodiac's company car.

"I was sound asleep," she says. "I knew it wasn't our car, but I thought they might phone first and ask when it was possible to pick it up. Later, I asked Don Crump why they did it that way, and he said, 'Maybe that's when people go to work.' To me, that wasn't good enough."

Ballard, of course, used Obodiac. He knew he loved his job and probably would have worked for less. In spite of all this, Emma Obodiac says she is not bitter. Stan was happy and he never complained. "The Gardens doesn't owe me anything," she says. "Stan was happy there. Ballard knew that. Stan . . . Stan, I think, was naive."

13

BALLARD

AND THE MEDIA

In Ballard's love-hate relationship with the media, he adores
the people who keep him in the newspapers and on the air and
spend a lot of time with him. You can write humorously about
Ballard. You can even make fun of him, as long as it is done in a
subtle enough way to escape his attention, which means you don't
have to be very subtle. Or you can pass on his message in a news
story. But don't criticize him.

You can knock the team, or the coach, or a particular player,
although if it's someone Ballard likes, it is better to do it gently and
not too often. But when you start pointing fingers at Harold, you are
in trouble. He will not talk to you, he certainly will not give you a
story, and he might even kick you out of the arena, if he really
dislikes you.

That's why, until recently, so very few prominent sports journalists in Toronto criticized Ballard. He was intimidating and too
valuable a source to lose. On a slow day you could call him up and
he would tell you anything. No matter how ridiculous, untrue,
hurtful, or unjustified, it would be reported and given prominence,
not just because Ballard is president and owner of the Leafs, but
because of the public image–"the colourful, outrageous owner of the
Maple Leafs." It could just as well be the "insensitive, abusive, and
incompetent owner of the Maple Leafs." But that wouldn't sell as
many newspapers, nor would it draw viewers to the nightly news.

Those he hates tend to see him more as the latter. But as recently as 10 years ago there were very few critics around. Ballard got along with almost everybody, because there was never a negative word heard or written. Pal Hal was seen as a crazy but essentially good-hearted guy who really wanted to be liked, and really wanted to win a Stanley Cup.

Some sycophants still exist. They choose to flatter Ballard and never ask a difficult question, because they are happy to accept the quick and easy story–a couple of words from the old guy, no matter how illogical, and their work is done for the day. Of the others, Ballard says, "They're not sportswriters. They're critics."

And he's right. To his way of thinking, sportswriters are the stereotypical cheerleaders–cigar chomping, hot-dog eating supporters of the team who do what they are told, never make him uncomfortable, and, of course, never express an opinion. Back in the good old days, they were even slipped a few dollars and given expensive gifts at Christmas to make sure they didn't waver from the party line.

One of the first reporters to fall from grace was Donald Ramsay of the *Globe and Mail* who at one time was Ballard's friend. Over the years, Ballard had given him many exclusive stories, but when Ramsay started criticizing Imlach and his coaches in 1979-80, Ballard cut him off. A few years later, when Ramsay was working as the public relations director of the Winnipeg Jets, he came over to Ballard in the Winnipeg press box, and figuring everything was forgotten, stuck out his hand and said hello. Ballard looked up from his seat and said, "Get away from me you fucking whore."

A little earlier Ballard had ended a long friendship with Frank Orr of the *Toronto Star*. Orr and Ballard had been close for many years. But one day, Orr wrote a column commending Gregory on doing a good job under difficult circumstances, meaning Ballard's meddling. Orr wrote, "When a man works for Ballard he does his job with as little fuss as possible. Every day, there's a crisis or a hassle often about minute subjects. Ballard is riding herd on the operation all the time and his public statements such as the knocks he's delivered against some of the team's athletes have made Gregory's job even more difficult."

That's all it took. Orr was sent to Coventry. Ballard also started spreading rumours about Orr, slanderous things that people laughed at, knowing it was a reflection of Ballard's vindictiveness and immaturity–at the age of 76 no less. At first, Orr thought Ballard would forget about the rift. But it never happened. And to Orr's knowledge none of Ballard's pals at the *Star* ever attempted to bring them together.

Among Ballard's media friends, no one has ever achieved the exalted status of Milt Dunnell. Dunnell is regarded as the dean of sportswriters in Canada, and over 40 years has built a reputation as the consummate insider, the friend and confidant of the most powerful figures on the Toronto sports scene.

In 1949 Dunnell was transferred from news side at the *Toronto Star* to become sports editor, a position he held until his retirement at 65. Since then he has continued to write his column, although he reduced his workload a few years ago. Now well into his eighties, he still writes three columns a week.

Over the years, Dunnell's friendships have earned him privileged information from such sources as Conn Smythe, John W. Bassett, the late John F. Bassett, who owned the Toros of the old World Hockey Association, and, of course, Ballard. Although Dunnell has on occasion mildly criticized people who work for Ballard, he has never pointed the finger at the owner. He reports Ballard's information and chooses not to comment negatively. That has preserved the friendship and helped it grow. When a magazine asked Ballard to rank the Toronto sports journalists a few years ago, he put Dunnell at the top with a grade A+++.

"You have to be a Sherlock Holmes to find any class people in the media," Ballard began. "But Milt Dunnell is certainly one. He's so far ahead of anyone else in the newspaper business it's a joke. He's forgotten more than the other dunces will ever know if they live to be a million years old."

Ballard's son Bill isn't as big a fan. He calls Dunnell "Milt the Tape Recorder," because Bill feels he reports his father's comments indiscriminately without questioning the accuracy of the information.

Another of Ballard's close media friends is George Gross at the Toronto *Sun*. But Gross has not totally escaped Ballard's wrath. When Imlach was in limbo while in hospital in 1981, Gross described McNamara and Nykoluk as Ballard's "yes-men" in a column. This offended the coach and GM because of their sensitivity. Ballard also was upset.

Ballard started telling people that Gross, who defected from Czechoslovakia 30 years earlier, had received a finder's fee for recruiting Crha, the Czechoslovak goaltender. Nykoluk spread that rumour around quite a bit, even suggesting Ballard was going to reveal this on television. He never did and Gross denies he received any money. But the two didn't speak for quite a while. Today, however, they get along well.

Gross's experience might be the exception to the rule, because some people in the media have been transferred, fired, or put out of business after upsetting Ballard. When Brian McFarlane, a host of "Hockey Night in Canada," publicly supported Sittler in his feud with Imlach, Ballard went to Ted Hough, then the head of the Canadian Sports Network, the company that produced the Leaf telecasts, and told him he wanted McFarlane removed from Leaf games. McFarlane was transferred to Winnipeg to be host of the Jets games.

Paul Palmer, an independent television producer, was forced out of business when he included Palmateer and Sittler in "Showdown," which was his production. Ballard forbade CSN from running the show on the Leaf telecasts, and since Toronto is the hub of Canada's most populated and wealthy region, Palmer lost enough money, about $100,000, to kill his business. The vice-president of Palmer's company, Gerry Patterson, said, "Hough wasn't going to challenge Ballard. Here was Palmer sitting with all that money invested in something still in the can."

Then there was Earl McRae, a journalist who had a sports phone-in show on the Toronto radio station CJCL, which held the rights to the Leaf games. When I was barred from the dressing room, McRae opened a show with a report, interviewing myself, *Globe* sports editor Geoffrey Stevens, and McNamara. All interviews ran unedited, after which McRae said he felt Higgins was a goon and the Leafs were doing him a disservice keeping him around. Most of the callers thought he had been too easy on McNamara. At one point, McRae replied, "My feeling was if the guy wants to hang himself, let him hang himself."

For whatever reason, Ballard and McNamara were outraged over the report. Ballard threatened to pull the next game off the air if McRae wasn't fired. McNamara told an executive of CJCL that McRae had "tricked" him during the show, but McRae didn't understand what he meant. McNamara's interview ran in its entirety.

CJCL didn't know what to do, because McRae was not part of the Leaf telecast. It was owned by Telemedia Broadcasting Systems, which in turn was a branch of Telemedia Communications Inc., which owned a network of stations, one of which was CJCL.

Finally, it was decided that McRae would take a two-week paid vacation. The game was carried, and by the time McRae returned the Leafs had been eliminated from the playoffs. About six weeks later, McRae was fired when the station underwent a change in format.

Ballard tends to treat agents much like journalists. If you don't cause trouble, which in the case of an agent would be doing a less than efficient job in representing your client, you might get along. After Bill Watters, the former president of Branada Sports Management Ltd., negotiated Boschman's contract, Ballard wrote on his cheque every week, after signing it, "Watters is a crook." When Don Meehan, the president of Newport Sports, negotiated Wendel Clark's first contract, making him the highest-paid Leaf rookie ever, the first thing Ballard said upon meeting Meehan was, "So, you're the crook."

At least one agent has been ejected from a Leaf practice. One day in early 1981, Ballard sat in the stands at North York Centennial Arena watching his team practise when a man in a suit and overcoat, carrying a briefcase, walked into the arena and sat down with two reporters, Orr and Suneel Joshi, who was then working for CFRB radio. Ballard turned to Curly Davies, who operates the arena, and said, "Curly, who's the fucking Indian."

Davies said, "That's Suneel Joshi. He works for CFRB."

"Not that Indian," said Ballard. "The other fucking Indian. Who let him into my practice?"

The man was Norm Caplan, an agent from Montreal. He was Jewish. When Ballard was told Caplan had received permission from Imlach to attend the practice, Ballard said, "Punch Imlach does not pay the bills around here. I pay the bills around here and I don't want any agents conducting business on my time. Tell him to open an office on Bathurst Street or rent a room somewhere. Just get him out of here." Davies took Caplan to his office where he remained until the practice was over.

One of Ballard's many contradictions is his love for publicity but his opposition to a book being written about him, authorized or otherwise. Many journalists have approached him over the years, only to be turned down or led on endlessly with maybes. When I decided to write his unauthorized biography in 1984 I was not on good terms with him. I had been critical over the years and at the time was barred from the press box. He wouldn't speak to me except to yell obscenities.

As a result, I sent him a letter informing him about the book and requesting an interview. A few weeks later, he came over to me outside the Leaf dressing room in the Chicago Stadium after a game against the Blackhawks and said, "Are you writing a book about me?"

"Yes."

"Well if there is one word, just one word–you'll get your throat cut!"

A few days later I received a letter from Obodiac, attempting to discourage me from going ahead. "A dozen people would like to do a book on Mr. Ballard," he wrote. "There are several publishers who would commission this. But two writers are doing books on Mr. Ballard. All material, most of it copyrighted, will be available to them."

To my knowledge nobody else was doing a book on Ballard, although Beddoes had thought about it. Two weeks later, a letter came from the boss himself, spelling mistakes and grammatical errors included.

> *Dear Mr. Houston:*
>
> *I understand that you are in the process of compiling material for an unauthorized biography of me. I would like to make you aware of two things.*
>
> *First, that an authorized biography of me with my full blessing and co-operation is in the works, in collaboration with a compotent [sic] and qualified writer.*
>
> *Also, if you go through with your plans–be warned that I will be waiting for the slightest opportunity to nail you with a lawsuit for any material that may be deemed slanderous and/or liable [sic]. And I know that with the limited amount of information that you really know about me, that the opportunity should present itself many times over. I've put up with enough crap from you and your paper and I warn you tha [sic] I am not going to give you the least little break if you choose to publish such a book.*
>
> *Cordially,*
> *Harold E. Ballard*
> *President*

From Ballard's perspective the book was probably as bad as, or worse than, he expected. It probably didn't make him feel any better when the publisher bought space on a billboard to advertise the book just outside the window of his Gardens apartment on Church

Street. Wisely, Ballard did not talk about the book and did not denounce it publicly.

There was a confrontation, however, a few weeks after it was released. I was at the Gardens covering a practice when Ballard appeared, which prompted the other reporters to walk over and talk to him. I followed and then decided to ask a question to test his reaction. When he saw me, his face turned red, and then the sparks started to fly.

"You've got a lot of nerve to talk to me! Who told you you could talk to me!" he raged. "Go on, get outta here."

"I'm just doing my job," I said, which was something I found myself saying quite a bit when I was around Ballard.

"You don't work!" he thundered.

Then he started to come after me, fists up, getting ready to swing, face turning purple by now. At the last second a couple of reporters stepped between us. His parting words were, "They should have smothered you when you were born!"

During that winter there was constant harassment. After a game, he would yell out, "You fucking son of a bitch" or some other choice endearment. I was covering a governors meeting where he saw me and said: "What are you doing here? Go on, get outta here! You're nothing but a disease!"

Then near the end of the 1984-85 season, we had a major confrontation. Again it was at a Leaf practice, this time at the North York arena. By this time I was getting sick of his bullying. About half-way through the practice, Ballard walked in with King Clancy at his side. When he saw me, it was the usual, "What are you doing here?!"

"I'm covering the practice. What does it look like I'm doing?"

"Go on, get outta here!"

"You don't own this place. It's a public arena," I said. "I'm doing my job."

"You don't work! You're the stupidest son of a bitch I've ever known!"

"I'm stupid?" I said. "You've got the worst hockey team in the league, and I'm stupid? You happen to be the stupidest son of a bitch I've ever known!"

Ballard was taken aback and didn't say anything for a few seconds. Then he said, "Where did you get that coffee?!"

Outside the dressing room the trainers kept a large urn of coffee for anybody who might be around, a coach, a scout, or a reporter. When I told him, he roared, "That's not your coffee! Who told you you could have it?!

"Do you want some money for it?" I said.

"Yeah."

I took a dollar out of my wallet, went over to him, and threw it at his feet. As Ballard bent over to pick it up, Clancy stepped in and said in his high voice, "No, Harold, you can't take the money! That's his money!"

Then Ballard put his fists up and started coming after me again. But before he could reach me, Clancy, who seemed about half Ballard's size, stepped in front of him and held him back with two hands.

"Don't hit him, Harold!" screamed King. "Don't hit him!"

Alan Eagleson once said that Ballard could tell the Toronto Media it was the first of the month when it was really the end of the month, and that they would report it as such, never thinking for a second to question what he had said. That used to be the case, and unfortunately still is to a degree.

In January 1988 he told the *Star* about firing two security guards who were drunk on Christmas Day. "Nobody's gonna believe this," he said. "But these are the first people I ever fired. No I didn't fire Punch Imlach, despite anything you've read. I told Punch I was transferring him to a desk job. Punch said he had been hired to manage the hockey club and refused the change. That ended it."

Ballard was right. Nobody was going to believe it, especially Kelly, Gregory, Neilson, Nykoluk, and Peter Thomson, who he tried to fire, and many others. But Ballard's version of reality is eagerly consumed by his friends in the media. It's good copy even if it isn't the truth.

For a long time, Ballard was referred to as a "former national speed skating champion in 1928 and 1932." Not only was he a title holder, he told us, but he set records in the 200-, 440-, and 800-yard classes. Not true. He speed skated a little in the 1920s but never won anything of significance and certainly never set any records. People who knew him back then say he wasn't much more than a fan.

In the late 1920s, Ballard raced hydroplanes, little outboard motor boats called sea fleas, on Lake Ontario. It was often reported Ballard set a Canadian speed record of 63 miles per hour (101 km per hour) in the 1920s in a 75-horsepower boat on Rice Lake in the

Peterborough area. "It was a fair speed," Ballard used to say. A fair speed 'perhaps for the 1940s, but in the 1920s there were no 75-horsepower motors and there was no speed record of 63. Nowhere in any year does the Canadian Boating Federation's record book include a mark of any kind belonging to Harold Ballard.

Ballard used to say that his uncle, George Ballard, played football for the Hamilton Tigers of the Big Four. This was mentioned in my first book. But when it came out, I received a call from Hugh Scully of Ottawa, who said George Mercier Ballard, the quarterback of the Tigers, was *his* uncle and "Harold Ballard is a cousin I don't need."

In 1977, there was Ballard's fabrication about the circumstances of Neilson's hiring. Neilson was given the job on a Friday night in June shortly after Red Kelly was told he was fired. Gregory instructed Neilson not to tell anybody he had the job, because "Ballard likes to announce these things himself." Neilson said there was no problem with that, because he was leaving the next morning for a long vacation in Africa and Europe. He was flying to Nigeria to meet his friend, Dunford, and then they were going to make their way up into Europe.

Several weeks later, somewhere in Europe, Neilson stopped at a public library to see if his appointment had been announced. Sure enough, just a few days earlier, Ballard had told the Toronto newspapers that he had personally talked to Neilson in Johannesburg the day before. "I could hear him as clearly as if he was in Cookstown," said Ballard.

The first paragraph of the *Globe* story read, "The telephone jangled beside Harold Ballard at 7:45 yesterday morning. South Africa calling. At the very far end of the line was a man who said he could coach the Toronto Maple Leafs. . . . From Johannesburg, Roger Neilson said yes to Ballard's job offer." Neilson, of course, had been nowhere near Johannesburg, and he had not spoken to Ballard.

A few years later, after Ballard said he was leaving his money to charity, he departed with Yolanda for a vacation. He said they were going to the Cayman Islands. The Ballard children were, understandably, hurt by their father's attack and said so.

To get Ballard's reaction, the *Star* sent a reporter to the Caymans to find him. But it turned into a wild goose chase. He couldn't find Ballard in the Caymans. When he called the Stavro residence in Palm Beach, he was told Ballard had just left for the islands. Back he went, but still there was no Ballard. When he returned to Florida the second time, he went to the Stavro home. But again he was told that Ballard was in the Caymans. It later turned out that Ballard was in the hospital with heart trouble.

During Ballard's stay in hospital, sports reporters who felt they were on good terms with Ballard were in something of a competition to be the first one to talk to him after he had left hospital. Dunnell, of course, had been on the telephone with him several times. But after he was released, the *Sun* reached him, and in addition to hinting that McNamara would be fired, he told the paper that he was taking a leisurely nine-day Caribbean cruise. "I'm leaving tonight," he said.

The *Sun* played his story up in a big way, using the entire front page of the sports section to display a picture of Ballard superimposed against a map of the Caribbean with lines showing the route and ports of call. In fact, Ballard returned straight home to Toronto.

In November of 1986, with the team off to one of its usual good starts, Ballard walked into the coach's office after a game, while several reporters waited outside, and said, "What a bunch of pigs." Nobody replied except for the CBC reporter who said quietly, "Yeah, and pigs are attracted to garbage."

And just a few days later, many of the same reporters sat at Ballard's feet and listened to him reminisce about Clancy who lay in hospital dying. For several days Ballard's picture was in the newspapers, often on the front page. He would be seen sitting in the stands at the Gardens, alone, without his old sidekick. Sympathetic stories were written daily about how difficult it was for Ballard to cope, and about the good old days with Clancy, the little Irish Leprechaun.

Ballard would tell them how close they were in the early 1930s, when Clancy played for the Leafs. In fact, nobody from that era can remember them being friendly at all. It wasn't until the 1970s that they became inseparable. Ballard would also tell the reporters that he was the one who had appointed Clancy vice-president of Maple Leaf Gardens Ltd. In fact, Stafford Smythe had done it in 1969 at the same time he fired Imlach. Clancy had been Imlach's pal and always said that the day Imlach left the organization he would go with him. But with the promotion, he decided to stay.

When Clancy died a few days after being admitted to hospital, Ballard announced publicly that he would never again sit in his north-end bunker. Too many memories, he said. He had it elaborately covered over with a dedication, "In memory of King."

But a few weeks later, a column appeared in the *Sun* with the news that Ballard had changed his mind. He would return to the bunker. It had been all the letters, dozens of them from fans, imploring him to return to his old place. Ballard, not wanting to let them down, had relented.

In fact, there was really nowhere else for him to go. Because of his diabetes, the circulation in his feet and legs was bad and he couldn't walk very well. By then, he was moving around in a shuffling motion. The arena escalators didn't take him high enough to make it to the press box or the private boxes. And he wasn't going to sit in the stands.

After Clancy had been buried and the story concluded, many journalists, one of them a good friend of Ballard's, felt he had used King's illness and hospitalization as a means of getting into the newspapers and before the public. Certainly the grieving was sincere, but he had done it in a very public way, eager to pose for pictures and grant interviews. He did this for hours. The one consolation for the death of his friend was the amount of attention he received for more than a week.

In a dispute that started in January of 1986, Ballard ended up receiving more attention than he wanted. It started because of his attitude toward women in journalism which had been clearly articulated in his interview with Frum. He not only disapproved of women in the business of journalism, but he wouldn't let them into the players' dressing room at the Gardens. This went against the spirit, if not the exact wording, of the NHL media bylaw. Still, for years Ballard had successfully barred women.

In January, Helene Elliott, a hockey reporter for *Newsday* of New York, decided to challenge the ban. To bar Elliott and not be accused of breaking the league bylaw, Ballard and his lawyer, Arthur Gans, used a strict interpretation of the bylaw that reads, "Those clubs which follow a policy of excluding female reporters from the room shall be required to provide separate interviewing facilities for all press media, male and female."

In simple terms, the Leafs barred everybody, male and female, from the dressing room. Instead, the players were brought out to an adjoining room for interviews after games, thus equal access. But this was unacceptable for the players and the media. It prevented a reporter from talking to a particular player alone, which can be done in the dressing room. And when the team was on the road, it denied the players their privacy. They had to leave the room for a public area, a hall usually, sometimes with only a towel wrapped around them, and answer questions.

Scott Morrison, the hockey writer for the *Sun* and the Toronto chapter chairman of the Professional Hockey Writers Association, sent letters to the NHL head office stating the dissatifaction of the Toronto writers. But nothing was done by the league. Finally, the hockey writers and sports editors from the three Toronto newspapers met to discuss the problem. It was decided they would test the ban–essentially the same thing the *Globe* had done three years earlier.

So in February of 1987, after the Leafs had defeated the Los Angeles Kings 5-4, about 20 reporters walked into the dressing room after the game. The reaction from the players was one of shock and amusement.

"What are you guys doing here?" said one.

"Is this Christmas?" asked another.

The reporters and players chatted for perhaps a minute before Ballard stormed in. In seven years, I had seen Ballard furious many times, usually at me, but I had never seen him as upset as he was that night. But instead of turning on the reporters, he berated Bob Stellick, brother of Gord Stellick, who had replaced Obodiac as Leaf public relations director. Stellick had been powerless to stop us, but he faced the full force of Ballard's wrath.

"What are these assholes doing here!" Ballard roared." Come on, get 'em the hell out of here! If you like working here, get 'em the hell out! Get the whole fucking bunch out. Grab 'em by the ass and throw them out! Take that camera and push it on the floor!"

Ballard was still screaming when Stellick asked the visitors to leave. As they walked out, not a word was said by anyone, so I decided to use the old line, "We're just trying to do our job."

"You don't work!" Ballard roared. "Get the fuck out of here and don't come back, you four-eyed cunt!"

A few minutes later, Ballard slapped a camera that a *Globe* photographer, Jeff Wasserman, had raised to his eye to take a picture, yelling, "Get out of here with that camera. Go on, get out."

That night Morrison released the following statement:

There are 119 major professional sports teams in North America. One hundred and eighteen allow reporters in the dressing room following games.

Since January of last year, the Toronto Maple Leafs have refused to extend reporters that courtesy. Several appeals to Harold Ballard, the most recent two days ago, and to NHL president John Ziegler to rectify this situation have been rejected.

It's the feeling of the [Toronto chapter] that our rights, but more so those of our readers, have been denied. For a major professional sports league, this is an extremely unprofessional working situation and one we feel obliged to try to change.

After the incident, the NHL moved quickly. In addition to pressure from the league, Brophy talked to Ballard and explained that the players did not like the procedure either. The NHLPA, in fact, voted unanimously to support the writers in getting back into the dressing room. Finally, at the June meetings Ballard announced that access would be granted to everyone. The league bylaw was rewritten to state that entry to the room was required.

Reporters continued to treat Ballard gently, of course, steering away from the tough questions. Ballard was never much good at fielding a question of any substance. In February of 1988, a few days after he had returned from Florida, he attended a practice at North York. Reporters sat around Ballard, writing down his silly comments about Brophy being the best coach in the league, when Ken Daniels of CBC Television asked Ballard if he thought his team needed more scouts.

"Who has more scouts than us?" Ballard shot back.

Daniels could have mentioned any team in the league, but instead he said Calgary and Edmonton, both strong and successful franchises.

"Yeah?" Ballard asked. "And what have they done?"

△ The Leafs, 1931-32. The powerful 1931-32 World Champion Leaf team featured the famous "Kid Line" of Jackson, Primeau, and Conacher, but had tremendous bench strength in the line of Baldy Cotton, Andy Blair, and Ace Bailey. Their backline was every bit as prominent with King Clancy, Hap Day, and Red Horner helping Lorne Chabot to a 2.41 goals-against average.

(*Courtesy Hockey Hall of Fame*)

△ The 1933 Leafs were so confident of Stanley Cup victory that they prepared their world championship photo before the series had even begun. But, as Yogi Berra later said, "It ain't over 'til it's over," and after the Rangers took the Leafs in four games, nothing was left of their hopes but this ill-advised picture. *(Courtesy Hockey Hall of Fame)*

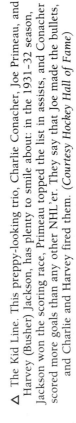

△ The Kid Line. This preppy-looking trio, Charlie Conacher, Joe Primeau, and Harvey (Busher) Jackson, has plenty to smile about: in the 1931–32 season, Jackson won the scoring race, Primeau topped the list in assists, and Conacher scored more goals than any other NHL'er. They say that Joe made the bullets, and Charlie and Harvey fired them. (*Courtesy Hockey Hall of Fame*)

▷ Charlie Conacher. Toronto born and bred, this 6-footer was an all-round athlete from a family of talented sportsmen. One of the most feared wingers in hockey, the "Big Bomber" won the Art Ross Trophy twice, and was selected for five all-star teams. (*Courtesy Hockey Hall of Fame*)

"ACE" BAILEY BENEFIT GAME, TORONTO, FEB 14, 1934, NATIONAL LEAGUE ALL-STARS VERSUS TORONTO MAPLE LEAFS

R HEWITSON   B O'BRIEN   H KILREA   E SHORE   C CONACHER   W COOK   C SANDS   L CONACHER   A BLAIR   A SHIELDS   H COTTON   N STEWART   H JACKSON   C JOHNSON   T DALY   M RODDEN
              F SELKE   M DUTTON   C DAY   R SMITH   L DANDURAND   L PATRICK   F CALDER   C SMYTHE   D IRVIN   H MORENZ   F CLANCY   J WARD
G HAINSWORTH   K DORATY   L AURIE   W THOMS   N HIMES   A LEVINSKY   F FINNIGAN   J PRIMEAU   R HORNER   B BOLL   H LEWIS   J JOLIAT   A JOLIAT   C GARDINER

△ The Ace Game. When Ace Bailey was upset in a career-ending encounter with Boston's Eddie Shore, ice-men gathered at Maple Leaf Gardens to play for his benefit. So it was that the NHL All-Star game was born. On 14 February 1934, showing a lot of heart, the greatest men from around the league played the Toronto team, losing the game 7–3, but winning the hearts of fans everywhere.

(Courtesy Hockey Hall of Fame)

△ Leafs over the boards. This famous frozen moment in time shows the 1946–47 Toronto Maple Leafs bounding over the boards to greet their teammates in celebration of another Stanley Cup victory. Seen (left to right) are: Garth Boesch, Harry Watson, Bill Ezinicki, and Cal Gardner.
(Courtesy Hockey Hall of Fame)

▽ Syl Apps, a McMaster University graduate, captained the Leafs for three years, from 1945 to 1948. The Stanley Cup was not the only silverware in his collection: he won the Calder in 1937 and the Lady Byng in 1942.
(Courtesy Hockey Hall of Fame)

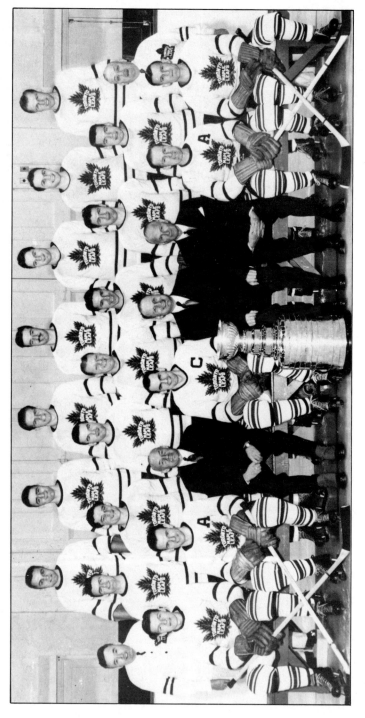

△ The 1947–48 Toronto Maple Leafs were well equipped to handle the bashing and grinding style of hockey that was played in the NHL of the late 1940s. When the forward lines of Watson-Apps-Ezinicki and Lynn-Kennedy-Meeker were given any trouble, backliners Jimmy Thomson, Garth Boesch, and Wally Stanowski would take care of it. After finishing in first place, they swept the Detroit Red Wings in four straight, giving Syl Apps his last taste of Stanley Cup champagne. (*Courtesy Hockey Hall of Fame*)

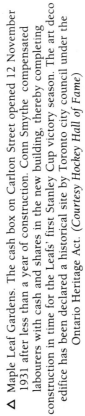

◁ Maple Leaf Gardens. The cash box on Carlton Street opened 12 November 1931 after less than a year of construction. Conn Smythe compensated labourers with cash and shares in the new building, thereby completing construction in time for the Leafs' first Stanley Cup victory season. The art deco edifice has been declared a historical site by Toronto city council under the Ontario Heritage Act. (*Courtesy Hockey Hall of Fame*)

▽ Bill Barilko looks at home here in the cooler; in the 1947–48 campaign, he won the "penalty race" with 147 minutes on the gripe bench. He was a rough, tough kid who played five NHL seasons and collected four Stanley Cup rings for his trouble. Barilko was never a man to back down from even the toughest of men, like Gordie Howe, seen here, sharing the glory in the penalty box. (*Courtesy Hockey Hall of Fame*)

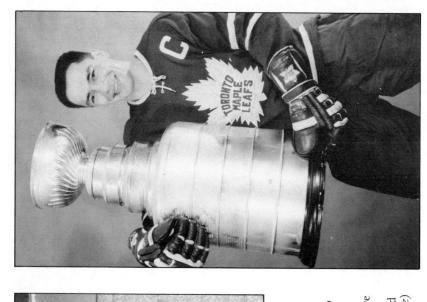

△ Frank and Red. Frank Mahovlich and Red Kelly hold the distinction of winning two Stanley Cups with two different teams. Red picked up two rings with Detroit and added four more while playing with the Leafs. The Big M played on four Cup winners in Toronto, and later helped the Habs to two Cup victories in the early seventies. (*Courtesy Hockey Hall of Fame*)

△ George Armstrong played 21 seasons with the Toronto Maple Leafs and wore the captain's "C" for 11 of them, earning him the well-deserved nickname "Chief." Army's steady play helped the Leafs to four Stanley Cup victories, and gave him an honoured place in the Hall of Fame. (*Courtesy Hockey Hall of Fame*)

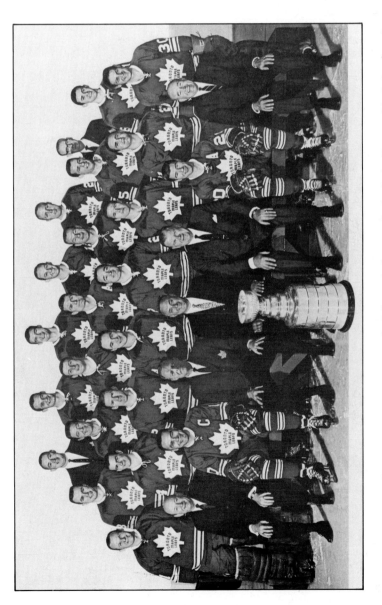

△ The 1966-67 Leafs. Nineteen sixty-seven marked the end of an era for both the Toronto Maple Leafs and the NHL. The Leafs won their last Stanley Cup that year. It was also the last year of the "original" six-team league. (*Courtesy Graphic Artists Photography*)

△ Harold Ballard and Bunny Ahearne compare their relative prosperity and good fortune. Theirs may not be the finely tuned bodies of professional athletes; nonetheless, they are happy to be inductees at the 1977 Hall of Fame induction ceremony. (*Courtesy Hockey Hall of Fame*)

▽ Punch Imlach views the Leafs from the press box, 30 December 1979, during his first season back in Toronto as general manager. (*Photo: Barry Davis, courtesy Globe and Mail*)

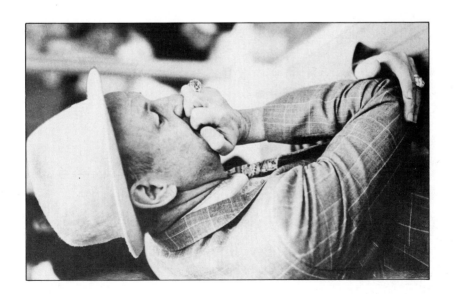

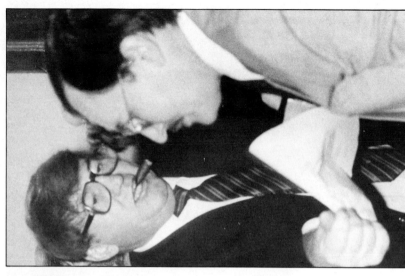

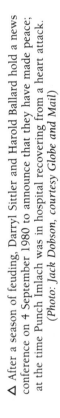

△ After a season of feuding, Darryl Sittler and Harold Ballard hold a news conference on 4 September 1980 to announce that they have made peace; at the time Punch Imlach was in hospital recovering from a heart attack. *(Photo: Jack Dobson, courtesy Globe and Mail)*

△ Leaf coach Mike Nykoluk, enraged over articles written by *Globe and Mail* sports columnist Al Strachan, physically ejects Strachan from the Leaf dressing room (13 January 1984). *(Photo: James Lewcun, courtesy Globe and Mail)*

◁ The newest Leaf, first draft choice Wendel Clark, poses with Harold Ballard at a news conference on 26 August 1985 to announce Clark's contract agreement with the club. (*Photo: Hans Deryk, courtesy Globe and Mail*)

▽ As the Leafs endured the worst season in the history of the club, disgusted fans held a "Bag Night" in December 1984, showing up with bags over their heads to show their embarrassment for supporting the team.
(*Photo: Tibor Kolley, courtesy Globe and Mail*)

△ Leaf general manager Gerry McNamara issues instructions to coach John Brophy and assistant coach Garry Lariviere (18 November 1986). *(Photo: Tibor Kolley, courtesy Globe and Mail)*

▷ A pensive John Brophy watches the team practise at training camp, 15 September 1987. *(Photo: Tim McKenna, courtesy Globe and Mail)*

△ 22 September 1988. Bill Ballard (centre) poses with his brother, Harold Jr., and his sister, Mary Elizabeth Flynn, outside Old City Hall in Toronto, where a date was set in provincial court to hear his trial for allegedly assaulting Yolanda Ballard. (*Photo: D. Nethercott, courtesy Globe and Mail*)

▷ Yolanda gives Harold an affectionate pinch on the cheek while they attend the Leafs' opening game of the 1988–89 National Hockey League season, 9 October 1988. (*Photo: Tibor Kolley, courtesy Globe and Mail*)

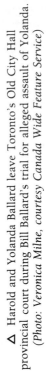

△ Harold and Yolanda Ballard leave Toronto's Old City Hall provincial court during Bill Ballard's trial for alleged assault of Yolanda. *(Photo: Veronica Milne, courtesy Canada Wide Feature Service)*

▽ Gord Stellick, below a picture of George Armstrong when he was captain of the Leafs, announces that Brophy has been fired and that Armstrong is to be his interim replacement, 19 December 1988. *(Photo: Tibor Kolley, courtesy Globe and Mail)*

14

McNamara's
Band

As the NHL draft approached in June of 1985, nobody knew which player would be selected first overall. In most other years, one particular 18-year-old stood out, or at least was identified as the top pick. In 1984, there had been Mario Lemieux, the young phenom from Laval of the Quebec league. A year earlier, Minnesota had made it clear they were taking Brian Lawton, a high-school player from the Boston area.

But in 1985 there was no consensus. Craig Simpson, a centre from London, Ontario, who played for Michigan State, was one everybody was looking at. Out West there was a big defenceman with the Calgary Wranglers, Dana Murzyn, who some compared to Larry Robinson. And then there was defenceman Wendel Clark of the Saskatoon Blades, which had been a very poor team that year.

Clark was a hard-rock farm boy from Kelvington, Saskatchewan, who loved to hit, loved to fight, and could score goals. Defensively he was undistinguished, so poor in fact that his coach had moved him up to left wing part-way through the season. And he wasn't all that big at 5-foot-11 and 187 pounds.

But he had charisma. It was rare to see a player with refined offensive skills, specifically a big shot, playing with such straight-ahead aggressiveness. He was strong, genuinely tough, and could hurt people. That made him a valuable commodity.

The Maple Leafs, by virtue of another dismal season, 20 wins, 52 losses, and 8 ties, had finished this time with the worst record in the league, thus ensuring their right to select first in the draft.

There was speculation they would take Simpson, a classy kid, a good student, and a skilful player. He had led his team in scoring, was an all-star in the Central Collegiate Hockey Association, and was selected to the National Collegiate Athletic Association all-America team. The league's Central Scouting Bureau ranked him number one. Others felt Murzyn would be taken by Toronto because more than anything the Leafs needed help on defence, particularly size, and Murzyn was 6-foot-2 and weighed 200 pounds.

As draft time approached, Simpson remained the favourite, even though his parents had expressed concern about his playing in the Leaf organization, given its reputation and that of the owner. About a month before the draft, McNamara had met with the Simpsons and it had not gone well. They told McNamara about their worries. McNamara was defensive. "The meeting was a little edgy," he said later. "I was confident enough to present our position and they were confident enough to present theirs."

A few days before the draft, however, Simpson went to McNamara and told him he would be "pleased to be part of the organization." So the Simpson rumours started again, although many still felt it would be Murzyn. On draft day, in fact, CBC Television predicted during its coverage that the Leafs would take the Calgary defenceman.

For the first time, the draft was held outside Montreal, ironically enough, in Toronto. That Saturday in June as the moment approached for the Leafs to begin proceedings, the spectators and prospective draftees started filling the bleachers at the Toronto Convention Centre. The drama continued to build. Would it be Simpson or Murzyn? Several times the camera focussed on the good-looking Simpson and his attractive girlfriend. Finally, it was time. McNamara, sitting beside Ballard at the Leaf table, leaned to the microphone and said, "The Toronto Maple Leafs are very happy to select Wendel Clark from Saskatoon."

Even McNamara's wife was surprised, a friend said later.

A fair-haired young man with a round face and broad shoulders stood up. He smiled and looked at his father, who had tears in his eyes. Les Clark gave his son a quick pat in the back. Wendel shook Don Meehan's hand and then walked down to the floor to put on a Leaf sweater.

Many that day thought the Leafs had made a mistake. But they hadn't. Clark would become the most important player to join the organization in more than a decade. In a matter of months he would become probably the leading athlete in terms of popularity in Toronto. He would be his team's leader and its hope for success in the future.

On a team that for so long had been passive and unaggressive and easily pushed around, Clark offered something quite different. He fought anyone, usually the biggest and toughest player on the other side, and it wasn't often that he lost. By January, after 35 games, he had been in 14 fights. When he wasn't in the penalty box, he was on his way to a 34-goal season. But more than the fighting and goal-scoring, what Toronto fans liked most were the robust checks. Clark hit people, and usually cleanly.

Brian Sutter of the St. Louis Blues noted that after fights Clark didn't say anything. He did not issue threats. In an age when so few hits were delivered without a high stick, and fights usually ended in verbal exchanges as the antagonists headed to the penalty box, Clark just skated away. He seemed like a player from the old days, a "throwback" to another era.

Clark was about the only good thing in the otherwise disappointing 1985-86 regular season. The Leafs were just as bad and just as unpredictable. They had a 23-game stretch where they played .500 hockey with a record of 9-9-5. That was followed by a 5-15-0 slump and then a winning run of 8-6-2 followed by four consecutive losses to end the season. For the year, they were 25-48-7, but they made the playoffs because the Red Wings had endured the worst campaign in their history.

More than anyone, the frustration showed on Dan Maloney, the head coach. He had retired as a player in 1982, but stayed on as Nykoluk's assistant. When Nykoluk was fired in 1984, Maloney moved up to take his place. Again it was a predictable Ballard move. Maloney had no experience as a head coach, but it was easier to anoint him than to bring in a qualified replacement.

Maloney had asked for an assistant coach, and his choice had been Walt McKechnie, an old friend who had played for the Leafs during Imlach's second regime. McKechnie was easy-going, and probably would have been a good balance to the intense and sometimes temperamental Maloney.

But McNamara refused to hire McKechnie, mainly because Floyd Smith disliked him. When Smith coached the team in the 1979-80 season, McKechnie had been one of those opposed to Imlach and his coaching staff. McKechnie, in fact, had been among the dart throwers. Once during practice Smith had put the team through a drill in which three players skated down the ice, passing the puck and then shooting on the goaltender. The players had been accustomed to Nielson's more sophisticated practices, so as McKechnie left the ice, he said. "That was just great Smitty. The next time we get a three on zero in a game, we'll know exactly what to do." Everybody laughed.

No, the Leafs would not hire McKechnie. Instead, for the 1984-85 season, on the advice of Smith, McNamara looked to a man in his fifties who had spent more than 30 years of his life playing and coaching in the minor leagues–John Brophy.

If ever there was a man ill suited to be an assistant coach, it was Brophy. He had a reputation as a tough disciplinarian and motivator. The idea of Brophy befriending the players, taking their problems to the coach, and mediating between the 34-year-old Maloney and guys in the dressing room was laughable. There was no good cop-bad cop relationship here, just two who were bad–and one worse than the other.

Their first season together was disastrous, the proof of which was the Leafs' picking first in the draft: their second season wasn't much better. Wisely, Brophy excused himself 11 games into the season to take the job of coaching the farm team in St. Catharines.

Yet, as bad as it was, there were encouraging signs. Having finished so low for so many years, they had acquired a group of young players selected high in the draft. There had been defenceman Gary Nylund in 1982. The next year centre Russ Courtnall was picked. He was followed by defenceman Al Iafrate in 1984 and then Clark. One of the most exciting players, along with Clark, was left winger Steve Thomas, a good young goal scorer who had won the rookie-of-the-year award in the American Hockey League.

Thomas had played for the Marlies but was never drafted, probably because of his size, 5-foot-10, 180 pounds. But he was strong on his skates and had a great shot. At the urging of Frank Bonello, the general manager of the Marlboros, McNamara signed him to a contract.

Up front the Leafs had talent. Tom Fergus, acquired from Boston, centred Vaive and Thomas. Then there was the Hound Line, so called because Clark, Courtnall, and Gary Leeman had all attended Notre Dame College in Saskatchewan as teenagers and had played for the Hounds. The third line consisted of Peter Ihnacak between

Miroslav Frycer and Walt Poddubny. But there were still problems on the blueline and in goal. Jim Benning and Nylund were slow in developing, although in Nylund's case he had missed most of his first two seasons with torn knee ligaments. Iafrate should have been in junior hockey. Salming was getting old.

McNamara had made two trades to get veteran defencemen but they weren't good deals. He had sent John Anderson to Quebec for Brad Maxwell, who had been ineffective with the Nordiques and was no better with the Leafs. Then, left winger Stewart Gavin was moved to Hartford for Chris Kotsopoulos, who played fairly well in Toronto, but McNamara could have acquired him for less. Worse than the defence was the goaltending. More had been expected of veteran Don Edwards. Ken Wregget, at the age of 21, had played 30 games, but wasn't ready for the NHL.

Still, there was enough to stir playoff excitement as the Leafs prepared to meet the Blackhawks. In the regular season the Leafs had lost only two of eight games to Chicago. In the playoffs, they didn't lose any, sweeping the Blackhawks in three games. Credit for the triumph was given to the "kiddie corps." Thomas led the team in scoring with four goals and one assist. Wregget was outstanding in goal. Clark played aggressively and scored the critical goal in the second game when they were behind 4-2, which started a comeback. And defenceman Bob McGill did an excellent job on Al Secord in front of the net.

When it was over, there was a sense that Maloney had outcoached Chicago's Bob Pulford and Roger Neilson, who was Pulford's assistant. There was a degree of irony to this, because Pulford, whom Maloney played for in Chicago, and Neilson had had the greatest influence on Maloney during his career. The pupil had bettered the teachers.

In the second round, the Leafs were in tough competition against a gritty and strong defensive team in the Blues. The series went seven games before the Leafs, with several injuries to key players, lost the final game.

Yet despite the defeat, there was reason to be optimistic. The young players were developing. Courtnall had his first good season, with 22 goals and 38 assists in 73 games. With Clark, Thomas, and Vaive there was plenty of firepower. Most encouraging was the progress of Maloney. After two years of apprenticeship, he had learned his trade. The line changes were crisper. He got the match-ups he wanted. There was preparation. There was also a genuine camaraderie on the team. If Thomas scored, Clark was the first to give him a high-five, and it was reciprocated. The Leafs were growing and gaining confidence. They were a young and happy team on the way up.

Then it started to turn sour–the togetherness, the hope, the morale. Tragically, a back ailment would disable Clark. Nobody was to blame for that, although people close to Clark, including his parents, felt that the team's medical staff had failed to handle the situation adequately. But Ballard and McNamara would be at the root of other problems and it would ultimately cost McNamara his job.

In some ways, the situation in the spring of 1986 paralleled that of 1979, when Neilson had completed his second season. At that time, the team needed stability. Instead it got Imlach. Now, seven years later, the Leafs were at another crossroads. The team should have carried on from its playoff success and maintained the continuity.

Maloney was without a contract and wanted a two-year deal at about $85,000 a year. It was a modest request, and would not have been a big deal with any other organization. But from somewhere Ballard had twigged to the idea of one-year agreements. That's all he talked about after the playoffs, one-year deals for McNamara and Maloney. Said Ballard that spring, "I've learned from experience that you don't hire a guy for five or six years, then find you have to dump him after two years and have to keep paying him."

From Maloney's position, a one-year contract, with no raise, was not enough security. It was important, he felt, for the players to know that the coach was supported by management for at least two years. But whenever Maloney went to McNamara, McNamara said that Ballard wouldn't allow anything more than a year. As the days passed, Maloney's situation remained unresolved.

At a news conference to announce the moving of the St. Catharines franchise to Newmarket, when Ballard was asked about his coach, he said, "I'm in no hurry to sign him. He's the one looking for a job, not me." Finally, Maloney did something unprecedented during the Ballard years. He told Ballard to find somebody else. He quit. "I was prepared to negotiate, but there were no negotiations," Maloney said. "Two years would have done it."

Maloney stayed unemployed exactly one day. John Ferguson, the general manager of the Winnipeg Jets, was looking for a coach, and immediately hired him. At a news conference to announce the appointment, Ferguson said, "I like his work ethic, the way he has matured and the way he runs practices." Then, in an obvious jab at the Leafs, who had kept a man for two years while he learned the job and then let him get away, Ferguson said, "He's been taught a great deal, working in Toronto."

It is debatable how much effort was exerted by McNamara to get Maloney the two years he wanted. Bob Goodenow, an agent based in Detroit, recalls a meeting in McNamara's office that illustrated not only McNamara's limited support of Maloney but also his attitude toward spending money. Goodenow had asked for a one-week conditioning program as part of a client's new contract. It costs about $500, and Goodenow says most general managers readily agree to it. But not McNamara.

Said Goodenow: "He put his head down, and he started rummaging through the drawers of his desk. Then he pulled out a piece of paper and started waving it in the air. 'You see this,' he said. 'This is a $17,000 bill from the Fitness Institute in Toronto. I've got a coach who's a physical fitness nut. But it doesn't do us any good. We spent $17,000 and we didn't get anything for it. We're paying these guys to be pros. They should know how to get in shape and take care of it themselves. No, I'm not agreeing to any clause like that.'

"I thought to myself," said Goodenow, "here he is cutting the legs off the coach right in front of me–Maloney quit a week later. And not only that, he's taking hockey back to the 1940s. I have a little feeling for the Toronto situation. It's depressing."

A Gardens employee who worked in the hockey office during this time said McNamara made no effort whatsoever on Maloney's behalf: "McNamara, in my opinion, hung Maloney out to dry." Vaive probably spoke for most of the players when he said, "Things were going so smoothly. Then this happened. Dan did a heckuva job and it's going to be a big loss."

It was, indeed, a big loss, but not for McNamara. A few months later, he went to Ballard and negotiated his own deal–a four-year contract with a raise, bringing his salary up to about $150,000 annually.

Shortly after Maloney's move to the Jets, reporters at the NHL June meetings in Montreal asked McNamara who would coach the Leafs. McNamara gave perhaps his most remembered quote. "I'm not a wealth of information," he said, which journalists viewed as the understatement of the year.

For finding a new coach, there were prerequisites. The man had to be already part of the organization, and Ballard had to like him. His qualifications and his ability to coach and to relate to young players were not important considerations. John Brophy fit the description. Hiring Brophy was the second half of McNamara's most damaging miscalculation. First he let Maloney get away, and then he replaced him with a man who would be the subject of the most controversy since the days of Imlach.

Whatever his abilities, however, it was difficult not to like John Brophy. He was friendly, had a good sense of humour, and was unpretentious, which was refreshing in a business pervaded by big egos and overwhelming pride. He was a Maritimer, from Antigonish, Nova Scotia, and one of eight children. His mother died when he was five, and because his father was a railroad man and away a lot of the time, Brophy had to live with his uncle for a considerable part of his childhood. Hockey became an escape and eventually something close to an obsession. It was his life, first as a player and then as a coach.

He was never good enough to play in the NHL and was barely adequate as a minor-leaguer. But he was rough, more specifically, dirty, and he lasted 21 years, mostly in the old Eastern Hockey League, which was famous for its bloodthirsty fans and somewhat homicidal players. More than a fighter, Brophy was a stick man, and over the years he became famous–and hated–as one of the meanest men ever to play the game.

Ray Miron, who coached a team in the Eastern league, once said, "He wasn't what you'd call a really good hockey player. But he was tough. A lot of people were scared to death of him."

Don Cherry also played in the minors, although never as far down as the Eastern League which ran along the Atlantic Seaboard of the United States to places such as Long Island (where Brophy played many years with the Ducks), New Haven, Connecticut, and Charlotte, North Carolina. Cherry says: "We used to hear about this guy in the Eastern League. It was like you heard about King Kong off in the jungle somewhere."

Brophy stories grew over the years to become part of the lore of the game. Eli Gold, a radio broadcaster in Birmingham, Alabama, worked with Brophy on several different teams and remembers a game in which Brophy broke another player's leg because the player had laughed at him. "Brophy was a defenceman and not a great skater. One night this little guy buzzed around him and scored a goal," Gold said. "He pointed at Brophy and laughed. The next time he came down the ice, Brophy chopped him down with a two-hander across the shin. It broke his leg. While the guy was laying in the corner, Brophy skated over to him and said, 'Now laugh, big man.' "

When a player who was new to the league viciously fouled one of Brophy's teammates he was told by Brophy he would be killed if he returned to the ice. Not sure there would be a second warning, the player went to the dressing room, removed his equipment, and was never heard from again.

Brophy was in vicious stick fights during his career, but the only time he says he feared for his life was when he went up against Bobby Taylor, the former flanker for the Argonauts who played minor-league hockey in the winter. As Taylor remembers it, Brophy cut him in the face and then he retaliated. That was the beginning of a blood bath. The referee and linesmen stood back as both started swinging their sticks wildly, wielding them like battle axes, connecting on the face and head, over and over.

"It's the only fight I can remember where I thought my life was on the line," Brophy said. "We got cut up pretty good. Taylor is a scary person. A nice guy, but a scary person regardless."

Said Taylor many years later, "Yeah, I remember that fight, but he never cut me again."

It goes without saying that Brophy was hated in other cities. There were times when he needed a police escort to the games, because fans had put a price on his head. Often his team bus would be assailed as it pulled up beside the arena. One night after the Ducks had played a particularly rough game in New Haven, Brophy was in the shower in the basement of the arena when a fan stuck his arm through the window and fired a shot that just missed him, ricocheting around the shower stall.

But Brophy survived all of this, and by the time he was appointed head coach of the Leafs in 1986 he appeared to be a dapper, almost courtly, 53-year-old. He had pure white hair, which had started turning gray when he was in his early twenties, thus his nickname, the Gray Ghost. Deep scars on his face attested to his violent past. But he dressed well and acted younger than a man approaching his mid-fifties.

As a coach in the minors, he brought with him from his playing days an obsession with winning, whether it was a fight or a game. He ruled with an iron fist and was a "motivator," the hockey euphemism for a tough and aggressive disciplinarian. He had been known to lock disorderly or disobedient players in dressing rooms or kick them off team buses in the middle of nowhere, in the middle of the night.

He brought this same coaching finesse with him as an assistant with the Leafs. When Al Iafrate showed up at training camp 30 pounds overweight Maloney handed him over to Brophy, who worked him so hard that Iafrate took off and fled to his parents home in Detroit, until Maloney went there to bring him back.

When Brophy took over the Saints from Alexander, the team had a record of 4-12. But with Brophy behind the bench, the Saints went 34-25-5 and took third place in the Southern Division, falling one game short of advancing to the AHL final. It had been a typical Brophy team—mean, with fighters such as Kevin Maguire and Val James, and strong defensively.

But there was a down side to Brophy, the coach. Before joining the Leaf organization, he had been replaced as coach of farm teams belonging to the Calgary Flames and the Canadiens, two of the best clubs in the NHL. Why had he not kept his job in either place? He wasn't viewed as a good coach, at least not for young players who were to be taught and developed for the NHL. Serge Savard, the Canadiens' managing director, once said privately that hiring Brophy to coach the Leafs was the worst mistake the club could have made.

But there was no evidence that the Leafs had any concern about Brophy. Ballard said, "I think he will be a great man for discipline. I think if a fellow plays for him, he'll be treated very fairly, but if he doesn't play for him, Brophy will have no time for him." McNamara told a friend that the Leaf front office could now boast the most intimidating lineup in the league, starting with the coach and moving on up to the general manager and then the owner.

But the Leafs played poorly under Brophy. Not that it was all his fault. The team's chemistry started to change. Players with leadership ability and character were traded away. Others were lost to free agency. For this, McNamara was to blame.

It started with Gary Nylund who had been drafted third overall in 1982. He was big (6-foot-4, 210 pounds), a good skater and seemed headed for stardom. Two operations on the same knee in his first season slowed his development. Still, he had improved in the 1985-86 season and played his best hockey against the Blackhawks in the playoffs, hitting people and clearing the area in front of the net. At the end of the 1984-85 season, Nylund had one year remaining on his contract—the option year, that paid him $110,000 a season. At that point, he had hoped to renegotiate. Teams try to sign the players they value before they play out their option. It's safer that way. You keep them happy and they're probably more productive. And there's always the risk of losing them if they become free agents.

In August 1985, McNamara sent Nylund a letter, saying he hoped he was having an enjoyable summer, and outlining the Leafs' new offer, which was a two-year contract with a $5000 raise. Nylund viewed it as too little and called his agent, Roland Thompson of Guelph, a partner in the company Murray and Thompson Sports Representatives and Advisors.

Thompson had not received a copy of the offer, even though the Leafs knew he represented Nylund. Thompson says that this was a standard procedure by the Leaf management, but not an intelligent one.

"The problem was the manner in which the Leafs perceived agents," Thompson says. "They tried to go around them and leave them out of the process. I don't know whether this was incompetence on McNamara's part, or he was taking directions from you know who. But it got agents' backs up."

Nylund wanted a $25,000 raise. That would have brought his salary to about $135,000, which was still well under the NHL average. But McNamara refused to negotiate. It was take the $5000 increase or leave it. Nylund chose to leave it and entered the 1985-86 season without a new contract. Several times during the winter Thompson went to McNamara and suggested they negotiate a deal. Nylund was having his best season and was beginning to show the promise scouts had seen in junior hockey.

Said Thompson: "I don't know how many times I went to Gerry and said Gary's playing pretty well. Let's get something done now. He said, 'Not during the season. That's our policy. We can't make exceptions.' "

When the season ended Thompson suggested again that they begin negotiating. McNamara, however, told him he was too busy, but asked, "Are you going to the Memorial Cup?" When Thompson said yes, he was, McNamara said they could meet there.

At the Memorial Cup Thompson spotted McNamara early in the tournament, sitting alone up in the stands. He approached him and asked about Nylund's contract. Again McNamara said he was too busy. "See me in a couple of days," he said, which Thompson found odd because he figured things would get busier as the tournament went on. Still, he went back to him in two days as agreed, but again McNamara said, "I'm too busy. Meet me at the NHL draft."

By now it was obvious to Thompson that he was getting the run-around, and Nylund was getting worried. He wanted to stay in Toronto, but his contract was to expire on 30 June which was just weeks away. Thompson kept trying. At the draft, he contacted McNamara again. Incredibly, McNamara told him he was "too busy."

Then, two weeks later, on 24 June, Nylund received a letter from McNamara. The wording was identical to the one sent a year earlier. McNamara hoped Nylund was having an enjoyable summer and "please find enclosed your standard NHL players contract." Like the earlier offer it was for two years (one year plus an option). But this time there was no raise. Despite Nylund's promising season, McNamara had rescinded the $5000 raise.

Nylund was incensed. He called Thompson, screaming over the telephone, "What the fuck's this guy doing?" It was at that point that Nylund and Thompson realized they would have to start looking elsewhere. When the 30 June deadline passed, making Nylund a free agent, Thompson sent letters to the other 20 NHL clubs. He also set up a meeting with McNamara in July with Nylund in attendance. At that meeting, McNamara offered a three-year deal (two plus an option) with a $10,000 raise. Given what had happened up to then, plus the hard feelings, Thompson and Nylund refused to consider the offer. "No way," said Thompson. "We can't do it."

"Go ahead and go shopping," replied McNamara, "because I know I'll get a great player in return if you do."

McNamara was referring to the compensation clause in the collective bargaining agreement. Because Nylund was under 25 and had played fewer than five seasons, he was classified as Group One. That meant if he signed with another team, the Leafs would receive compensation in the form of a player or players. This was determined by an arbitrator designated by the league. The Leafs would submit what they thought was fair compensation and Nylund's new team would put on the table what they were willing to offer. There would be no compromise. The arbitrator would rule in favour of one side or the other. It was risky for the team signing a player, because it might end up losing in arbitration and be forced to part with a top player.

As a result, only six NHL teams expressed interest in Nylund. Finally it came down to two–Chicago and Edmonton. Oiler president Glen Sather asked Wayne Gretzky about Nylund and Gretzky said sign him. By August, another factor had entered the picture. The league and the players were negotiating a new collective bargaining agreement and players were advised not to re-sign until an agreement was reached, which happened on 26 August. But on that very day McNamara decided to take two weeks holidays. Thompson and Nylund threw up their hands. Despite a final Leaf offer of four years starting at $130,000, Nylund would not accept it. By then, the Blackhawks had put up $150,000 a year (U.S.), and Nylund was fed up with McNamara. "By then Gary was absolutely turned off," Thompson said. "He phoned me and said let's take the Chicago offer."

On the day Nylund signed, a Leaf spokesman said the club was disappointed, because Thompson had never got back to them for a final offer. Thompson couldn't help but laugh. McNamara had had more than a year to cut a deal with a player who had been happy in Toronto and wanted to stay and whose contract demand had not been unreasonable.

Many of the Leaf players felt losing Nylund had been a mistake, including Russ Courtnall, who says, "He was a big guy and with a bit of help he was going to come around and play well. I think he didn't play up to his capability or to what everybody expected, but he had two serious knee injuries, and he added a lot of toughness to our team. He was a good team guy too."

McNamara's arrogance and ineptitude did not stop with losing Nylund. At that point, the Leaf's could have avoided arbitration by making a trade with the Blackhawks. They were offered players such as winger Curt Fraser and defenceman Keith Brown.

Instead, McNamara opted for arbitration and then submitted an unrealistic proposal. He wanted Ed Olczyk, a big forward who had played two years for the Blackhawks. Like Nylund in 1982, he had been third overall in the 1984 draft. But the similarities ended there. Following a rookie year, in which he had 20 goals and 30 assists in 50 games, Olczyk improved in his second season to score 29 goals and earn 50 assists in 79 games for third in team scoring. He was a young star, and the chance of the Leafs' being awarded him for Nylund was less than remote. Not surprisingly, Toronto was awarded the Chicago offer, centre Ken Yaremchuk and defenceman

Jerome Dupont, both of whom failed to make the team and were sent to Newmarket. Dupont eventually quit hockey. Yaremchuk has become a minor-leaguer.

Having been awarded two players, both of whom were earning about the same as Nylund, in U.S. money, McNamara would pay double for losing Nylund. It would have been cheaper to give him the raise he wanted. Ballard said on the day of the arbitration ruling: "We lost a Class-A guy for two guys who will play in the minor leagues."

McNamara, on the other hand, blamed the arbitrator, Judge Edward Houston of Ottawa. He felt that Houston was unqualified to rule on such matters and expressed his concern to the NHL. He also held Thompson responsible. "Once it took place Gerry blamed all of it on me," Thompson says. "He said I went and talked behind his back to other clubs about Gary. Through Gord Stellick, I was told not to show my face around the Gardens."

McNamara also attempted to freeze out Thompson, who represented other players on the Leafs, such as Derek Laxdal and Dan Daoust. The Leafs wouldn't return his phone calls when he attempted to negotiate, and one player (Dan Daoust) wondered if he might have to change agents to get a new contract, which, of course, was what McNamara wanted. Finally, to get Daoust a new deal, Thompson's partner, Bob Murray, had to come in and do it. Commenting on the Nylund-McNamara situation, Thompson says, "I don't mind negotiating with general managers who are hard and tough, but in McNamara's case, the irrationality was frustrating."

If it was possible, McNamara disliked people in the media more than agents. Not surprisingly, his relationship with Toronto reporters had deteriorated significantly over the years. He intensely disliked the two beat writers at the *Sun,* Scott Morrison and Jim O'Leary. During training camp, O'Leary had made a fairly innocuous comment to the effect that the only thing Kaszycki had done right up to then was to get a guaranteed contract from McNamara. That was enough for McNamara to stop talking to him. Once during a practice, when McNamara saw that O'Leary had poured himself a cup of coffee, he posted a sign on the dressing room door saying the coffee was only for the Leaf staff.

Morrison had enraged McNamara by lampooning him in reports. It was harmless stuff, but that didn't matter. He stopped talking to Morrison. He railed about the "jerks" in the media. Of Morrison, who at the time had a beard, he would tell the people in the office, "I'd like to grab that little jerk and rip his beard off!"

He hated Wayne Parrish, who had moved to the *Sun* from the *Star* to become sports editor, because of critical things Parrish had written about Ballard. And he refused to speak to anybody from the *Globe*. At the *Star,* both hockey columnists, Milt Dunnell and Jim Proudfoot, felt that McNamara was basically paranoid and had little to do with him. The Toronto media had always been agreeable to meeting McNamara to air grievances and attempt a normal professional relationship. But McNamara refused. He was genuinely convinced that he had been badly mistreated.

When the Leafs got off to a good start in 1986-87, leading the division by November with a record of 6-2-3, McNamara seemed to think he was in a strong enough position to pay back the people who had attacked him. He felt that his team had arrived, that it was on its way to a winning season.

Over the years, he had avoided radio and television, for the most part, and wasn't quoted much in the newspapers. So when he went on the air between periods of a televised Leaf game with host Ron Maclean, it was the first time that many viewers saw him. It also provided an opportunity for McNamara to present himself as a normal, well-adjusted person, happy with the success of his team and thankful that everything had finally come together.

Instead, the viewers saw an angry, resentful man, who talked about settling scores, getting even, paying back his enemies. It was a disturbing performance even for those who knew him. The interview started off well, but quickly degenerated. McNamara's face started to redden and perspire. There was a forced smile. He started to talk faster. The uneasiness, the nervous "heh, heh" laugh, and the paranoia, reminded some of Captain Queeg, the Humphrey Bogart character in the film, *The Caine Mutiny.* "Did he bring the ball bearings?" asked one reporter as he watched the interview from the Leaf press room, a reference to the metal balls Queeg rattled in his hand during the court martial.

McNamara started by saying that the rebuilding of the team had been a long and painful experience. Then he quickly moved to the subject of Toronto sports journalists. "Mediawise," he said, "Everybody accepted [the rebuilding] at the time. But as you know, and everybody in the country knows, it hasn't happened that way. The media has taken a pretty good run at me, and a pretty good run at the hockey club."

At this point he became more tense and agitated. "I can tell you, ah, heh, heh, I don't take too many things lying down. I never have. I never will. And I can tell you I'm going to have my day."

Then Maclean interjected with: "When the reviews were bad you said 'To heck with it, I'm not going to read them.' Now that you're winning, aren't you curious?"

"No, I'm not really," said McNamara. "Because it doesn't make any difference what they say. First of all, when I look and see a piece in the paper, if I happen to read it, I take a look at who's writing it. And I know quite a bit about all these reporters, much more than they think I know about them. And I look at the credibility of those reporters, and I can tell you I can't find too much credibility in a number of them. So I look at myself and I say what do I worry about? I'm still here. Some of those guys aren't here any longer and they're not writing hockey any longer. They're missing. And right now they're missing a good thing."

Maclean attempted to get McNamara away from the subject of media by discussing the young players on the team.

"Once again, this didn't happen over night," McNamara said. "Our scouts have done an excellent job, have been beating the bushes for five years.

"Once again, the media jumped all over those people and were really unfair–especially a national paper that heads out all over the country.

"Those scouts are out there on the road and they read about how bad they are, and it's a tough thing. It's tough to swallow.

"You know, it's the old story. When I get wound up some day we'll, heh, heh, take the gloves off and we'll go at it pretty good. I'd like to do that maybe in the future. I don't think tonight I'd like to do it, but I've got lots of ammunition, believe me, and I'm not going to take it sitting down.

"I mean there are lots of people. I see them around here. One thing I can tell you, there's a lack of crows in the air these days. For whatever reason, they might even maybe put a limit on them that you can take, because there are not many in the skies these days. There are lots of people eating crow believe me. One in particular has a claw stuck in his throat, because I see a big lump there.

"And I'm going to get pretty nasty, I can tell you, and don't think there's anybody who can get as nasty as I can."

Again Maclean tried to lighten things up: "Don't you think while you're winning it might be best to just enjoy it, and–"

"It's got nothing to do with winning!" McNamara loudly interrupted. "This team is a good team. It's all the things that happened. All these players who came along–not one has gone through without being heavily criticized, and that's including Wendel Clark.

"Us taking him in the draft, we were heavily criticized for taking him in the draft. All you have to do is look back in the papers and read what they said previous. You don't see them saying that anymore.

"For some reason or other, those people have slunk, or probably slithered into the background. And we don't see them anymore. And I know this–they're going to take runs at me, but I could care less. I weathered the storm, believe me I have–"

At this point, McNamara had to stop because it was time for a commercial. When they returned, Maclean tried again to steer him away from the media. "I'll give you one more thought on that," Maclean said. "But then I'd like to talk about some positives. But go ahead."

"Well Ron, I just think that, all you people if you're watching and I don't know whether you're interested in what I'm saying or not, but you wait and see the number of runs they're going to take at me now.

"But that's okay. I've come through the worst of it. I've weathered it pretty good. And my family has weathered it pretty well. It's been extremely tough on my family. But that's okay. It's time now for me to get my shots in, and I can tell you that nobody knows how to do it better than I can. If they think they have a pacifist by the tail they don't."

In a louder voice, he said, "I mean, watch the papers. They can take as many runs as they want. I'll tell you I'll get my innings in, I'll–"

Maclean tried one more time: "If anybody is good at getting shots, you've got two people who can handle shots. Allan Bester and Ken Wregget were two of your draft choices who were not ready in 1984, but boy they are in 1986."

"But who said they weren't ready?" asked McNamara, still loud. "*We* said they weren't ready. But we were in a position where we had to play them. All those yahoos who spoke about–all the goaltending experts, you know, quotation marks, who said we were ruining these kids. Here we are. I predicted four years ago, I think it was four years ago, that these two kids were the goaltending future for the Toronto Maple Leafs."

Maclean then asked about Vincent Damphousse, the rookie who wasn't being used much. McNamara said Damphousse was close to becoming a very good player. He ended the interview by making one last observation about the media: "You can't ruin a player no matter what all the experts say. I don't care what the experts say."

McNamara was right about one thing. The media did take "runs" at him. The next day, Parrish wrote, "the resentment, the vitriol, the hatred. . . ." Ken McKee, the broadcasting columnist in the *Star,* commented:

> Gerry McNamara had a grand opportunity the other night on Ch. 11 to do something about a public image that, to put it kindly, is less than positive–his and his Maple Leaf organization.
>
> He did not. Fact is, he probably made it worse. Some fans I know were flabbergasted. They seldom see Big Mac, or hear from him. He is, by choice, publicly silent and invisible.

There was probably another reason for McNamara's low profile. Because of his refusal to communicate with the media, he had neatly avoided answering questions over the years–particularly when the team had been on one of its many losing streaks. That job was left to the coaches, Nykoluk and Maloney, who could never count on a word of support from their general manager in a newspaper article. McNamara was never available.

A lot of what McNamara had said in the interview was either inaccurate or ludicrous–or both. The media, print and broadcast, got along well with the players. In fact some people thought the beat writers had not been tough enough, given the record of the team. Maloney and Brophy also had good relationships with the media. They never complained publicly about the coverage. On the road they occasionally went out for dinner with the writers.

In McNamara's first two years as general manager, journalists for the most part had been fair, complimentary even, noting that he had made some good trades and drafted well. Both of these conclusions are debatable, but that was the perception of some people at the time.

McNamara's accusation that the media had criticized the Leafs for selecting Clark in the draft was wrong. There had been speculation about their taking Simpson. And on the day of the draft the Pittsburgh Penguins, who picked second and selected Simpson, said they rated Simpson ahead of Clark. But there was no reproof in reporting that. And Clark has received consistently good notices in the press since the day he joined the Leafs.

The videotape of McNamara's interview quickly became a collector's item around the league. Copies were made and distributed to general managers and agents. McNamara's friend, Lou Nanne, asked for one, and laughed heartily when he watched it. Agents, who had trouble with McNamara, laughed too. When a broadcaster called a general manager a few days later, he was harangued from the other end. "That's what a general manager is supposed to do, isn't it?" he said with laughter. '

But one person had been favourably impressed–from McNamara's perspective the most important. Ballard gave him four stars and warmly complimented him. His general manager had put the "pigs" in their place, and for a job well done he was rewarded a few days later with his new four-year deal. In a matter of weeks, Ballard regretted the decision. The team started losing badly and made the playoffs only because of the North Stars' late-season swoon. McNamara, of course, blamed Brophy and attempted in March 1987 to get him fired. He appeared on television about that time and criticized Brophy, fingering him for the collapse. "We should have been home and cooled out by now," McNamara said.

That did not sit well with Ballard, who had supported Brophy when McNamara wanted him dismissed. A few weeks later, Morrison asked Ballard if McNamara's long contract would be a problem if Ballard decided McNamara should be replaced. "It doesn't worry me. I've gotten rid of guys before," said Ballard, adding, "I don't think he should be sitting in the office all the time. He should be out seeing what the scouts are looking at."

Others besides Ballard had noticed that McNamara neglected scouting. Since the Leafs had the fewest number of full-time scouts of any team in the league, it made sense that McNamara should spend as much time as he could assisting his staff. He had risen through the scouting ranks, after all. But he did very little scouting. Instead, he accompanied the team on its road trips. At home, he was usually in the office when he wasn't sitting in the stands, watching the team practise.

Still, McNamara argued that he had a good team. Despite their poor showing in the regular season, the Leafs came alive in the playoffs, upsetting the Blues in the first round before losing to the Red Wings in seven games. Despite the problems, there still seemed to be a nucleus of talented players who got along well together. Two of them were Rick Vaive, who had an off-year but still ended up with 32 goals and 34 assists in 73 games, and Steve Thomas, who in his second NHL season had 35 goals and 27 assists in 78 games.

But before the next season began, McNamara traded both, along with McGill, a mediocre defenceman but a strong player and a team leader. By numbers and statistics, it wasn't a bad deal perhaps, but many believe it destroyed the team's camaraderie and character, which to this day has not been restored. Thomas was the main reason for the trade, and his situation had similarities with Nylund's. It involved an agent, in this case Meehan, who like most player representatives had difficulty dealing with McNamara.

"You have to remember," says Meehan, "that as far as I was concerned, McNamara dealt with me on the basis of contempt, simply because I represented the players and would act in their best interest. But never did I insult McNamara, never did I prove to be brazen or arrogant. Simply because I represented players and took an independent position, he dealt with me on the basis of contempt."

In a short period of time, Meehan had become enormously successful. His clients included Wendel Clark, Pat LaFontaine, and Chris Chelios. He was much more skilled in his line of work than McNamara was in his–and earned considerably more money. Despite this, or perhaps because of it, McNamara disliked him.

Once when Meehan was negotiating Clark's contract, a day and time had been set for a meeting with McNamara at the Gardens. Meehan drove into the city from his office in Mississauga only to be told by McNamara that he was "too busy" to meet him.

Said Meehan: "I told him that on the next occasion he would either meet me at my office or somewhere in between. He said, 'Oh no, I can't do that. I can meet you tomorrow at the Gardens.' I said, 'That happens to be unacceptable from my point of view.' He was too busy golfing half the time, in the summer anyway. When he was 'too busy' it related to golf, not business."

Thomas had grown up in Toronto, and playing for the Leafs had been his dream. He had made his way up through the Marlboro organization with the Markham Waxers and then the Marlies and, in 1984, signed a three-year contract with the Leafs. His first year with the St. Catharines Saints of the AHL was impressive. Always a good goalscorer, he picked up 42 goals and earned 48 assists in 62 games. He was a first-team all-star and selected rookie of the year.

The following season, he was called up to the Leafs after 15 games, and went on to get 20 goals and 37 assists in 65 games. In the playoffs, he was the team's leading scorer with 6 goals and 8 assists in 10 games. He was definitely one of their brightest young players. After the season, Meehan attempted to renegotiate. Thomas had earned only $25,000 in the AHL and then $80,000 with the Leafs. He was looking for something close to $125,000 a year. McNamara offered $95,000, $30,000 if Thomas played in the minors.

Said Meehan: "I would have been prepared to negotiate up to $125,000, including bonuses, but the $95,000 wasn't anything close to what we wanted. I got back to them and said, 'Look, we'd like to negotiate.' The answer was no. That was as far as they would go."

So Thomas, like Nylund before him, opted to play out his option. That season Thomas performed very well, finishing with 35 goals and 27 assists in 78 games. Although Meehan had advised McNamara by letter that Thomas was prepared to negotiate a new contract at any time, they never heard from the Leafs.

"If my analysis of the industry is accurate, most clubs would have come along and said you're having an outstanding year. Let's sit down and talk," Meehan says. "But there was no discussion, no approach, no nothing."

In May, the Leafs finally made a proposal. A new contract would pay Thomas about $175,000 a year. McNamara viewed it as a fair offer, and many observers agreed. But Meehan and Thomas saw it differently. For two years Thomas had been probably the poorest-paid Leaf, despite being one of the best players. In the NHL, $80,000 was about as low as you could get. Had the Leafs renegotiated a year earlier, bumping his salary up to $125,000, then something could have been done with the $175,000 offer. But Meehan felt his client had to be given consideration for the two previous seasons. As a result, they went high, asking for $250,000 a year.

In most salary negotiations, each side is prepared to move, and certainly Meehan was. This was only an opening bid. But again McNamara refused to negotiate. It was a take-it-or-leave-it proposition. "There was never any negotiation," Meehan said. "That was the way he operated." By now Thomas was furious, McNamara had not accorded him the courtesy of negotiations, and, although he wanted to stay in Toronto, he came to a decision that he might have to leave.

At one point, Meehan attempted to go straight to Ballard. But through Crump, Ballard told him that negotiating contracts was the responsibility of his general manager. On 27 August, Meehan tried one last time. He sent a letter to McNamara, part of which read, "It appears your position is inflexible, and if you maintain your position, without any opportunity for negotiation, I've been instructed by Steve that he wants to be traded to another team. If you wish to negotiate the matter further, I'd be prepared to meet with you."

By offering to negotiate, Meehan felt that he had reached out at the eleventh hour. But there was no reply. A week later, Thomas called a news conference to announce he had requested a trade, and the next day the Leafs accommodated him, sending him to Chicago, along with Vaive and McGill, for Olczyk and Al Secord.

Looking back on that summer, Meehan says: "I have negotiated many times, and by that point in time I was pretty substantive in the business, with a substantive clientele. But I had never had that kind of impasse with anyone. All relationships with McNamara were from an adversarial position. He couldn't really deal with anybody in good faith, without dealing on the basis that it was personal–that it was a personal vendetta against McNamara. And as such, he would refuse to acknowledge you. He wouldn't communicate to you in any way."

In Vaive's case, he had been unhappy in Toronto. In February 1986, he had been stripped of his captaincy, when he slept through a morning practice at Bloomington, Minnesota. The Leafs could have done it quietly, by waiting until the team returned home and then perhaps allowing Vaive to resign. Instead, Ballard and McNamara announced Vaive's demotion on the spot. Ballard, of course, put him down, and said he had been an irresponsible captain. All of this left Vaive bitter, although he continued to play well, and carried on his leadership role.

Vaive, Thomas, and McGill were missed, and, although losing Nylund a year earlier to free agency had been a mistake, many believe that McNamara's most costly error of the previous 18 months had been in letting Maloney get away.

Brad Smith, a former Leaf, says: "When we had Maloney I really felt we were heading in the right direction. We had a lot of good players and if the coaching situation had been left alone, and a few of the trades hadn't been made, I think you'd see a pretty good hockey club here right now."

But when McNamara was fired in February of the 1987-88 season, these things were rarely mentioned. Arguably, McNamara had outsmarted himself by doing little to keep Maloney as coach and then replacing him with Brophy, whose questionable coaching ability and strong friendship with Ballard contributed significantly to McNamara's imminent downfall. Instead, McNamara's greatest sin, according to Ballard, was in wasting money by recruiting forward Miroslav Ihnacak, who defected from Czechoslovakia and signed a lucrative contract with the Leafs. Ballard would grumble that it had cost him $1 million, which of course was inaccurate. Ihnacak's contract had been in the $600,000 range. Still, it was a lot of money for a minor-leaguer.

For years, McNamara and Imlach had tried the quick fix by bringing in players from Czechoslovakia. There had been goaltender Jiri Crha, Martin Maglay, a teenage goaltender who wasn't good enough to play major junior hockey, defenceman Slava Duris, and Ihnacak's brother, Peter, who was the best of the bunch, but still just a journeyman. The money used for these players would have been better spent on upgrading the coaching and scouting.

But in the Miro Ihnacak case, at least McNamara had attempted to improve the team. It had been an error of commission on a record that was full of errors of omission. In six and a half years as general manager he had ignored the waiver draft, except once in 1984 when he claimed Jeff Brubaker from Edmonton. Other teams were active in the waiver draft. In 1987, for example, 13 teams participated, but not the Leafs, despite finishing the previous season with the fifth worst record in the league. It costs money to claim players, however, so he saved Ballard money.

During McNamara's years, the Leafs lacked depth and were short of role players. But McNamara rarely signed free agents. The few he did pick up included Marian Stastny, who was finished by the time he arrived in Toronto, Brad Smith, who was useful, and Dave Semenko, who fit into Stastny's category. To make room for Semenko on his protected list, he dropped Kevin Maguire, an aggressive forward and just the kind of player the Leafs needed. A few days later, Maguire was the first to go in the 1987 waiver draft, to Buffalo.

The farm team under McNamara wasn't adequately supplied with players. At least once, McNamara and his staff failed to accurately rate the players on their minor-league team. It was decided that defenceman Craig Muni wasn't worth keeping, so he joined the Oilers, played regularly, and won a Stanley Cup.

In themselves, none of these things amounted to much, but in combination they were damning evidence of incompetence or at least failure to do a thorough job. The organization always seemed a step behind the others. When the Quebec Nordiques were in Czechoslovakia getting out Peter and Anton Stastny, two young stars, the Leafs were scouting Crha and Duris. When other teams were scouting Europe, the Leafs stayed away. The Leafs rarely signed a free agent, and those they did sign were invariably over the hill.

As hockey approached the 1990s, McNamara and Ballard seemed lost somewhere in the past. Contempt and hatred of agents was an attitude they carried forward from the 1960s–and it hadn't worked then. Bullying the media had always been a losing proposition, something other organizations had learned years before. McNamara never learned.

The media had sometimes been unfair. And some agents had been tough. The trick was to get along. But McNamara had never been interested in even trying. When he was fired, he told a reporter he was proud that he had never given in.

15

FAMILY

TIES

The deterioration of the Ballard family started not long after Dorothy was buried in December 1969. When Ballard returned home from the funeral, he said to Harold Jr.: "Well, it's over now." Harold interpreted that to mean that everyone was on his own. Before long, Ballard had moved to the Gardens.

Of the two, Dorothy played by far the largest role in raising the children. Ballard was often away with Stafford at hockey games, or on the road, and it was left to Dorothy to run the household. She was also active in the Cancer Society and the United Church. Punch Imlach once said, "I think Dorothy pretty much raised the kids by herself and did a damn good job."

Looking back on his childhood Bill Ballard says, "He wasn't around that much. I don't think he had the strength or patience to adapt to what you're supposed to do, to be a Father Knows Best type. It just wasn't in him."

Despite his active social life and involvement in sports, Ballard was a loner. He had few close friends. Spending time with his family in a normal domestic relationship was all but impossible. On Sunday afternoons, Ballard went to Marlboros games at the Gardens. When he returned home, he generally went upstairs to sleep while Dorothy prepared dinner. But often he wouldn't sit at the table. Instead he'd go to the kitchen, get a quart of buttermilk, a can of sardines, perhaps some peanut butter, and a piece of cheese, and he'd stand there and eat it. "It almost seemed to me that he was trying to irritate everyone," Harold Jr. says. "He wouldn't join in. He wasn't a joiner."

Harold Jr. says his mother was strict but protective. One summer, when Bill and Harold Jr. were children, they were caught by a neighbour in his garden, pulling out his stakes. The neighbour took them to Dorothy and insisted they be disciplined. She said they would, but when the neighbour insisted it be done in front of him, she said, "They're just little boys. Didn't you do anything like that when you were a child?" When the neighbour said no, Dorothy replied, "Well you must have been a suck." The children laughed.

Harold Jr. remembers his mother as tolerant and understanding. But his father, well into his forties by then, had difficulty handling the turmoil of a household that included three small children. "He couldn't handle the confusion or the spats," Harold Jr. says. "He would step in after being away two weeks and would think that everything was helter skelter, which it was not. My mother was quite used to it."

Most of Ballard's time at home was spent in the garden. That was his hobby and his major interest outside of sports. It wasn't the children. "He didn't take his nose out of the garden very often," Bill Ballard says. "But I rather liked it that way. I was different from most kids I guess. I didn't want parents hanging around watching me play baseball and football. I'm quite happy if they're at home watering the lawn. If they keep out of my way, I'll keep out of their way."

Harold Jr.'s most vivid recollections of his childhood with his father were at the cottage. Ballard, who was a tremendous swimmer, would carry his sons, one on each shoulder, out into the bay for miles. Or he would take them out in the boat and dump them, forcing them to swim to shore.

One of the annual occasions the boys dreaded, but now recall fondly, was the camping trip with their father. Over a period of five or six days, they would cruise on Georgian Bay in Ballard's motor launch. The incessant banging of the hull against the waves would almost make them sick. "It was like going on a boat ride that never ended, up and down, up and down, all over Georgian Bay," Bill says. "It was like five or six days of nonstop torture." When they got to their destination, usually an island, they were soaked and tired. Then they had to fight off mosquitoes. Harold remembers his father, who was an insomniac, staying up all night, staring into the fire.

Thinking back, Bill says he doubts if his father was really interested in spending time with his sons or providing any memorable experience. "I think he just liked driving the boat," Bill says. "I don't think he cared if we lived or died, to tell you the truth."

In a profile of Bill Ballard for *T.O. Magazine* in June 1987, Paul Kaihla noted that as a teenager Bill was supremely self-confident. He would anoint himself "King" during the summer months at the cottage; his friends were his subjects and he gave them numbers that signified their relative importance. Radio personality Robbie Evans was "Three." Evans told Kaihla: "Whenever his dad would have a party up there, Bill would slip a couple of bottles of liquor out of the case for his own teen parties. Then he'd call one of us in and give us a command–'Three, get here; go stash this.' As payment, he'd promote us to a higher rank and let us drive his motor scooter or his car. I was driving like a professional by the time I was 12." To this day, Bill's closest friends still call him King.

Of the three children, Mary Elizabeth is most like her father in terms of disposition and ambition. She is fiery and quick-tempered. As a child, she was an accomplished pianist, not because she was blessed with natural ability, but because she was determined. At five in the morning, she would be up practising before school. "She was full of drive, just like Dad," Harold Jr. says. "If she wanted something, she went for it. If she didn't have a lot of talent, she made up for it in effort. She's a very, very hard worker at anything she does."

Ballard doted over his daughter, but Harold Jr. says his father's attitude changed drastically when she started dating. The coolness seemed to be the result of jealousy, and the feeling that no-one had the right to impose on his family. When Mary Elizabeth met and eventually married Allan MacLean, a junior executive for Ford at Oakville, Ontario, in the 1960s, Ballard would have little to do with him. "He never recognized Allan," Harold Jr. says. "He never gave him the time of day."

At the University of Toronto, Mary Elizabeth studied music and received a degree in occupational physiotherapy. After the failure of her first marriage she returned to school and earned a Masters of Business Administration from York University. About this time, she met Michael Flynn, a young executive in the trucking business. Today they have three children and a house in Forest Hill, a posh Toronto neighbourhood.

Of the two boys, Bill was the favoured son. He was an athlete and did well in school. Ballard was always saying Bill was a chip off the old block. "He was a great promoter of Bill," Harold Jr. says. "It was Bill this, Bill that, which I agreed with. Bill was always successful in school and everything he pursued."

Harold Jr., unlike his brother and sister, was introspective and quiet. He was never able to please his father. Artistically inclined, he went to the Ontario College of Art, but was put down by his father, who said "only flakes go to art school." Harold Jr. says, "He was always belittling me or knocking me down. I was never tough enough. He was always saying you could never do this, you could never do that. After a while, you start to believe it about yourself."

In the fall of 1972, Harold Jr. was enrolled at Waterloo Lutheran (now Wilfrid Laurier) University where he shared a house with other students. When furniture was needed, he constructed some using a circular saw borrowed from his father. A few weeks later, he took a day off from school to be in court on the day his father was sentenced for his convictions of fraud and theft. As Ballard was led out of the court house, he stopped and spoke briefly to Bill and told him to look after things while he was away. When he saw Harold, he said, "Why aren't you in school?" Harold Jr. told him that he wanted to see him before he went to prison. Harold says the last thing his father said to him before being taken away was, "Where's my circular saw?"

After Harold graduated from Waterloo Lutheran, he worked in the Gardens ticket office. But there were arguments with his father, and he quit. Later he worked for a car dealer in North York. When he married a Lebanese woman, who was three years his senior and a divorcee with two children, Ballard refused to accept her. He continued to tell people his son was single, referring to him as a "playboy." In early 1980 Harold Jr. told Mark Bonokoski of the *Sun*, "I don't feel like his son anymore, just a separated entity. He probably won't talk to me anymore but, then again, I have to ask myself if that's any different than before."

When Ballard appeared on CBC's "The Fifth Estate" and defended his proclivity for racist and anti-Semitic remarks, Harold Jr. told Bonokoski, "I've heard my father's racial remarks. I've heard them all my life and it hurts me to think the media plays upon them so much."

Harold Jr. had just started his job with the North York car dealership: "Here I was trying to make a start in a new career, working for a decent man who also happens to be Jewish. I couldn't look my employer in the eye." For a while Harold Jr. dropped his surname and went by Harold Garner, which was his middle name.

Bill, on the other-hand, was the achiever. He was loud, extroverted and a wise guy. Like his father he was hot-tempered. At Waterloo Lutheran Bill was student council president, and played centre for the football team. After university, he attended Osgoode Hall Law School, from which he graduated in 1972 *magna cum laude*. At Osgoode, he was captain of the York University Yeomans football team and the Osgoode Hall debating team. His friend Peter Larsen used to think he would someday be prime minister.

Bill's graduation from Osgoode came during Ballard's trial; when Ballard was convicted, he made Bill vice-president of the Gardens and left him in charge. Most people believe Bill did a good job at the Gardens. He brought in young people he knew from school and gave them key positions, but they weren't accepted by Ballard, and eventually they left. The Gardens, after all, was Ballard's territory, and he wasn't about to concede any amount of control to his son and his son's friends. As Kaihla noted, there was a huge gap between the business ideas of Ballard, the 19th-century robber baron, and his law-degree-toting son.

When Ballard got out of prison, he started attacking Bill, yelling at him in front of people, calling him a "dummy" or a "stupid fucking asshole."

Finally, there was a spectacular confrontation in 1976. Ballard had been in Detroit for a Leaf game, and then returned to the Gardens, where a reception for equestrians was being held in the Hot Stove Lounge. For some reason, it enraged Ballard that Bill was there. Ballard started screaming at him, "What the hell are you doing here? This isn't your reception. Get out of here!"

Humiliated, Bill followed his father to his office where the two had a fight. Bill screamed at him, asking why he had embarrassed him. He started throwing things, trashing the office. Then Gregory came in to break it up. Neither Gregory nor the participants feel comfortable talking about the incident. However, Bill did leave the Gardens shortly after that, resigning from his post as vice-president. He refused to set foot in the arena when his father was in town until the spring of the following year.

Bill had a job waiting for him when he left. In 1973, he set up a concert promotions company. With his access to the Gardens, this was a natural. It was something Tom Smythe had done before his father, Stafford, had died.

Bill and Peter Larsen went in with Michael Cohl and David Wolinski, who owned and operated a small company called Cymba Productions above the China House Restaurant on Eglinton Avenue in Toronto. Thus, Concert Productions International was formed as a Gardens subsidiary, with Bill as chairman, and Larsen, Cohl, and Wolinski as partners. In 1974, they bought the company from the Gardens, and a year later Larsen cashed in his shares.

It is generally understood that Cohl is the driving force in the company. He is often described as "ruthless" and "aggressive." Bill is the legal counsel and, of course, is the son of the Gardens owner. With Bill's influence, CPI established a quasi-monopoly on the arena and quickly grew to become Toronto's largest rock promotion company. It's biggest competitor nation-wide was Donald K. Donald in Montreal. Donald once told Matthew Fraser of the *Globe and Mail*, "We were vicious competitors. Cohl was a brash young upstart and he had some clever ideas. But, because I'm no wimp, I started to kick ass too."

After a major war, the two sides came to an understanding. CPI would get Toronto, which included a deal with the Canadian National Exhibition grandstand, and Donald would get Montreal. In the rest of the country, they would share the market. Said Donald in 1984, "Michael doesn't come into Montreal unless it's to buy a smoked-meat sandwich at Schwartz's, and I don't go into Toronto unless it's to buy some popcorn at one of his concerts."

By 1984, CPI was one of the largest promotional companies in North America, grossing $56 million and presenting more than 200 concerts a year, as well as some sporting events. In June of that year, CPI expanded into the merchandising business by purchasing a New Jersey–based company called Krimson. This gave CPI the merchandising rights to the Jacksons' 1984 summer tour. By selling Jacksons T-Shirts, buttons, and posters, CPI earned about $63 million, boosting the company's total earnings for the next year to $117 million.

Then, in December 1987, CPI made the biggest deal of its 15-year history, and not surprisingly it was with a Canadian brewery. Long into sports, breweries were now turning their attention to other means of entertainment such as rock concerts. It was, without question, a good deal for Ballard and Cohl, who had bought out Wolinski a few months earlier. In return for selling 45 per cent of

CPI to John Labatt Ltd., they received about $20 million. The holding company owned by Ballard, Cohl and Labatt's was called BCL Entertainment, the initials standing for the three partners.

In bringing in Labatt's, Ballard and Cohl retained control of the company but now had the financial backing needed to expand. Labatt's, too, got what it wanted: a foothold at the Gardens, and a partnership with a man who might some day control the arena and the hockey club.

Bill's cut was about $10 million, thus making him a wealthy man. By then he was married to an attractive Dutch woman, Renée Belonjé. Soon there was a baby girl. Described by a Canadian Press reporter as "boyishly handsome" at 41, he seemed to be living a charmed life. But by the mid 1980s, there was a major distraction in Bill's otherwise perfect life.

16

BALLARD

v. BALLARD

In the beginning, the Ballard children were not alarmed by Yolanda. They knew she had a record, but their father was not exactly the epitome of good conduct and virtue either. Besides, he was strong and robust and still sharp, despite his eccentricities. Harold Jr. says, "More than anything, we wanted him to be happy. That was the most important thing."

Yolanda filled a void in Harold's life. By 1986, he was pretty much alone, having survived many of his contemporaries. Robert Sedgewick, a stabilizing influence on Ballard, died from heart disease in 1984. His oldest friend, Harry (Red) Foster, with whom he raced motor boats in the 1920s, passed away the same year. The biggest blow, of course, was the death of Clancy in 1986.

Ballard's health also was starting to decline. In 1984, he lost 60 pounds, reducing his weight from 240 to 180, on doctors orders, he said. He had insulin blackouts from not adhering to a proper diet. He sometimes binged on chocolates and ice cream. In 1986, he had prostate gland surgery. "I'm going to have an operation where they turn you into a girl," he said. And he was beginning to suffer chest pains.

Because of his diabetes, he had serious circulation problems in his feet and legs. Rather than walking, he shuffled. By 1987, he sometimes used a wheelchair. Without Yolanda, he would have required a full-time nurse. As the relationship continued, he began to rely on her more and more. "Besides," said a friend of Ballard's, "he needs somebody to yell at." And, of course, they had so much in common. They were wilful, determined, and manipulative. Neither had much education. Both tended to be vulgar. "When you think about it," says a Gardens employee, "they were meant for each other."

There was one main difference. Yolanda loved the status and material things that wealth provided. Yolanda had a particular fondness for shoes. As a result, the children nicknamed her Imelda, as in Marcos. When Ballard was in hospital in Florida with his heart trouble in 1988, for example, his American Express credit card was used extensively at exclusive shops. There was one charge from a Gucci shop in Palm Beach and two more from Gucci in Bal Harbor; there were 12 charges to Joseph's Shoe Salon in Miami Beach and one to Lord and Taylor, a clothing department store in Miami–all in a period of about three weeks. Ballard, on the other hand, wasn't interested in expensive clothes or a high social standing. He liked hanging out with denizens of the arena, and of course the hockey people. He had hated Upper Canada College when he attended as a teenager. He had made sure his children didn't go to private schools, although Bill thinks the cost involved probably had more to do with this than anything else. "Harold isn't stingy," Bill says. "He just doesn't like to spend."

Early in the relationship, Yolanda was accepted as part of the family. In the summer, Bill, who had a cottage near his father's at Thunder Beach, would come over with his wife, Renée, and their infant daughter. Harold and Yolanda would play with the baby and T.C. Puck would frolic with Bill's dog. Sometimes the family would get together for barbecues and dinners, and Yolanda's two children, Bill and Ana, were often included.

Gradually, however, these occasions disappeared. Harold Jr. says one of the early influences on the Ballard children was Sedgewick. He was deeply suspicious of Yolanda and avoided her whenever possible. Harold Jr. says, "Sedgewick didn't want anything to do with her. When she came along, he was out of there."

As time went on, the children felt that Yolanda was attempting to isolate them from their father. When they called they heard somebody pick up the other line. Ballard himself accused her of listening in to telephone conversations.

They noticed it was difficult to see their father alone. Yolanda was always there, and when she wasn't she was close by, often listening in, according to Bill and Harold Jr. Several times, Bill says, he caught

Yolanda with her ear to the door of Ballard's office, while he was talking business with his father. When Yolanda would come in, Bill would say, "What's the matter, Yolanda? The doorknob burn your ear?"

Harold Jr. remembers a scene at the cottage, when he was talking to his father on the veranda. During the conversation Harold Jr. noticed something odd in one of the flower pots. For an instant he thought it was an animal. Then he looked closer and realized it was Yolanda's blonde hair. "She was lying down, hiding behind the flowers, listening to our conversation," he says. "But you could see her hair. She couldn't get her hair out of the way."

Most disturbing for young Harold was the sight of Yolanda wearing his father's wedding ring: "I went in and sat down. Then I looked over and there she was with my father's wedding ring on, the one that was given to my father by my mother. I said, 'Yolanda correct me if I'm wrong, but is that or is that not my father's wedding ring?"

"She said, 'Well there have been so many things missing out of your father's office, I thought I'd put it on.'

"I said, 'Well, get it off. Give it back to my father. How could you do that?' "

Like her father, Mary Elizabeth can be blunt, and after a while she didn't hide her dislike for Yolanda. The children were at the family cottage one day when, as Harold Jr. remembers, "out of the blue" Mary Elizabeth brought up Yolanda's record and then said, "The only reason you're around here is to try the same thing."

As Harold Jr. recalls, "Yolanda went wild. Then she started crying, as she always does when she doesn't get her way, and then appealed to my father for support." She did receive Ballard's support, and that ended Mary Elizabeth's relationship with her father.

Earlier, Mary Elizabeth had asked Ballard if he would allow her son Matthew's hockey team to play a game in the Gardens. The NHL season was over but the ice was still in the arena. Ballard had done this in the past for people he didn't even know, and initially he had said yes.

As the day of the game approached Mary Elizabeth had not received a confirmation. When she called her father at the Gardens, he wouldn't talk to her. "Tell her I'm in Chicago," he said to an employee, which is his usual reply when he doesn't wish to talk to somebody.

She drove to the arena. When she met Gord Stellick, who was the assistant general manager at the time, she was told that Ballard didn't want to see her. After talking to Shanty MacKenzie, the building superintendent, she learned that her son's hockey game had been cancelled.

Furious, and determined to meet her father, she walked into his office and waited for him. Almost two hours later, he appeared and what resulted was a blistering exchange. According to Harold Jr., Ballard told Mary Elizabeth her children were hers and not his and he wanted nothing to do with them.

Bill attempted to continue his relationship with his father but says he found it difficult. In November 1986, there was a brief confrontation during Clancy's funeral when Ballard stumbled. Bill went to help him, but Yolanda moved in ahead of him. Words were exchanged.

After the funeral, Yolanda and Ballard went to the Cayman Islands, and days later the three Toronto newspapers received a telegram stating, "Enjoying the sun and all the fun the Grand Cayman Islands have to offer. Wish you were here." It was signed "Harold and Yolanda Ballard." Immediately the rumour spread that they had married, although the Leaf front office denied it. McNamara was quoted as saying, "Yolanda may have sent them (the telegrams). Maybe she wants people believing it." By then, Yolanda insisted that Gardens employees call her "Mrs. Ballard."

That summer, Yolanda threw a gala party at the cottage to celebrate Ballard's 84th birthday. Bill and Mary Elizabeth refused to attend, but Harold Jr. was there. He says that during the party Yolanda attempted to turn him against his brother and sister, telling him that they put him down and laughed at him behind his back. Just weeks later, the children learned that Yolanda had legally changed her name to Ballard. They were appalled and worried.

An even more disturbing event followed. It would result in a lawsuit against Ballard and stir speculation that he was finally ready to sell the arena and the hockey club. Ballard had met Michael Gobuty in about 1979. At that time, Gobuty lived in Winnipeg and was one of the owners of the Winnipeg Jets, the WHA team that would join with the NHL. In the 1978-79 season, Gobuty had acted as the club's lobbyist by flying to different NHL cities on behalf of the team. Although successful, Gobuty found his role diminished by the Shenkarow family which had a larger interest in the club. Gobuty attempted to buy out the Shenkarows but failed and then sold his 12 per cent before moving to Toronto in 1984.

Gobuty and Ballard made unlikely friends, largely because Gobuty had come from the WHA, which Ballard hated with a passion. But among the NHL owners and governors, Gobuty was one of the few who tried to get to know the Leaf owner. He hung out with Ballard and listened to his complaints and stories. "He tried a little harder to get to know Harold than the others," said an acquaintance of Gobuty's in Winnipeg. And Ballard was receptive. When Gobuty was in the midst of his power struggle with the Shenkarows, Ballard sent letters to the *Winnipeg Free Press,* praising Gobuty as an upstanding citizen and all-round great guy.

Gobuty started out in the garment business in Winnipeg in 1961. He moved into real estate and at one time owned the Assiniboia Race Track in Winnipeg and a men's leather clothing company called Gobuty and Sons. In 1986, Gobuty and CPI attempted to purchase the Jets and move the team to Hamilton. When they met with resistance by the other Winnipeg owners, CPI abandoned the idea, but later, according to Bill Ballard, Gobuty tried to make the deal on his own, without telling CPI. This infuriated Bill, who refers to Gobuty as a snake.

When Gobuty moved to Toronto in 1984, he was in serious financial difficulty. His race track had failed, Gobuty and Sons was in receivership, and his new business in Etobicoke, Canus Containers, a garbage can rental company, was in serious need of refinancing. His one bit of luck was a flourishing relationship with Ballard. He watched Leaf games with Ballard. His wife, Adrian, and Yolanda became close. The two couples spent time together at Ballard's cottage. In a court document, Gobuty referred to himself as "a close personal friend and constant companion of Ballard." The friendship was "equivalent to a close bond between father and son."

Ballard also became Gobuty's saviour, although he had helped him many times in the past as well. In the early 1980s, he had guaranteed a line of credit at the Canadian Imperial Bank of Commerce for Gobuty and Sons for $100,000. A few years later, he guaranteed another loan, this time for $150,000, from the Standard Chartered Bank of Canada. In 1986 there was a third guarantee, for a loan of $1 million from Standard Chartered. And then, in July 1987, Gobuty approached Lloyd's Bank of Canada for a line of credit in the amount of $5 million to prop up Canus. This, too, was supported by Ballard's guarantee.

In August of 1987, according to Gobuty, he began discussing with Ballard a "friendly takeover" of the Gardens. During this time,

Gobuty contacted Larry Luby, who was a manager in the North American Corporate Banking Division of the National Bank of Canada, and told him of his plan to buy Ballard's Gardens shares. Gobuty says that when he asked if National Bank was interested in financing the takeover, Luby was enthusiastic.

So, in September, Gobuty requested credit from the National Bank for $2.5 million. For this he again received Ballard's personal guarantee. Later, it would be disputed whether the loan was to pay Gobuty's debt to Lloyd's, or to be used in a takeover of the Gardens.

The loan was guaranteed on 9 October, the second day of the NHL season, when Gobuty and Thomas Reber, vice-president for North American Banking at National, met Ballard in the stands at the Gardens while the team practised. Ballard was presented with the National Bank guarantee and he signed it.

In a letter dated exactly one week later, Gobuty wrote:

Dear Harold,

Please find enclosed the guarantees that you signed for me. These have enabled me to regain my respectability in the community and for this I am forever grateful. Now in your words, "Business is Business".

I have arranged to purchase your 81 percent share in Maple Leaf Gardens for $35 a share which is approximately $104,000,000 cash.

Harold, as you know Maple Leaf Gardens and the Toronto Maple Leafs are you! In order for me to follow in your footsteps, I need your guidance in what I am attempting to do. Your friendship to me is more important than monetary gain. If you say no to me I will still respect and value your friendship as I have done for years.

Should you consider my offer, there are many conditions I would like to be in place.

1. You stay on as president and governor for as long as you wish.

2. You draw the same salary for life.

3. You sign all the cheques.

4. You maintain your residence in the building.

5. You guide me as your protege in the running of the facility.

6. *The Russians will NOT play in Maple Leaf Gardens for as long as I am involved.*

Respectfully yours,
Michael Gobuty

About this time, the National Bank sent a letter to Ballard confirming the loan guarantee. When it was seen by Don Crump, the National Bank was advised that Ballard "will not be responsible for any amounts advanced pursuant to the guarantee." A follow-up letter from Crump suggested that Gobuty's account at the bank be frozen.

The bank responded by demanding that Gobuty immediately repay $2.115 million already loaned plus interest. When the money was not forthcoming, the bank launched a lawsuit against the borrower, Gobuty, and the guarantor, Ballard, for the unpaid amount. Thus ended the friendship between Ballard and Gobuty.

It still isn't clear if Ballard did indeed plan to sell to Gobuty. In Ballard's original response to the lawsuit, his lawyers stated that he guaranteed the loan "because of his trust of Gobuty and as he wished his friend to have an opportunity to play an active role in MLG [Maple Leaf Gardens]" and that a "material factor" in the dealings between Gobuty and the bank "was Gobuty's representation that a friendly takeover of MLG would soon take place and that National would be part of the takeover." However, this assertion disappeared in a re-draft, which says the signing was "in reliance upon his friendship and because he believed Gobuty had substantial means and only needed temporary assistance."

Under cross examination for discovery several months later, held at the Gardens to accommodate Ballard, Ballard strongly denied there was any takeover plan: "As far as I'm concerned, it's a total lie."

"You weren't aware of that?" asked lawyer Hilary Clarke, who represented the bank.

"No, it's a lot of garbage."

Later Ballard said, "I knew he was interested in it, but I never knew he had gone as far as trying to promote it." Ballard was asked what his response had been to Gobuty's interest. "I didn't say anything. I said there was no chance. There's dozens of people that want to have it. I've got lots of letters upstairs requesting to do business to sell Maple Leaf Gardens."

Several months later, intriguing information was uncovered during cross examination of Gobuty by Ballard's lawyer, John Chapman of the law firm Miller, Thomson, Sedgewick, Lewis and Healy. It was revealed that Gobuty had signed a certified cheque in the amount of $75,000, payable to Yolanda and to be drawn on Gobuty's account at Lloyd's Bank. The date on the cheque was 11 September 1987, which was about six weeks after Gobuty had secured Ballard's guarantee on the loan from Lloyd's, and a little less than a month before Ballard guaranteed the National Bank loan.

During the cross examination it was revealed that Crump had asked to see the list of cheques written on Gobuty's Lloyd's account. But when Gobuty provided the list, the cheque made out to Yolanda was not included. Chapman said to Gobuty: "It's missing from the list, you'll agree with me there."

GOBUTY: There's a blank. It doesn't mean it's a missing check. Don't put words in my mouth.

CHAPMAN: And exhibit No. 3 was the list that you provided to Mr. Crump when Mr. Crump wanted to know where the money went.

GOBUTY: Yes, Mr. Chapman.

CHAPMAN: And 49 [the cheque number] is not there.

At that point, Gobuty's lawyer conceded there was a blank between 48 and 50. Chapman then asked Gobuty if cheque 49 was on Gobuty's personal line of credit with Lloyd's Bank.

GOBUTY: If I wrote a cheque on Lloyd's Bank, which I did, it would be on my line of credit with Lloyd's Bank, yes, Mr. Chapman.

When Chapman asked the purpose of the $75,000 cheque, Gobuty was told by his lawyer not to answer. Gobuty then asked for a short recess. When the cross examination resumed, Gobuty refused to answer the question. Next, Chapman asked: "Mr. Gobuty, was this money paid to Yolanda in return for her assistance in helping you get these guarantees?"

Gobuty was told by his lawyer not to answer. Later Chapman stated, "And Mr. Gobuty I'll put it to you that you intentionally hid this payment from Mr. Crump when you provided the list of cheques to Mr. Crump." Again Gobuty was told not to answer the question.

The next crisis for the family occurred just after Christmas with

Ballard's now-famous declaration that he would leave his money to charity. Ballard was quoted as saying, "Bill never will move in to run the Gardens and the hockey club. Bill has his own business. The worst thing that could happen would be for my three kids to take over. It just wouldn't work. They have fought among themselves ever since they were kids. My daughter is the worst. Bill sometimes asks when I intend to move on. He's kidding, but sometimes he sounds serious."

Ballard then said he expected a charity to operate the Gardens: "The Gardens and the hockey club will be run by a trust that represent charities, some of which already are very important to me. It will be up to each charity to name a trustee. Some of them might even be present Gardens directors. . . . Lawyers are working on the arrangements."

The story was treated as something very important, but in some ways the reaction of the children, specifically Harold Jr., was more interesting. From young Harold's remarks, the public, for the first time, was made aware of the animosity between the Ballard children and Yolanda. In a *Star* article, he blamed her for inciting Ballard against them. "It's awfully upsetting," he said. "It's news to me that we all hate each other." Of Yolanda, he said: "I don't like the fact that Yolanda wears my dad's wedding ring. I don't like her calling herself Mrs. Ballard. And I don't like her asking me to get my share certificates out to show her."

Harold Jr. was referring to his stock in the family holding company, Harold E. Ballard Ltd. From time to time Yolanda would ask Harold Jr. to produce his share certificates. This made him uncomfortable and suspicious. Bill and his brother had been trying to stay on good terms with their father. Bill someday wanted a chance at running the arena, or more to the point, operating a new facility that would replace the Gardens. But both deny that money was the motivating factor in trying to maintain the relationship. They would eventually receive millions of dollars from HEB Ltd. anyway. Harold Jr. says, "He's my father and I love him. I don't need a lot of money. I didn't want to see him get hurt."

With the controversy of the will still raging, Ballard headed off to Florida with Yolanda. Two days later, he became ill. On 3 January 1988 he was taken to a hospital in Palm Beach, complaining of chest pains. Then he was moved to the Miami Heart Institute, where it was determined he had suffered a heart attack.

At the heart institute Ballard and Yolanda rented a VIP suite with two bedrooms at $500 (U.S.) a day, so Yolanda could stay with him. One day, dressed in a terrycloth robe, she told reporters, "Harold's not going to die. He's going to live to 102, plus, plus, plus."

When Bill learned of his father's illness, he flew to Florida to be with him. But according to Bill, Yolanda attempted to keep him away from his father, and made it difficult to see him. Bill says that at various times at the hospital she accused him of using drugs and attempting to harm his father. A sign was posted on the door of the suite stating no one was to be admitted but his wife and children. "She named the kids on the sign," says Bill. "They were hers."

Shortly after Bill arrived, he said, Yolanda got into an argument with a nurse, who was attempting to give Ballard his medication. "She was saying, 'I'm his wife.' I walked up and said, 'It's irrelevant if you're his wife, and you *aren't* his wife. The doctors have to give him his medication.' And then she did a big flip and the nurse went down the hall and got the doctor. He rushed by her and gave him the medication."

Despite Ballard's age, he made steady progress. His breathing improved, there was a reduction in the fluid in his lungs, and his blood pressure started to come up. By early February he was released. Still, he was weak and tired. He was thin and he moved slowly. It was a startling change in a man who, until the summer of 1984, had been big, vital, and energetic, with a straight back and a quick step. Now he shuffled, head down, or used his wheelchair. He spoke slowly.

More than the heart trouble, Bill said the doctors had told him diabetes was the cause of the decline. "His heart's fine," Bill said after his father's release from the institute. "It's the diabetes. It eats away at him, both mentally and physically. That's why on some days he's normal and other days he looks like he's on the planet Uranus."

The extent of Ballard's deterioration was evident a few weeks later in March 1988 during examination for discovery in the National Bank lawsuit. Under questioning from Clarke, Ballard could barely remember the circumstances of his signing Gobuty's guarantee. He said Reber wasn't present, and he didn't know the name of the law firm representing him.

CLARKE: Mr. Ballard do you recollect signing any personal guarantees for Mr. Gobuty?

BALLARD: How do you mean recollect?

CLARKE: Do you remember signing any guarantees for him for his indebtedness?

BALLARD: Well I signed . . . whether they represented a guarantee or not I don't know. He just asked me to sign them for him.

CLARKE: So you do recollect signing certain documents.

BALLARD: That's right.

CLARKE: But you don't know the contents of these documents.

BALLARD: No.

CLARKE: And how many of these documents did you sign?

BALLARD: That I don't remember, but I think it must have been three or four of them.

CLARKE: On each of these occasions when you were asked to sign them did you ever make an inquiry of Mr. Gobuty as to what they were all about?

BALLARD: No.

When Chapman asked the reason for the line of questioning, Clarke said it was to determine the "sophistication" of Chapman's client. Clarke then asked the identity of Rosanne Rocchi, who was Ballard's lawyer from the firm of Miller, Thomson.

BALLARD: I believe she works for the law company.

CLARKE: For a law firm?

BALLARD: Yes.

CLARKE: What law firm does she work for?

BALLARD: MacKinnon . . . what is it?

CHAPMAN: Miller, Thomson.

In June, Ballard was strong enough to attend the NHL's annual congress, but in July he suffered a relapse. Initially, he was taken to Wellesley Hospital, but when it became apparent that surgery would be needed, he was moved to Toronto General Hospital.

At this point, Mike Wassilyn, a significant member of the Gardens' cast of characters, entered the picture. At the arena, Wassilyn was known as Yolanda's loyal friend and protector. For years Wassilyn, who is in his late thirties, has been a fixture on

Carlton Street. He calls himself a "ticket host," which is his euphemism for ticket scalper. On most days he can be seen to the right of the main entrance of the arena on Carlton Street. That has been his turf for years, but he also has free access to the building, including Ballard's apartment. They are the best of friends, Ballard and Wassilyn; Wassilyn refers to Ballard as "one of the greatest men God ever put on earth."

Harold Jr. says: "Mike calls himself a street person. He says he was born on the street and raised on the street. My dad likes guys like that, and he has known Mike since he was a little kid. But because Mike is a scalper, dad doesn't like to be seen with him."

Wassilyn grew up in downtown Toronto but lives in the Guelph area. Over the years he has been involved in harness racing as an owner and driver. In July 1987 he was charged by the Ontario Racing Commission with lack of effort, affecting the outcome of a race, and preventing another horse from winning at Elmira Raceway. Others were charged as well in what turned out to be the longest-running investigation by the ORC into alleged race-fixing in 15 years. Eventually Wassilyn was suspended.

During the investigation and hearing, Wassilyn's behaviour was at times strange and erratic. Once he had to be removed from the office of ORC chairman Frank Drea by security guards, after he had burst in demanding to see Drea and had intimidated Drea's secretary. During the hearing, the proceedings were interrupted by constant outbursts from Wassilyn.

One day Wassilyn showed up dressed in a terrycloth robe and padded headgear, carrying boxing gloves. "Why don't you tie my hands and my legs up too?" he said to Drea. "You've been beating up on me all week."

"Let the record show that at 11 o'clock Mr. Wassilyn appeared in rather bizarre attire," Drea said. "It would appear he's in some kind of prize fight."

"You threatened me," Wassilyn said.

"And let the record show that he appears not to be in control of himself," Drea said, who asked Wassilyn's representative, David Alderton, to control his client.

At one point, Alderton told Wassilyn, "Shut up or I'll smack you."

When Ballard was taken to Wellesley Hospital, Harold Jr. was at Wassilyn's home helping him build a fireplace. During this time he says Wassilyn told him some wild stories, including his plans to buy the Gardens with Ballard's help. Later, according to Harold Jr.,

Wassilyn said that Ballard intended to appoint him assistant general manager of the team. He also told Harold Jr. continuously that Yolanda was a wonderful woman of saintly conduct.

Harold Jr. says he told Yolanda to call him if his father required surgery, but heard nothing, even though he says she was on the telephone to Wassilyn every day. Then on Friday afternoon, 22 July, Wassilyn told Harold Jr. that he had a sudden feeling that Harold's father had died. The same rumour was spreading through the Toronto Stock Exchange. Harold Jr. finally got through to his father just as he had been sedated for surgery.

"How're you doing?" Ballard said.

"How's everything going down there with you?" asked Harold Jr.

"Oh, very well. How's your work going?"

"Oh just great."

"Well, that's fine. Great talking to you. Thank you."

Then Ballard hung up. Minutes later he went in for a quintuple bypass. When Harold Jr. arrived at the intensive care unit at Toronto General after the surgery, a nurse said to him, "Your mother's here." Harold said that his mother had been dead for 20 years.

At Wellesley, the hospital officials had known the Ballard family. Dorothy had nursed there for years. Hugh Smythe was an old friend of the family, although not a great fan of Ballard's. But at Toronto General, the Ballards were strangers. Yolanda gave her name as Mrs. Ballard and the nurses assumed she was the mother of Bill and Harold.

The hospital gave Yolanda a room, because there were vacancies on that floor, and she stayed with Ballard around the clock. She hired a maid, a young girl named Denise. Prowling about in her pajamas in the middle of the day, Yolanda watched Ballard like a guard dog. David Allen, the hospital's public relations director, says Yolanda was helpful in discouraging visitors and making sure that Ballard took his medication. The two sons, however, say she went out of her way to stop them from seeing their father. They say she accused them, in front of people in the hospital, of being on drugs and of attempting to harm their father.

Said Harold Jr.: "She was running up and down the hallway saying my brother was on drugs and all this kind of stuff, and that he was here to hurt him. She did this to keep him away. She had the medical staff convinced the kids would do nothing but upset him.

"One day when I showed up, I was told there was no admittance at all for the children. And here she was walking around in bedclothes telling people she was Mr. Ballard's wife. By then Bill had just about had it. He was running around like a nit in a pit. I thought he was going to have a nervous breakdown."

Others who were close to Ballard had difficulty getting in as well, except Wassilyn, who did have access. A Gardens employee and old friend of Ballard's says: "I think everyone was having trouble, except the scalper. I thought that she did not want him to see the regular people. She would make up stories against them. I mean she told one of the doctors that I was trying to kill him. I just walked up to her, in front of the doctor, and said, 'You mean to say I'm going to kill him?' I'm sure the doctor felt she was ridiculous."

Donald Giffin, a Gardens director and long-time friend of Ballard, says no one should have been allowed in during the recovery. "He had major surgery and was very sick," Giffin said. "No one should have been getting in except medical staff. Yolanda was there, being a special nurse so to speak. And of course the children wanted to see their father."

The next dispute occurred on Ballard's 85th birthday, 30 July. By this time, Bill, exhausted from his battles, had gone on a fishing trip, leaving instructions to Harold Jr. to keep a close eye on their father. Since it was Ballard's birthday, Harold Jr. arrived at the hospital in the early afternoon. Yolanda refused to let him in, suggesting he come back about four that afternoon. As Harold turned to leave, Yolanda told him not to take the elevator but instead a back exit.

"Then I saw the little fat girl, Denise, running down the hall, waving her hands," Harold Jr. says. "It was then that I realized they were bringing in a birthday cake for Dad."

When Harold asked about the cake, he says Yolanda admitted there was going to be a small party that afternoon at four o'clock, and he could attend. But when Harold returned, a little before four, the party was over. Wassilyn had been there. A photograph had been taken of Ballard and Yolanda together and sent to the Toronto newspapers. In the caption, Yolanda was referred to as Mrs. Ballard. But nobody from Ballard's immediate family had been there. Mary Elizabeth no longer spoke to her father. Bill was fishing. And Harold, from what he could tell, wasn't welcome. He looked into the room and said, "Yolanda, you're a cunt."

Then suddenly, a few days later, Yolanda fell from grace. Ballard wanted her out of the hospital, out of the Gardens, and apparently out of his life. According to Harold Jr., his father said: "She's driving me crazy. She's pushing me around and I'm sick of it. I can't make a call. Tell them [the hospital staff] I can't make a call. Tell them I don't want Yolanda in here and tell them I don't want that little girl in here!"

Harold told his father that many of his friends including Rosanne Rocchi, one of his lawyers, had been trying to see him and were confused as to why they were not allowed in.

"Well tell them to get down here right now," Ballard said.

On 8 August, Rocchi and Crump met Ballard in his hospital room to inform him that the $75,000 cheque paid to Yolanda by Gobuty had been found during the investigation of the lawsuit by the National Bank. Ballard interpreted this as a payoff for getting him to guarantee Gobuty's loan. He was furious and told Crump and Rocchi he wanted Yolanda kicked out of the Gardens and the locks changed. "Throw her clothes out on the street," he said.

Suddenly Yolanda burst into the hospital room and asked them what they were talking about. She was told it was private business. When she ordered them to leave, Ballard turned around and told her to get out. Then Bill and Harold Jr. barged in and there was complete chaos. A senior nurse who was in attendance felt she had no choice but to order everyone out. When she asked Ballard who he didn't want in his room he told her Yolanda.

One of the results of the meeting was a decision by Ballard to run notices in the three Toronto newspapers several days later disavowing responsibility "for any debts, charges or expenses incurred by or on behalf of Yolanda MacMillan, also known as Yolanda Babic."

One day after the meeting, 9 August, Yolanda called a police officer to the hospital and asked him to accompany her to the Gardens. When she got there, however, she was told by an arena security guard that she was no longer welcome. Another development occurred earlier that day, when Ana, Yolanda's daughter, was supervising the moving of Yolanda's furniture into a condominium at the corner of Carlton and Jarvis streets. Ballard had purchased the unit several years earlier, but it had never been occupied. The plan was for Yolanda and Ballard to move in after his release from the hospital. Instead, the furniture remained on an elevator during a stand-off between Bill Ballard, who refused to allow it to be moved into the condominium, and Ana, who wouldn't leave. Eventually, the furniture was taken back to the Gardens.

Also that day, the *Globe* learned of Yolanda's ouster from a source who phoned in the tip. There was also a rumour that she was being investigated by the Ontario Securities Commission for insider trading of MLG Ltd. stocks. That turned out to be inaccurate, but the banishment of Yolanda was confirmed by Bill.

The next day, 10 August, the Ballard story ran on the front page of the *Globe* along with another hockey report, this one about Wayne Gretzky, who had been traded to the Los Angeles Kings. Hockey people found it somewhat amusing that Ballard shared space on the front page with the biggest NHL story of the year, although in this case Ballard had not solicited the attention.

The *Globe* report angered Ballard, partly because it was written by me, but also because it appeared as though Bill had gone to the media with a family matter. In fact, Bill only confirmed what I already knew from the phone tip. For these reasons, and others, the separation of Ballard and Yolanda lasted only two days. The sudden reversal shocked the two sons, but not the people who knew Yolanda and Ballard. Said a Gardens source at the time: "Bill and Harold tried a power-play and it backfired. I can't say I blame them. But the woman has 900 lives and anybody who gets near her gets burned."

In addition to the report in the *Globe,* there were other reasons for the reconciliation, the most important of which was Ballard's dependence on Yolanda. It was either Yolanda or a nurse, and it was better for his manly image to have Yolanda, whom he perceived as a glamorous blonde, looking after him.

This twist in the plot, of course, was reported in the newspapers, which were paying considerable attention to the feud by then. In a banner story in the *Star,* Yolanda told Dunnell that there had never been a falling out. "Harold and I never have been apart," she said. "The only separation has been in the brain of Bill Ballard." She added: "There is only one good Ballard, the one I live with." Yolanda also mentioned that she had purchased a small number of MLG Ltd. shares because she thought it important that she attend the board of directors meetings.

A few days later, Ballard was released from hospital, but instead of going to his Gardens apartment, he was taken to a suite at the Loews Westbury Hotel across the street from the arena. The idea was to remove him from the fighting between Yolanda and the sons. "We elected to put him in the Westbury, out of reach of the daily goings on," said Giffin.

When Ballard moved into his hotel room, Giffin noticed that Toronto General had sent along its own nursing staff, security, and public relations people. When he asked why, he was told that Ballard was something of a record holder, having survived a quintuple bypass at the age of 85. Toronto General believes Ballard is the oldest man in Canada to have survived five bypasses.

Ballard was back home at his Gardens apartment a few days later, and it didn't take much longer than that for Yolanda to get back in the news again. This time she called the police to have four old handguns removed from the apartment. Until police officers clarified the story, there were rumours about a violent argument, threats, and perhaps even shots being fired. As it turned out, the pistols were relics, probably not even usable. But Yolanda had found them in the apartment and was terrified.

By now, the soap opera was reaching new heights of absurdity every day. It was described as Toronto's version of "Dallas," and indeed in a few weeks there would be a mystery to rival "Who Shot J.R.?" In this case, it was "Who Punched Out Yolanda?"

It started on 6 September when Bill visited his father in his Gardens office. For several weeks, Bill had found it difficult to get through by phone. Yolanda screened the calls and, according to Bill, also monitored them. On that particular day, Bill was showing his father pictures of his daughter. When Yolanda appeared, words were exchanged between her and Bill. After that there are two versions of what happened.

Yolanda claims that Bill punched her in the face as he was leaving, bruising her around the left eye, and then kicked her in the stomach after she had fallen. Bill says that words were exchanged and then Yolanda came after him with her hands up as if to scratch him. He says he grabbed her hands to stop her from hitting him, and then as he opened the door to leave, kicked out with his leg to keep her away, as one would fend off a vicious dog.

Said Bill: "I turned around and grabbed her hand and said, 'Just keep away from me, my brother and sister, and just leave us the fuck alone.'

"She said, 'Look Harold, he's trying to assault me.'

"I said, 'If I get around to assaulting you, bitch, there won't be enough left to put in a fucking hotdog.'

"I turned around, and she came at me again. I didn't kick. It was like 'get away'. I didn't hit her. I'll take a lie detector test. I didn't hit this bitch."

Bill said that when he left the office, there were no marks on Yolanda. But there was later—a very visible black eye and a bruise on the stomach. The same day, Yolanda went to Toronto General Hospital to have her wounds attended to. She returned the following day, complaining of nausea. Pictures were taken and she filed a complaint with the Toronto police. The result was a charge against Bill of assault causing bodily harm. But at a news conference to announce the signing of the Leafs' first draft choice, Scott Pearson, Ballard denied any knowledge of the incident. "Is that so?" he said. "She's big enough to look after herself. So keep your microphone in your ass."

Ballard's office is more or less L-shaped, and it would have been unlikely for him to have seen anything that happened at the door from where he was sitting behind his desk. The view is also obstructed by a pillar. Sergeant Rusty Beauchesne of the Metropolitan Toronto Police Department's 52 Division said, "From where he was sitting, I don't think he could have seen anything."

One of the results of the charge was a $1 million civil suit for damages by Yolanda against Bill, claiming serious internal and external injuries. In the statement of claim, she gave her residence as Maple Leaf Gardens.

As a show of solidarity, Mary Elizabeth and Harold Jr. accompanied Bill when he appeared in court on the day a date was set for his case to be heard. Outside, they posed for pictures. "Here we are," said Mary Elizabeth, "the battling Ballards," a reference to Ballard's remark that they were always fighting.

In November, the *Sun* did a two-part series on Ballard. During the interview with Jean Sonmor, Ballard referred to his daughter as a "reptile" who "doesn't deserve any consideration." Of Bill he said: "He had no brains. He'd still be eating out of garbage cans if it weren't for Cohl." He also said he suspected Bill was a cocaine addict. Yolanda was quoted as saying, "I've been the one who's tried to keep the family together."

In the weeks that followed, what remained of the tenuous relationship between the father and his two sons disappeared. When Harold Jr. attempted to talk to Ballard before a game in December, Ballard refused to see him. By January 1989, neither Bill nor Harold Jr. were speaking to their father. By then Bill had been barred from the Hot Stove Lounge, where he occasionally had lunch. "He's lost in orbit," Bill said. "He doesn't care anymore."

The assault charge was heard in provincial court from 26 to 28 June. For his defence Bill hired Clive Bynoe, a Toronto lawyer who has built much of his reputation on defending police officers. Over the years he has represented dozens of Metro policemen on behalf of their union, the Metro Toronto Police Association, many on criminal charges.

Bynoe's strategy was to discredit Yolanda, the Crown's star witness. He hoped to portray her as a golddigger who had attempted to isolate Ballard and alienate him from his family. He hoped to question her in court about her past, particularly her guilty plea to perjury in 1981. He wanted to show that she was of dubious character and could not be believed on the witness stand.

Bynoe employed a private investigator, who conducted interviews in Toronto, Windsor, and Chatham, including some with police officers. From one interview he learned that prior to her relationship with Ballard Yolanda had attempted to meet Steve Roman, the multi-millionaire chairman of Denison Mines Ltd., who like Yolanda was of eastern European descent. Yolanda, apparently, had been turned away by an executive in Roman's company.

Among the information gathered by the investigator were the details of Yolanda's assault on Ron Jones. Jones, however, did not want to testify. He had been harassed by Ballard since the incident and feared losing his job. But on the Friday before the first day of trial on Monday, he was subpoenaed by Bynoe. When Ballard heard about it later that day, he telephoned Jones.

"What's this about a summons?" Ballard asked.

"I was subpoenaed by Bill's lawyer," Jones said.

"About Yolanda scratching you?" Ballard asked.

"I don't see what it has to do with the case," Jones said

"Well, you'd better look for another job," said Ballard.

Jones wasn't surprised to hear that Ballard wanted him out but he was bitterly hurt. The 45-year-old Jones, a cheerful, heavy-set man, had worked at the Gardens since the age of 14. He was married with two children and had been a loyal employee. Just days before being told to leave, he had gone up to Ballard's cottage and spent the day cutting the grass, weeding the gardens, and getting everything in shape.

In an interview later he said, "I had everything just right at the cottage and then I come back and find out that I've been fired." The Gardens local of the Teamsters Union was outraged over Ballard's threat and filed a grievance. Maintenance worker Harry Abbott, one of the union stewards, said in an interview, "I don't think Ballard runs the arena anymore. I think she [Yolanda] does. But whoever it is, everyone is totally demoralized. . . . Many of them wish he would die. It's so bad that during the winter they all cheer for the visiting team." Abbott also said that there was no sympathy for Ballard in his battles with his children. "He's reaped what he has sown," Abbott said. "And he's sown nothing but hate all of his life."

On a hot and humid Monday, the two feuding sides as well as friends and observers assembled in a courtroom at Toronto's Old City Hall. They included Dick Duff, Michael Cohl, Sylvia Train, who had been Harold Ballard's long-time friend but was now a strong supporter of the children, Dick Beddoes, a close friend of Ballard's who is writing a book about him, Yolanda's daughter, Ana, Irwin's daughter, Candice, and Denise, the little helper from Ballard's hospital stay. By the time the trial started, the courtroom was just about full.

Yolanda, dressed in a white suit, with her hair swept up and back, was the first to testify. She spoke forcefully, but gave rambling unclear answers to the questions, offering instead long tirades against Bill and his brother and sister, sprinkled with plenty of colourful name calling. Her emotions ran the gamut from sorrow and tears to anger and table pounding. Her testimony often evoked guffaws from the courtroom. At one point, Judge Walter Bell warned the courtroom would be cleared if the laughter continued.

Under oath she said Bill Ballard "was extremely vicious, mean and cruel" and regularly called her names such as "bitch, slut and tramp." She accused him of attempting to poison her and Ballard. "He was going to get me good," she said. "He threatened me several times that he was going to kill me. 'I will kill you, you bitch,' he said." Yolanda said that when Ballard was in Toronto General Hospital recovering from heart surgery, Bill showed up appearing as though he had been "smoking up or smelling up."

She claimed that the crux of the problem between her and the children was "power and greed," adding that the children were jealous because "if I stayed, there might be something there for me." Of the alleged assault, she said, "It wasn't a punch. It was a vicious and malicious smash in the face. Only a vicious animal would attack a woman!" She added that the hit had impact because Bill "has a big mitt."

As entertaining as her performance was, the real theatre was still ahead in Bynoe's cross examination. Yolanda knew that Bill had hired a "high-priced" lawyer whose defence would be to attack her, so she braced herself for what was to come. During the Crown's questioning, she had been keyed up, but in the cross examination she took that a step further, to extreme histrionics.

When prosecutor Sal Merenda chose not to object to Bynoe's line of questioning, Yolanda voiced her own loud objections, crying, pounding with her fist, and gesticulating. She referred to Ballard as "my Harold," as "a great and wonderful man," as "this famous human being who I had admired." She stressed that she loved animals and children. At one point her false teeth almost fell out, for which she apologized. After the first morning of the trial, Linda Barnard of the Toronto *Sun* said, "I've never seen anything like this in my life."

Bynoe began by asking Yolanda to confirm that she had met her ex-husband William MacMillan while he was in law school.

"Yes," said Yolanda. "And we have two wonderful children."

"You then went down to Chatham, Ontario. Is that right? Is that where you resided?"

Suddenly Yolanda blew up. "Is this relevant to the punch and bruising! Because that's what Harold will be . . . is this all necessary Your Honour? Is something that happened 20 years ago–let's see, he left me in 1967, my ex-husband, that's about, what 22 years ago–is this relevant to smashing and beating and killing!? Trying to kill me and threaten my children!?"

Tears welled up in Yolanda's eyes.

"Is this relevant sir? I know that you are a competent and brilliant attorney, otherwise Bill Ballard wouldn't have you, and it's thanks to his father's money that he can well afford to pay you, sir. You look like a decent guy. I think we are going to get along."

"Well," said Bynoe, "I'm afraid a lawyer's job is just to ask questions and not answer them, see. That's a rule we have in our courts. Now then you moved to Chatham, Ontario?"

"Yes."

"While you were in Chatham, Ontario, I gather you started raising your two children. A boy by the name of William?"

"Yes."

"And a girl by the name of Ana?"

"Yes."

"Now then, did you meet a lawyer there by the name of Robert Irwin?"

Heatedly Yolanda said, "I didn't meet a lawyer there by the name of Robert Irwin! I had known the Irwin family for many years! And again I ask Your Honour, is this relevant—what happened 15 or 20 years ago. I mean whatever happened 15 and 20 years ago is still 20 years ago. Whatever happened, I am sure that it will be hard to recollect. Yes I did know a family very well. In fact the young lady [Candice Irwin]—oh, she is not here at the moment. I have raised her, her mother died and I have raised that lovely child as I am raising another youngster [Denise the helper] that is in this courtroom."

Bynoe pressed on. "Now then," he said. "At some stage I gather you met—"

"This is relevant, is it?" asked Yolanda loudly as she pounded the stand. "Mr. Sal Merenda? I was told that only things that were relevant and pertain to the case. Mr Justice? Or Judge Bell? Perhaps I just elevated him to Mr. Justice, and he is a kind, decent man I'm sure. Is this relevant? Because Bill Ballard told me he was going to smut, smear, garbage. If this is the kind of case this is going to be, then the press is going to have a heyday because I've got some wonderful things on Bill Ballard with witnesses, sir. So, as long as we put the rules straight. We are going to dig back. And he has tried to get my ex-husband here, who wouldn't come. If we are going to make this a dirty, vicious, vehement [sic] . . ."

Suddenly she stopped and slapped her hand to mouth. Her teeth had almost fallen out.

"Pardon my teeth—because of the bang-up—flopping out. If we are going to make this dirty, then this little girl that doesn't have the money to pay for all the detectives that I'm sure Bill Ballard has had . . . I have nothing to hide and my Harold knows everything about the past. I have nothing to hide. I want to ask you, sir, just one question. Please forgive me Judge Bell— it is very important. Um, do you know why that assault and bodily charge was dropped [to common assault]? Because one more time this little girl—"

"Madam, just a moment madam," said Bynoe.

"I didn't want Hal to go through a big court trial," she said weeping. "It is not because of the lawyers and the judges. I again—again—gave these children a chance. Firstly, my Harold, he couldn't go through something called a preliminary, sir, and then a jury trial. Why was this done? I did it one more time for the health and welfare of my Harold. And it's not because you look over us, this kindly soul or that his lawyers did anything, or you. I, one more time, dropped that—that which Harold will never forgive me for."

Now Yolanda was standing.

"I have to live with this wonderful human being who won't

forgive me for dropping that bodily assault or whatever it is," she continued. "Because, again, I thought of his health–his health and welfare. And to live and to outlive the maggots and the vultures that can't wait for this precious man to die, sir. Forgive me for rambling on, but I was the one who dropped–"

"Would you please sit down," said Bynoe. "You're getting a little. . ."

Later Bynoe asked her if she had taken acting lessons as a young woman.

"Ahhh," said Yolanda. "You sir are going to take, bring out the . . . Yes. What's that got to do with human feelings? I'm not an actress. I am a person with feelings. Women that cry are good, kind, emotional women. That doesn't make an actress. I took a little course, went nowhere, obviously. Obviously went nowhere. Raised children. Didn't go on the stage. But everything has been twisted and turned, sir–"

"By you?" said Bynoe.

"Pardon me?"

"By you?"

"What are you saying sir?"

"And directing," asked Bynoe. "Did you direct as well as act?"

"This is going to be a trashy trial isn't it?" said Yolanda.

At one point she said to the judge, "Your Honour, Bill Ballard is smirking and making me nervous."

When Bynoe asked Yolanda about Marion Lloyd, one of the conspirators in the phony will scam, Yolanda said, "Judge Bell is this really relevant? Because if it is then I will answer in my own way as I can, and it is not going to be misguided and preconceived and whatever–as theatrics or whatever. You're looking at a person that's been battered and bruised. What has this all got to do with all the other garbage?"

Finally, Merenda spoke up. "Your Honour, perhaps you can direct the witness please?"

Said Bell drily, "I was waiting for you to make some objection."

The questions that upset Yolanda the most were the ones pertaining to Irwin. When Bynoe asked her if she had shared a bank account with Irwin at a Canadian Imperial Bank of Commerce branch in downtown Toronto in 1987, she said no. When Bynoe asked her if she had lived with Irwin at the house on Dundonald Street, she sighed and said, "I feel sorry for you Mr. Bynoe."

"Thank you," replied Bynoe.

Despite Yolanda's objections, Bynoe was allowed to introduce information about her past as part of the defence. He was able to show that there was a precedent for the defence in challenging the conduct of a witness. This would not have been accepted if Yolanda had been the accused.

Bynoe told Bell, "It is the theory of the defence that this alleged assault is part of a deliberate, preconceived, well-entered, well-planned enterprise on the part of this woman with respect to the acquisition of funds ultimately from the father of the accused. I'm sure Your Honour is well aware that this is a witness and not an accused, and I intend to cross-examine her with respect to discreditable conduct and associations unrelated to the testimony that she gave in this case as a ground for disbelieving her evidence."

Bynoe delved into such things as Yolanda's attack on Jones. Asked about the incident, she accused Jones of allowing Ballard to fall because he was a friend of Bill Ballard. She said, "He has been very, very good friends with Bill Ballard, and I feel it was deliberate. And when I saw Mr. Ballard fall, as a good companion, a friend, as a mother instinct, I said, 'You did this purposely,' as I would if he had dropped a little baby, sir, I would attack. I would attack."

"At the time, you had both your hands out in front with your nails out, now isn't that right?" asked Bynoe.

"Pardon me?"

"You just demonstrated by having your hands out in front like claws."

"No. I don't have claws. These are, by the way, Your Honour, not real nails. I had chewed my nails right down to the bone with constant worry about Mr. Ballard. So I had a very little bit of nail. But yes, Your Honour, I will not deny the fact that I would do the same if my children had dropped him. I would do it if you had dropped him. I would do it if anybody dropped Harold E. Ballard, or dropped a baby that I was taking care of."

Said Bynoe: "So that you would really attack anybody . . ."

"No–"

". . . that you thought had wronged Harold Ballard."

"No. You're not going to make me into a vicious person, sir, because you can't be a vicious person and be around Harold E. Ballard. I'm sorry, I'm a protector of his, as I am with my children. I did reach out and I may have . . . I may have scratched him. I was livid with concern."

In response to Yolanda's accusations of Bill Ballard using rough language around her, Bynoe asked her if she swore. Yolanda told him that she used the word "fuck" in a friendly and inoffensive way. "I do tend to use it, but in a nice way," she said. "Not that I think it's ladylike. But when I do, I really rip it off."

Of the incident that led to Bill Ballard's assault charge, Yolanda said she had been in Ballard's apartment, which is adjacent to the office, while Bill talked to his father. When Ballard called to her and asked her to show Bill out, she followed Bill to the doorway. Bill then "started his profanities." Yolanda testified that Bill said to her, "I'll see you dead. You're a slut. You're a bitch. You keep that old fucker alive."

Yolanda said that she replied, "I'll keep your dad alive until he's 102 plus."

Then she claimed Bill called her a "cunt face," before hauling off and slugging her, the result of which was "a vicious, swollen, bashed eye."

Yolanda continued, "While I was down he kicked me in the stomach," after which Bill fled "like a deer."

When asked about the $75,000 cheque from Gobuty, Yolanda admitted receiving it, claiming it was payment for her personal jewellery, although it was never explained why she felt the need to sell her jewellery when Ballard was looking after her. She tearfully confirmed the hospital incident in which Ballard had ordered her out of his room.

The next day, the Ballards were on the front pages of the three Toronto newspapers. A photograph of Yolanda and Rocchi was on the front of the *Star*. The *Sun* ran a picture of Ballard getting out of his limousine at Old City Hall, waving his cane menacingly at the media like a pirate brandishing his sword. The headline in the *Globe* read, "Ballards 'like vultures' companion tells court," referring to Yolanda's opinion of the Ballard children. In the *Sun* it was "Yolanda tells of 'vicious attack.' "

Ballard did not testify on the first day of the trial. Instead, he waited in his wheelchair for Yolanda in an office in the building. As he left later that day he was in better spirits than in the morning when he had duelled with the media. A reporter asked him if he would testify, and he said, "Well I'm not here for a birthday party." Another asked him what he was going to say about the incident. Ballard was just about to reply when Yolanda whispered to him loudly that he shouldn't discuss the case. Impatiently Ballard turned to her and roared, "Will you shut the fuck up!?" Yolanda did. They got into the car and drove away.

Tuesday afternoon, Ballard showed a little more affection for his companion when he took the stand. He said he would have been dead long ago if not for her constant care. For the most part his testimony was disturbing. His belligerence and his accusations against Bill as well as his other son and his daughter illustrated a distrust and an intense hatred for his children. In an earlier time, Ballard's public remarks had been comical if not tasteful. Now they were pathetic and tragic. He refused to admit he could see Bill in the court room. "My eyes are bad," he said. He accused his children of attempting to steal money from him and of even trying to poison him. "We were scared they were going to bring some kind of poison in," Ballard said. He said Bill was "nuts" and that he had tried to kill Yolanda. "He made it quite evident he was going to kill her or put her away," Ballard said. "That's when I knew he'd gone nuts." Ballard said he didn't want to see his children again, and added that he had never wanted them around him in the first place.

From Bynoe's perspective it was essential that Ballard be discredited as a witness. A day after the incident, Ballard had publicly denied any knowledge of it, and added that Yolanda was old enough to look after herself. About three weeks later, Yolanda's lawyer, Allen Rachlin, taped an interview with Ballard for evidence in the $1 million civil suit brought against Bill by Yolanda. In the interview, Ballard reiterated that he had not seen the alleged assault. "Evidently something happened, but I couldn't see from the angle I was sitting at from my desk," Ballard said on the tape. "I couldn't actually see if he made contact."

But in court, Ballard changed his story. Now he said that he had seen the assault clearly and he was ashamed of his son for doing it. "I think it's a bloody disgrace to the name of Ballard," he said. "I was goddamned ashamed of any son of mine doing that."

Under oath, Ballard said, "I was the only one there. All of a sudden he up and slugged her in the jaw–a dandy. Then when she fell down he gave her a helluva kick in the gut. Then he disappeared like a deer."

Bynoe, however, suggested to Ballard that he hadn't seen anything, and could no longer distinguish between truth and fiction, because he had been "brainwashed" by Yolanda. "You don't know what you're talking about," Ballard snapped. "You'd better get your facts straight before you suggest that!"

When Bynoe suggested that Ballard had invited Bill into his office that day, Ballard replied, "I've never invited him into my office."

"And that Bill showed you pictures of his daughter."

"I forget," Ballard said.

"And that when Bill heard Yolanda in the next room he said, 'Are your ears burning?'"

"That's a lie!" Ballard said.

"And that when Bill and Yolanda went down the hall they were out of your sight."

"That's a lie!"

"You couldn't see down the hall."

"That's a lie! Whoever told you that's a liar!"

"Is it not true Mr. Ballard that within a few minutes of the incident you said that you had not seen anything?"

"You're a liar!" thundered Ballard. "You never saw it! You're just making up stories!"

At that point, Bynoe produced Rachlin's taped interview with Ballard. "Would that refresh your memory?" Bynoe asked. "No," replied Ballard.

A few seconds after the tape played, Ballard complained that he couldn't hear it. Bynoe handed him a transcript of the tape and placed the recorder beside him. After listening to his conflicting statement, Ballard suggested that he had been under the influence of medication when he gave the interview. "Don't forget I just got out of hospital and those guys have you full of hop for a while," he said.

Earlier in the cross examination, Ballard also denied his brief falling out with Yolanda. Asked about the meeting with Rocchi and Crump in his hospital room, he said, "I know nothing about it."

When Bynoe reminded him that he had become upset with Yolanda, he said, "I don't remember that."

"You were so angry that you said to throw her clothes out of the Gardens," said Bynoe.

"That's a lie," said Ballard.

"And to change the locks on the Gardens, the condominium, and the cottage."

"That's a lie!"

"And that you placed notices in the newspapers—"

"That's a lie!"

When the cross examination ended Ballard was helped into his wheelchair. He was pushed down the hall by a Gardens employee, as he waved his cane at the reporters. Because of the time spent on Yolanda's testimony and cross examination, the case would be adjourned the next day. The trial would not resume until September 1989. There was no conclusion to be drawn other than that the Ballard family no longer existed. For two days before the public the disintegration was made complete. There had been no smirks or gestures from the prisoner's dock during Ballard's testimony. As Ballard was assisted from the witness stand, the favoured son sat silently, staring straight ahead.

17

THE

WHITE-HAIRED GHOST

By the spring of 1988, John Brophy was at the peak of his influence in the Leaf organization. After the dismissal of McNamara, Ballard had decided that a committee of Brophy, Stellick, and Duff would manage the team for the duration of the season. Brophy was already coach and now he had significant input into player personnel decisions–and he was close to Ballard. The next logical step was his appointment as general manager.

Brophy's friends in the media were rooting for him, and when the team played its last game, the *Sun* reported that he would probably be given the job of general manager the next day. The very thought made some of the players almost ill. They didn't like him–they saw him as a bully who blamed them for his weaknesses as a coach.

Brad Smith says: "There are three kinds of coaches: there's a motivator, a strategist, and a teacher. He was basically none of these three. He had no plan for anything. There wasn't one game where he had an actual plan. And of course he couldn't teach anybody anything. It was always said that he worked hard. I didn't see that. But he did take a lot of pride in his job as coach of the Leafs."

Brophy was always thought to be a motivator, somebody who could get results through fear and intimidation. But Smith says the players were not afraid of him. "He took the tough-guy approach. But it never worked. Not once did he have a player scared."

Courtnall says: "John was a good coach in the minors, but in the

NHL I just think he was in over his head. He tried to compensate by being tough, and there were some wild times in the dressing room."

Brophy would yell and scream at the players. He'd call them names. He'd belittle them and humiliate them. But the results were marginal. At the time he was fired, his NHL record was 64 wins, 111 losses, and 18 ties.

Smith remembers the game in which Brophy berated Kevin Maguire, who had been called up from the minors: "After two periods, the team wasn't doing well and he came in the dressing room and started ranting and raving and screaming," Smith says. "He went up to Kevin Maguire and took a dime out of his pocket and told him he was so stupid he couldn't make a dime driving a cab. He said he'd better smarten up or he'd be back in St. Catharines. You can't insult people like that. It didn't motivate anybody. It just made us hate him."

Smith remembers another incident during a game in which the Leafs were playing well against Minnesota. "I guess he thought screaming was a motivational gimmick. He was complaining the guys had no intensity. He went up to Todd Gill, and screamed at poor Todd, and told him he had as much intensity in him as he did in his cock that night."

Although Smith did not agree with Brophy's way of coaching, he and others found some of Brophy's antics amusing. One night in Detroit, against his coaching rival, Jacques Demers, the players almost broke out laughing during one of Brophy's tirades.

"Brophy lived and died to beat Demers," Chris Kotsopoulous says. "He came in between periods ranting and raving. Then, right in the middle of his speech, he picked up a roll of tape, and said, 'And you fuckin' goalies, I don't want any of this.' Then he bent over and threw the tape between his legs. I guess he was trying to illustrate a puck going in between their pads. It was all we could do to stop from laughing."

There was a night in Los Angeles when nine of the players went out for dinner together. Brophy, McNamara, and Stellick were leaving as the players were entering the restaurant, but Brophy, whom the players nicknamed the White-Haired Ghost, came back and hung around. That night, everybody had too much to drink, including Vaive and Greg Terrion who roomed together. Vaive, in fact, got sick.

When Vaive and Terrion got back to their room, they both passed out. Later, Brophy came around for a curfew check. When he knocked on the door, there was no answer. Then he called security to have the room opened only to find Vaive and Terrion sound asleep.

Another player wakened by the commotion saw Brophy, who also might have had too much to drink, kicking the foot of the bed and yelling, "Get up you bastards." Neither one of them did, and it's not clear why he wanted them up.

The next morning, Terrion said to the player next to him on the team bus, "You wouldn't believe the nightmare I had last night. The White-Haired Ghost was sitting at the foot of my bed screaming at me to get up and fight."

Many remember the day in practice when Brophy picked on Val James, who had been called up from the Saints. James, a big black man, was a career minor-leaguer with no hope of playing in the NHL. He had been a loyal follower of Brophy's in St. Catharines.

That day at practice, Brophy wanted to show how a defenceman protects the front of the crease, so he instructed James to take a three-point stance. Then Brophy, in the role of a defenceman, began jabbing and slashing James, knocking him down. James would get back up, and then Brophy would knock him down again. "If he'd done that to me," said a Leaf player, "I would have taken care of the coaching problem with one swing."

Not all the Leaf players disliked Brophy. Some say he was a different person away from the game. His biggest problem, they felt, was communication. He was not articulate and therefore had trouble expressing himself. He was unable to get his message across.

"The older guys on the team knew where he was coming from," said a veteran Leaf. "The young guys are different. They didn't like him, because they weren't used to playing for a guy like him. But a lot of the older players felt the young guys had been pampered by McNamara, anyway."

These younger players were sometimes called "Gerry's Kids" because McNamara had drafted them and they had been pushed into the lineup at an early age. They included Courtnall, Iafrate, Damphousse, Leeman, and Wregget. Partly because of a lack of teaching, they were slow to develop, and some seemed to lack interest in doing so. But they were excused, because they were "kids." Said a veteran: "Suddenly, when they're 23 or 24 management discovers they can't play, or don't have any guts and trades them."

As much as some of these players hated Brophy, it's fair to say he disliked them equally. In a bar after a game, he would refer to Courtnall as "the little cocksucker." He had a particular contempt for Tom Fergus, whom he viewed as lazy and uncommitted. He wanted Salming off the team and couldn't stand Frycer.

The third element in the feud was the media, specifically the writers who covered the team. The players resented the lack of criticism directed at the coach. Some felt reporters had been compromised by their friendship with Brophy. Despite no discernible progress by the team in two seasons, he was rarely fingered as being responsible.

Courtnall says: "It's too bad the press in Toronto let it go so long, They got all over Gerry McNamara and they got all over the wrong guy. I think John was fairly friendly with the Toronto media. Gerry wasn't and it probably killed him in the end."

Smith says: "I like [the hockey writers]. But I'll tell you what, a few of them made him out to be some sort of kingpin, which I think was unfair for everybody. It's nice if the media is on your side and says nice things. But when I read the articles, I just said 'please. . .' "

But the players didn't go out of their way to communicate their unhappiness either. In 1979, for example, the Leafs were constantly complaining to the sportswriters, off the record, about Imlach and his coaches, and their remarks got into the newspapers without names attached to them. But in 1987-88 there was nobody willing to pin a picture of Brophy to a dartboard and start throwing. Even when the team was eliminated from the playoffs, many of the players expressed their support.

But the next day, perhaps after reading that Brophy might hold the dual responsibilities of the coach and general manager, the players unloaded on him. One of them said, off the record, "We'd all like to go out and shoot him between the eyes. He tore the heart out of this team."

Frycer said, "It's terrible here. The coach hates the players and the players hate the coach. He doesn't know anything about hockey." Commenting on the players who said they liked Brophy, Frycer said, "Ninety per cent of them are lying. But you can't blame them for saying that. They have a future here and can't afford to get into trouble. I don't have a future here."

Salming alluded to the role of the media when he said, "All we read is, he works hard and we don't respond. All I'm saying he has to take some responsibility. You hate us scum bags, but you love the coach."

Brophy's reaction to this was to go to Ballard and argue that Salming be retired, and, oddly enough, that Bill Watters be fired as the colour commentator on the Leaf radio games. Stellick felt all of this was a little wide of the mark.

Watters, after leaving the employ of Alan Eagleson in 1980, had built one of the largest agencies for hockey players in the business, his chief rival being Meehan. In 1985, Watters started doing radio work for Telemedia Broadcasting Systems on Leaf radio broadcasts. This was an obvious conflict of interest, because his company represented, at one point, 8 Leafs, and about 80 players on other teams. Still TBS didn't seem to mind, nor did Ballard.

But during the 1987-88 season, Watters heavily criticized Brophy on the air. He felt he was a bad coach, and said so. A few times he became particularly upset when Brophy pulled Wregget, who was a Watters client. Near the end of the season, there had been a confrontation in a bar in St. Louis when Watters told Garry Lariviere, who was Brophy's assistant, that he was a "fraud" as an assistant coach. Lariviere didn't respond, but it infuriated the coaching staff.

Still, it struck Stellick that the Leafs had better things to do than punish a colour commentator and a 37-year-old defenceman for a bad season. During the meeting nothing was said about Brophy's becoming general manager.

Stellick recalls: "At that point, it was a real unsatisfactory situation. H.B. had decided he wanted Broph over Gerry, but we didn't know what the solution was. At the end of the year, I think Broph thought he was going to be the guy."

As time went on, it became increasingly apparent that Brophy was not the guy. But Ballard didn't know what to do. He didn't know where to look, and his two closest advisers, Sedgewick and Clancy, were dead. Clancy's input in the past had been suspect anyway.

Then one day, Ballard went to Stellick and, typically, said, "Give me a list of players you want to get rid of." Stellick said there were some players who should be moved, but there were other more important things to address, such as why the young players don't progress and why a player such as Craig Muni escapes from the farm system.

"For the first time, we had an argument," Stellick said. "But I thought, what the hell, I'll get my ideas across." According to Stellick, Ballard told him he didn't agree with everything he was saying, to which Stellick replied, "Do you want me to tell you what you want to hear, as Gerry always did, or do you want me to tell you what I really think?"

Ballard suggested he put his ideas in writing, which Stellick did. He says his report consisted of seven or eight pages analysing all areas of the organization. Ballard read it, and a few days later Dunnell wrote a column in the *Star,* predicting that Stellick soon would be named the team's general manager. Stellick knew then that he had the job. "That was the tap," he says.

Stellick was just a month shy of his 31st birthday when he was announced as the new general manager in April, making him the youngest GM ever in the league. Later in the spring, at the NHL Awards Dinner, host Alan Thicke would make jokes about the youthful Stellick. "Gord Stellick was going to be here," he said, "but it's past his bedtime."

Stellick was a personable young man. He had an honours degree in economics from the University of Toronto, which was completed in summers and at night schools while working full-time at the Gardens.

At 17, he got his first job with the Leafs, through a school friend who worked in the press box as helper on Saturday nights and knew Obodiac. When somebody quit, Stellick's pal recommended him. Stellick saw it as the best job in the world for a boy who had followed the Leafs from the time he could read the sports pages.

From working in the press box, he learned how to operate the facsimile machine, which reporters used in those days to transmit their stories. This was a service called Can-Fax, and by the summer of 1977, Stellick and his brother, Bob, who was two years younger, were running the Can-Fax operation for all the major sporting events in Toronto.

Stellick's next move up the ladder occurred at Christmas of 1977 when Gregory asked him if he could come in Wednesdays and type up game notes for the press. Wednesday was a bad day for him because of a heavy class load, but he readily agreed.

Stellick showed himself to be increasingly useful in the hockey offices, doing everything from public relations to making calls during trade talks. Obodiac, who viewed him as a little too ambitious, referred to him in the Leaf fact book as "a college educated typist."

The next break came in 1980, when he was named Imlach's executive assistant, as well as travel secretary. For several years, he made all the trips, which meant hanging out with Ballard and Imlach, and later McNamara. During McNamara's term, one would invariably hear him bawl out at an airport, "Gordie, where's the luggage?" or "Gordie, where's the bus?" Stellick was the man with all the answers and was eventually given the title of assistant to the general manager.

By the time Ballard appointed him general manager of the farm team in Newmarket in 1986, Stellick had worked in just about all the administrative areas of a hockey club. But in the operational areas, he had no experience. He had done very little scouting and hadn't coached or played.

So when Ballard offered Stellick the job of managing the Leafs, there were those who advised him against it. Because of the small scouting staff, it was really a job for a man who could assess players with a large degree of accuracy. There was no indication Stellick could do this. Still, for a Leaf fan growing up in Toronto, the job was a dream come true. He knew the restrictions and the frustrations that would exist, and was aware of his limitations, but he said to himself, "I'm a high school kid from Georges Vanier, and now I have the chance to be GM of the Leafs."

But he had very little authority. Almost without exception, general managers are allowed to hire their own coaches. Stellick was not. If he had been given that authority, he would have fired Brophy immediately. Nor could he add substantially to the scouting staff, although he did bring in George Armstrong, after he had left the Quebec Nordiques organization, and Doug Woods, who had been fired by the Penguins as a scout, to work as a part-timer in Ontario.

But nothing was done to upgrade the coaching. Brophy had asked for a strength coach, someone who would be responsible for the conditioning of the players, and had suggested Curt Brackenbury, a former player and friend. But Stellick refused, for two reasons, he said. He didn't feel Brophy knew how to use the one assistant he had, let alone two. And if a second assistant were hired, Stellick would want him to take charge of more than just conditioning the players–game preparation and teaching for instance.

Stellick did add players to the organization through the signing of free agents. Forwards Dave Reid, Paul Gagné, and Craig Laughlin were picked up. Reid and Laughlin were checkers and could play aggressively. Gagné was a former first-round draft choice who had missed two seasons because of a back problem. He was slated for Newmarket, as was another free agent forward, Doug Shedden. In addition to adding depth to the Leafs, Stellick wanted the Newmarket team to be reasonably successful, so there would be a winning environment for the young players such as defenceman Darryl Shannon. Stellick also re-signed Salming to a one-year contract, despite his remarks about Brophy. Frycer, however, was traded to Detroit for defenceman Darren Veitch.

Agents noticed a new attitude from Leaf management. Herb Pinder, who negotiated Veitch's contract, liked Stellick. He found him reasonable and fair. Stellick gave Wendel Clark a three-year contract worth $250,000 annually despite Clark's suffering from a back problem. He was criticized for this, because there was no guarantee Clark would play again. Still, the new general manager said, "Wendel Clark does not have to prove himself, he proved himself by coming in here, taking on the league, and getting us into the playoffs." It's fair to say McNamara would have handled things differently.

Another change was Toronto's participation in the waiver draft for the first time in four years. They picked up defenceman Brad Marsh from the Flyers, who was probably Stellick's best acquisition. Marsh was a stabilizing influence and a team leader. But to make room for Marsh on the roster, Stellick dropped the wrong man, defenceman Dale DeGray, who was strong and steady. Many felt the player to go should have been Rick Lanz, who was neither physical nor consistent.

But the biggest concern remained the coaching. Before the season started, Stellick and Brophy met several times, during which it was suggested to Brophy that he ease up and stop the yelling. And indeed, the palyers did notice a difference. Brophy held his temper and didn't criticize them after games.

The new John Brophy seemed to be getting results in the early part of the season. After 12 games, the Leafs had a good record of 8 wins, 3 losses, and 1 tie. They were tied for first place in the overall NHL standing, and were a game away from setting a team record for consecutive road wins.

But then they lost in St. Louis. When they returned home they lost again, this time to the Bruins, and in doing so looked frighteningly similar to the old Leafs. And so began the slide, and another disastrous season. As it turned out, nothing had really changed. The coaching was bad and the players unmotivated and uncaring. It was an ailing franchise, in worse shape, if possible, than at any time in the past.

One of the mysteries of the Leafs during Brophy's term as coach was the impressive starts in 1986, 1987, and 1988, followed by a terrible record for the remainder of the season. After 10 or 12 games, they would be ahead of the pack or near the top. And then they would fall apart.

Brad Smith, Courtnall, and others have theories on that. Smith says Brophy never had a "system"–a strategy that explicitly outlined how the team would forecheck, move the puck out of its zone, and set up the power play. That was one of the real differences Courtnall noticed in Montreal when he was traded there in November 1988.

"The Canadiens go out and play the same way every game," Courtnall says. "We know what we're supposed to do and we never change. When I was with the Leafs, we never stuck to one system. Throughout the year, we were trying to play like other teams instead of like the Maple Leafs. If the Canadiens were winning, we had to forecheck like the Canadiens. If the Flyers were successful, we were expected to play like them. It was confusing because we were always changing and we never found the game that was comfortable for us."

Smith believes the Leafs were able to compete in the early stages of the season because all the teams were basically on equal footing. Players had not yet adjusted to the style their particular coach wanted. It took time for every team to jell. But the Leafs never did. "The Leafs had a handful of talented players, so that helped," says Smith. "And when the gate opened at the beginning of the season, everybody was basically playing the same bad style of hockey. Teams don't get set in their ways, as far as playing a system, until 10 or 15 games into the season. And, of course, we had no plan, so we could play basically even with the other teams in the first few games, but then we got left behind."

Courtnall feels that Brophy was guilty of overworking the team's better players early in the season. By Christmas they were tired. Olczyk, for example, participated in the 1987 Canada Cup hockey tournament for the United States, and then immediately joined the Leaf training camp. Instead of giving him a rest, Brophy used him in eight of nine exhibition games. Olczyk and others also feel Brophy worked them too long and hard in morning skates on game days.

Sometimes the workout lasted more than an hour and instead of casual skating and a few drills, it was an all-out practice. Said Olczyk: "We used to joke and say, 'I guess we don't have anything to do tonight.' "

In assessing Brophy, a Leaf veteran said: "John, all his life, was used to coaching plug horses. In order to get 70 per cent out of a plug horse you have to work him to 120 per cent. But you can't work a thoroughbred at 120 per cent and still think you're going to keep him up there. The day they go downhill, boy, it's tough to bring them back."

Stellick was aware of Brophy's weaknesses, but attempted to make the best of a bad situation. When the team started losing, he made a trade, his most significant up to then, sending Courtnall to Montreal for John Kordic, who was a fighter. Brophy had wanted more toughness, but the Leafs continued to lose, and what followed was highly predictable. Ballard started hinting that Brophy would be fired. This occurred in the middle of November 1988, after the team had lost six in a row and had dipped to one game under .500. Ballard made it clear to Gross that he was thinking of making a change.

Asked if it involved the coach, he said, "Everybody else seems to be doing well after firing the coach." Did he have a candidate to replace Brophy?" "No, not yet. But as I told you, teams seem to be doing well after a coach is let go." Given that hearty endorsement, Brophy should have been fired immediately. But typically, Ballard could not make up his mind, and Brophy, undermined by the owner, waited, as the team continued to lose.

A few weeks later, Stellick, through the media, set a deadline for Brophy to meet. He implied that if the team did not do well in four divisional games, the coach would be fired. Brophy might have been a mediocre coach, but he didn't deserve that kind of pressure.

As it happened, the Leafs played a little better and split the four games. But then after a layoff of almost a week, they went on the road and lost twice, badly, 8-3 to the Kings and 3-0 to the Blues. When the team returned home, Stellick went to Ballard and pushed hard for Brophy's dismissal. But on the following Monday morning, a story in the *Sun* delivered a message from Ballard to Stellick. Ballard said, "I don't want to disrupt things at the present. I'm going to think about it for a day or two. Then, I might change things considerably. The coaching and the managing. The manager's a good guy, but maybe I need someone with a little more experience."

This was obviously done to keep Stellick in line. Stellick, after all, was more inclined than McNamara had been to challenge Ballard, and he was much more candid in the media. Indeed, many thought Stellick was too visible, given his job restrictions. He was a semi-regular on the Leaf midweek telecasts and was always available for radio and print people. This was good for the reporters, but not so good for Stellick when the owner didn't like what he was saying.

It was decided that Brophy would be given a reprieve until the new year. By then it was 5 December, and it didn't leave him much time.

Other than Ballard's unwillingness to dismiss his friend, the big problem was that the Leafs did not have a viable replacement. Paul Gardner, the coach of the Newmarket team, was not ready for the NHL, and no consideration was given to Lariviere. Outside the organization, there were some excellent people, including Dave Chambers, the head of York University's athletic department, and Bob Murdoch, who had done a pretty good job coaching the Blackhawks the previous season but had been fired to make way for Mike Keenan. But to hire from outside was unthinkable. That left George Armstrong, who had coached the Marlboros more than 10 years earlier, but he made it clear early on that he wanted no part of the Leaf coaching job.

When it was announced that nothing would change, Stellick was criticized in the media. During the summer, he had said several times that he had accepted Ballard's decision to keep Brophy, but would resign if he couldn't choose his own coach in the future. Ballard's response was that he, as the owner, would have the coach he wanted, and if Stellick didn't like it, "he can get the hell out."

Ballard avoided the media by making a quick exit to Florida with Yolanda. But when he returned after two weeks, during which the Leafs had won only one of seven games, the axe finally came down. Brophy was fired and Armstrong was commandeered as interim coach until the end of the season.

Ballard and Armstrong were and are old friends who go back together 40 years to when Ballard managed the senior Marlies and the 19-year-old Armstrong was his star player. Joe Primeau coached the team in 1949–50 and took it to the Allan Cup final in Calgary. On a day off, Ballard took the team on a bus tour that stopped off at a national Indian reserve in Morley, Alberta. When the Stoney tribe learned that Armstrong was part native Indian (Ojibwa), the leaders organized a ceremony. He was presented with a chieftain's head-dress and proclaimed "Chief Shoot the Puck." Armstrong told the delegation it was a great honour and he would try to live up to his name in the series against the Calgary Stampeders, which the Marlboros won.

After Armstrong retired as a player, he coached the junior Marlboros in the mid-1970s. They had great teams and won Memorial Cups in 1973 and 1975. But Armstrong didn't like coaching. He had a stomach ulcer and the pressure made it worse. Although he was easy-going, he didn't enjoy dealing with the media.

In 1977, Ballard had asked him to take over the Leafs from Red Kelly, but Armstrong turned him down. A year later he had had enough of coaching the Marlies and handed the job over to Bill White. Armstrong had held the dual roles of general manager and coach of the Marlies, and assumed he would stay on as manager. But when he went to pick up his paycheque, he discovered his name had been taken off the payroll. There had been no word from Ballard, no letter, no explanation. Armstrong said later, "I quit because I wasn't getting paid."

From there he went to the Nordiques to work as a scout. Over the years, he recommended players from Ontario such as Dale Hunter and Paul Gillis. When the Nordiques let him go in the spring of 1988, they said they wanted a younger man doing the job. At 58, Armstrong was not only up in age among scouts, but he also became the oldest coach in the NHL when he accepted the Leaf post.

After two and a half years with Brophy, playing for Armstrong was about as different as night and day for the Leafs, sort of like moving from boot camp to a country club. Many of the practices were optional. Some lasted only half an hour. Nobody worked too hard. Morning skates were sometimes optional. Armstrong was undemanding, uncritical, and brutally honest about his abilities.

He had said from the beginning that he didn't want the job and a few weeks after taking it suggested that the game had passed him by. Lariviere quickly assumed a position of co-coach, although still an assistant in title. He ran the practices, did most of the talking to the players, and had input into the changing of lines.

Many, such as Mike Walton, a former Leaf, found the situation ludicrous. He said before an old-timers' game in Toronto that the Leafs were "a joke. They have someone who doesn't want to coach. They haven't got a captain. It's ridiculous. There's no direction."

As the season went on, there was one embarrassment after

another. The Courtnall-Kordic trade looked worse every day. Courtnall continued to progress in Montreal, while Kordic was rarely used in Toronto. Shortly after joining the Leafs, he injured his hand and missed several games; then he was suspended by the league for high-sticking Keith Acton of Edmonton, a little player, from behind. He was unhappy with his lack of ice time and felt the fans were blaming him for the Courtnall trade. At one point he said, "I hate Toronto and everybody knows that."

Everything seemed out of control. At the top was a feeble and ailing owner, who refused to give his general manager any real control. The coach didn't want to coach. And many of the players didn't seem to want to play.

Early in the season, Stellick had asked second-year defenceman Luke Richardson, who wasn't being used, to play in Newmarket for two weeks to get in shape. Richardson refused. It seemed like a reasonable request and most general managers would have insisted, especially since Richardson could have been sent all the way back to the Peterborough Petes of junior hockey. Stellick was criticized for not being more firm.

On the team, there were consistent rumours about feuds, arguments, and sometimes fights. They were denied. When the team was in Los Angeles, Ken Yaremchuk, who had been called up from the AHL, got drunk and ventured out into traffic, apparently risking his life. According to a woman who was a witness to this, his teammates didn't attempt to help him. The Leafs again denied it.

In February, Iafrate suffered an emotional breakdown caused by the problems he was having on the ice and the stress of a divorce. He left the team and received counselling at home in Detroit, and returned two weeks later.

Said a Leaf player in March, "It's been a combination of 'Dynasty' and 'Dallas.' There was a good feeling at the beginning of the season. Then, with Brophy, there was 'Is he, or isn't he?' Then there were the trade rumours. Of course, it's had an effect."

During all of this Ballard was making his own headlines. There were his attempts to sell the Hamilton Tiger-Cats of the Canadian Football League, and then his opposition to designating the Gardens a historical site. Ballard threatened to tear down the arena and build a new one, which was ridiculous because it had been his home or favourite hang-out for more than 50 years.

Then there was his rather farcical appearance at Ontario provincial court in February for Bill's court case. The charge against Bill was reduced to assault from assault causing bodily harm, and the case was adjourned until June. Ballard, who was wheeled into court by Yolanda, said to the judge, John Kerr: "The only thing that I'm worried about, Your Honour, is that they're stalling on this thing until I croak, and then they'll be home free." Before he left, he added: "As long as you're in our corner, Your Honour, we'll do all right," and then invited Kerr to drop over to the Gardens for a drink sometime. Kerr, of course, said that he was obliged to remain impartial in such matters.

Despite the external distractions, Ballard continued to impose himself on the management of the team. With the Leafs 5-10-1 under Armstrong, Ballard, by way of Dunnell, announced in late January that Armstrong would be given a contract to coach for two more years. "I like him," Ballard said. "The players like him. From my conversations with him, I get the impression he can be persuaded to sign for a couple of more years."

The operative phrase was "I like him." Armstrong's interest in the job or his ability was not important. It put both Armstrong and Stellick in a ticklish situation. Despite Armstrong's making it clear that he would coach only for the remainder of the season, Ballard was pressuring him to stay. Stellick, meanwhile, wanted to hire his own coach but wasn't relishing another showdown with his boss. But Ballard continued to sing Armstrong's praises. He told the *Sun's* Dave Fuller: "He was the best captain this team ever had. He's a real student of hockey. And he knows how to handle players. Who else are you gonna get?"

When Fuller asked if Ballard had not compromised his manager in his search for a coach, Ballard said, "I'm the guy who signs the cheques, so it would be a good thing for me to know who I'm paying to coach. [Stellick's] got lots to manage. If he's looking for work he can go out and get some players who can help this team." Ballard kept on the Armstrong kick for the remainder of the season. Later, he suggested that he would bring in a couple of more assistants to help.

The best news of the season came at the end of February, when Clark decided it was time to test his back. "Finally!" said the headline in the *Star*, "Wendel's back."

After his fine rookie season, Clark had put together another strong year in 1986-87, scoring 37 goals and earning 23 assists, plus picking up 271 penalty minutes, mostly for fighting. He was, without question, the Leafs' best player and team leader.

That summer he was invited to the Canadian team's training camp for the Canada Cup hockey tournament. Clark played well in the scrimmages, but in an exhibition game against the United States he got into a fight with Chris Nilan, during which he landed on his lower back. The blow hurt him, and a few days later he was cut from the team.

By the time the Leaf training camp opened, the pain had subsided. He participated in the exhibition games, but in the first regular-season game, the dull ache returned to his lower back. To this day it remains.

Clark's back problem and the way it was handled brought into question another controversial element of the Leaf organization, that of the medical and training staff. Clark was seen by David Hastings, a long-time Leaf doctor who is an orthopaedic specialist but not a back specialist. Hastings could see no structural or nerve damage, so he told Clark he could play. The Leaf position was that Clark would have to accept the fact of playing with pain. He was not referred to a back specialist.

"I was told to play through it," Clark says. "But nobody can tell you how it feels. It may not look like it hurts, but nobody can tell you how it feels."

Clark does not have a high sensitivity to pain. In fact, he has a low pain threshhold, which means he can endure the discomfort of injuries and play hurt. But this time, although he tried, he couldn't do it. After missing 3 games, he came back and played for 5. He sat out for 23 games, returned for 17, and then packed it in for the season. His final game was at the Spectrum in Philadelphia in early February 1988. After taking a slapshot in the second period, he doubled over and skated off in pain.

This time, Clark decided to seek medical treatment on his own. He had already seen Hastings, and the club had no other support system. It didn't even have a qualified athletic therapist on staff.

Clark first visited a Chicago clinic that was used by Blackhawk players. Then he sought help from the Mayo Clinic in Rochester, Minnesota, where it was determined that he had a muscular problem. He was told to stay off his skates, to rest, and to work on rehabilitating the muscles in his back. "It didn't completely solve the problem," Clark said, "but it was one more piece to the puzzle."

By the summer, however, the situation had worsened. The tightness and pain had spread down into his legs, and was still in his back. Clark wondered if he would ever play again. "I couldn't sit in a chair for more than five minutes," he said. "I couldn't drive because I couldn't sit in a car for any length of time. I couldn't even stand still. To feel better, I had to stay on my feet and walk slowly."

At this point, some unexpected assistance came from a benefactor of some means. Depending on which financial publication is cited, Kenneth Thomson, chief executive officer of Thomson Newspapers Ltd. and the Thomson Group, the international publishing empire, is either the fifth or the eighth richest man in the world. Thomson, a Canadian, lives in Toronto and owns the *Globe and Mail*. He is also a Leaf fan and watches the games from a private box at the top level of the Gardens.

Years earlier, Thomson had helped Alan Eagleson, who had suffered from a sports-related back ailment, by recommending a doctor he knew in London, L. M. Nidoo, an acclaimed osteopath who drew patients from around the world.

When Thomson heard that Clark's condition had not improved he called on Eagleson to help him get in touch with Clark. Eagleson contacted Don Meehan, Clark's agent, and before long it was arranged that Clark would fly to London to see Dr. Nidoo. He received therapy for 10 days, during which time he stayed at Thomson's executive townhouse. Thomson picked up the bill.

Nidoo found a curvature of Clark's spine, and he also had to straighten the pelvis. He determined that the pain, which was on the left side of Clark's back, was a result of the cumulative effect of years of Clark's aggressive style of playing hockey. Because of Clark's low sensitivity level, he had played through serious injuries on the left side of his body. He had had tendonitis in the left shoulder as well as a groin injury. The body's automatic reaction is to compensate for pain: the muscles around the injured area tend to become immobile while other muscles take up the extra load. For Clark this meant that he was not skating and shooting properly and resulted in stress in his lower left back. Nidoo worked on easing the tightness and correcting the damaged tissue.

"Within weeks I could see the results," Clark said. "He gave me exercises to do and when I returned I went to a physiotherapist." In September, Stellick arranged for the Leafs to use a clinic called the Centre for Sports and Recreation Medicine, which was just up the street from the Gardens. Clark was treated by athletic therapist Chris Broadhurst for two hours a day, six days a week. During this time, he practised with the team but didn't play.

As the season progressed and the team performed poorly, pressure increased from management and the media for Clark to get back into the lineup. In January, the *Sun* carried an article predicting that Clark would return to the lineup for a weekend game. It was useless information, because Clark himself didn't know when he would return.

Perhaps the most ridiculous theory to come from the media was that Clark's practising with the Leafs was a distraction to his teammates–instead he should drive 30 miles north every day to Newmarket and practice with the Saints (and then drive 30 miles back to Toronto to be treated by the therapist–driving, of course, is great therapy for a bad back).

It seemed to many that the Leafs had more important problems to address than the "distraction" of Clark at practices. Not suprisingly, the most insensitive and inane remark came from Ballard, who intimated to the *Star* in February that Clark was using his sore back as an excuse not to play. "I sometimes think Wendel's swinging the lead," he said.

To anyone who knew Clark, the suggestion was preposterous. But to anyone who knew Ballard, the remark was in character. Historically, Ballard attacked his players when things weren't going well. Because the team had been without a captain since Vaive had lost the C, Clark was an easy target.

So, for a day, the Gardens zoo was back in business, as a scrum of reporters surrounded Clark for his reaction to his boss's comments. Clark handled it well, saying, "He's the one who's paying me, he's the one who wants me back as soon as possible. But I won't be coming back until I think I'm healthy enough and I feel I can contribute and keep contributing. I don't want to play one or two games, find out I can't play, and have tried it all for nothing."

Ballard's energy would better have been used toward improving the medical personnel of his club. For starters, the Leafs did not employ a qualified medical trainer. The team's head trainer was Guy Kinnear, whose trade is that of a marine motor mechanic. In the summer he works on boat motors in Midland, near Ballard's cottage. He got his job with the Leafs because of his friendship with Ballard, starting as an assistant trainer in 1967. They have remained close over the years and are co-owners of a runabout that Ballard uses only infrequently on Georgian Bay. Around the Gardens, Kinnear is called the vice-president because of his close relationship with the president.

In an era when clubs take the physical well-being of their players seriously, and include on their staff athletic therapists, physiotherapists, and even massage therapists, the Leafs are still in the dark ages, although Stellick moved them several years closer to the present when he set up a working arrangement with the Centre for Sports and Recreation Medicine.

Clark performed well upon his return to the line up on 1 March 1989, but he had not fully recovered and he played in pain. His back stiffened and near the end of the season he could not play regularly.

The team as a whole improved after Brophy's dismissal, but not by much. When Brophy was fired the record was 11-20-2 for a winning percentage of .364. Under Armstrong it was 17-26-4 (.404).

There continued to be a lack of direction and leadership, but there were signs that some of the younger players were developing. Leeman had an excellent season. Olczyk led the team in scoring for the second consecutive season, with 90 points. Right winger Daniel Marois had a good rookie season. Bester played well in goal. Damphousse was oustanding at times, but lacked consistency.

By mid-March, the Leafs had moved to within two points of the Blackhawks for the last playoff spot. But then they played two stunningly inept weekend games, one of which was against Winnipeg, a bad team, and the other with Philadelphia, which had been struggling. That, coupled with two Chicago victories, left them six points out.

But they came back again, defeating Vancouver, Detroit, and then Minnesota. That meant the playoff spot would be contested on the final game of the season in Chicago. The Leafs played well in the game and held a 3-1 lead in the third period. But they couldn't hold it. The game went into overtime and a giveaway resulted in Chicago's winning goal.

The next day, when the players packed up for the season, some of them criticized Ballard. One said there was no leadership from the top.

"Was the coaching any better with Armstrong behind the bench?" a Leaf was asked.

"No," he said. "Just different."

With the season over for the Leafs, Stellick still held onto the hope that he would be allowed to bring in his own coach for 1989-90. Despite Ballard's overtures, Armstrong had made it clear he did not want to go behind the bench for another year.

But Ballard was determined to get his way and stay in control, despite the continued deterioration of his health. In mid-April he was admitted to Toronto General Hospital and treated for a severe toe infection resulting from circulation problems in his feet.

While Ballard was in the hospital, Stellick received a call from Mike Kiley, a hockey writer with the Chicago *Tribune* who was curious about the Leaf coaching situation. Unwisely, Stellick told him that Armstrong definitely would not return as coach. Upon hearing this, Kiley called Gary Loewen, who covers the Leafs for the *Globe,* to ask him if this had been reported before. Nothing quite as unequivocal had been reported.

When Loewen asked Stellick about the comments, he was told they had been intended as background information and not for publication. Loewen then called Armstrong, who said: "It's settled in our minds. We have to go to the big boss. He's the guy who's going to call the shots. The thing is, I want to work. I like it here. Sometimes, when you work for somebody, you don't want to do what you're told to do."

Below a headline that read "Only Ballard Stands in the Way of Armstrong Stepping Down," Loewen wrote, "Club owner Harold Ballard has yet to give final assent, but George Armstrong will not be back as the Toronto Maple Leafs' coach next season."

When Ballard read the story from his hospital bed, he was furious. Stellick was continuing to work against his wishes, and he wasn't going to put up with it. A call was put in to Armstrong, and then he was on the phone to Dunnell with another scoop. In a banner story on the front page of the *Star,* Dunnell reported that not only would Armstrong stay on as coach of the team, but he also had been given the position of director of player personnel. "I'm gonna be the coach," said Armstrong. "That's been decided." As Dunnell correctly noted, Armstrong was now the second most powerful man in the Leaf organization, responsible for most of the duties previously handled by Stellick.

Armstrong's capitulation was a complete turnaround from the position he had taken earlier. He was viewed in the media as jumping at the chance for a considerable pay raise at the cost of betraying Stellick, who had been responsible for bringing him back to the organization. Still, it should not have been surprising. Armstrong needed a job and said privately to his friends, "How could I turn down a dying man?" In Ballard's mind Armstrong was in charge, and he made that clear to the media on several occasions.

But Stellick continued to carry out the general manager's duties, such as preparing for the draft and discussing trades. Armstrong showed only a marginal interest in what was going on, and showed up infrequently at the hockey office after the season ended. Still, the Chief was the "head potato," as Ballard put it, and on the day of the NHL draft in Minneapolis in June, Ballard insisted that Armstrong announce the Leaf selections–a responsibility that traditionally belongs to the general manager.

For Stellick, it was the ultimate humiliation. During the season, his credibility had slipped away as it became apparent that he had little real authority. The coaching situation had become a fiasco. His only major trade, the Courtnall deal, was looming as one of the worst deals ever made by a Leaf general manager. Now he had been essentially demoted without being told.

More than ever before, there was a mood of hopelessness in the organization. There was no leadership–only a sick old man whose visits to the hospital were becoming more frequent, only people in jobs they weren't qualified to hold–and those in jobs they didn't want. In the late spring of 1989, the fall of the Maple Leaf hockey club was complete.

18

Icons

of Ineptitude

The Leafs are in special company when it comes to losing. There has been nothing quite like it in major-league baseball although the Seattle Mariners have been pretty inept, with a winning percentage of .424 over the past 10 years. The Mariners, of course, were an expansion franchise in 1977.

Over in the National Basketball Association and the National Football League, there are several big losers. They include the Los Angeles Clippers of the NBA, and the Tampa Bay Buccaneers, the Indianapolis Colts, and the Detroit Lions of the NFL. These teams have actually had worse records than the Leafs over the past 10 years, although not by much. The Clippers' winning percentage has been .312, Tampa Bay's .332, Indianapolis' (Baltimore) .339, and Detroit's .368. The Leafs aren't far behind with .388.

In the NHL, only two teams have had poorer winning percentages since 1972-73, which was Toronto's first season with Ballard as owner. The two biggest losers are the Vancouver Canucks (.424) and the Detroit Red Wings (.410). The Leafs are ahead of both with a winning percentage of .433.

It's worth noting, however, that the Canucks were an expansion team in 1970, and although they have been bad for most of the years since, they did advance to the Cup final in 1982. In 1988-89, they had a respectable season. Like the Canucks, the Red Wings have been improving, although they fell back a bit in 1988-89. Still, for the past two years, they have finished first in the Norris Division.

The Leafs, on the other hand, have become progressively worse. Over the past 10 years, they were exceeded in competence by only one team (in successive incarnations), the Kansas City Scouts-Colorado Rockies-New Jersey Devils. But again, the Scouts-Rockies-Devils were an expansion team. Their percentage in 10 years is .357 compared to Toronto's .388. But in the past five years, Toronto is by itself at the bottom while other long-time denizens of the depths have moved up. The Devils, .406 in the past five years, and the Pittsburgh Penguins, .461, have both improved. The Leafs are .361.

Through all of this there has been one constant. Although it is often said that Ballard loves his team, and that "nobody wants a Stanley Cup more than Harold Ballard," both points are highly debatable. When Ballard really wants something, he is persistent and usually gets it. His record shows that his two greatest desires in life are money and publicity, and he has been diligent in acquiring both. So, if it's agreed he loves the Leafs and wants a Cup, why wouldn't he be just as committed to building a winning team?

The simple answer is that the team exists for his pleasure, and that does not necessarily mean winning. That is not to say he wants the Leafs to lose, but winning is not a priority. Making money and feeling comfortable are priorities.

There is something that makes him more comfortable, and is better for his ego, than having a championship team–the security of being surrounded by sycophants, whether they're old friends or people afraid of losing their jobs. This is what feeds his ego and makes him happy–to know that he is the boss, the big man at the Gardens.

He tried it the other way once, when he hired Imlach the second time around. But Imlach was his own man and called the shots–and Ballard quickly realized that he didn't like it. It was in November of 1981, when he fired Imlach and installed McNamara, that he ended any serious attempt at winning a Stanley Cup or even of having a winning team.

But he was happier. In this system, the front office staff, especially McNamara and Crump, made him feel important. They would sit with him and listen to his stories about the good old days, which inevitably got around to his hero, Hap Day, whom he rejected in 1957 but still worships.

In the past, the people in the front office created small problems for Ballard to solve, so that he would feel that he was an important part of the process. If, for example, Salming had a sinus problem, they might have gone to Ballard with the pressing question about what should be done. Should Salming (a) be taken to hospital? (b) be forced to play? (c) be suspended? or (d) be given a couple of days rest?

"A couple of days rest, Mr. Ballard? Of course. Why didn't I think of that? How right you are." Another crisis is averted by a monumental decision from the chief commander.

But one should never assume that Ballard knows anything about hockey. There are numerous stories that illustrate how limited his awareness is of the NHL and his team. For example, in the spring of 1984, when he decided he would have to fire Nykoluk, he met a friend at his cottage. During their conversation, Ballard bemoaned the state of the team and expressed sadness at the prospect of firing his friend Nykoluk. Moreover, he didn't know where to turn for a replacement.

"Why don't you bring in Pat Quinn?" asked his friend, knowing Ballard had liked Quinn when he played for Toronto in the late 1960s. Two years earlier, Quinn had been fired as coach of the Flyers. He had returned to school and was now looking for a job.

"Ah, he coaches the Flyers," Ballard said, "They'll never let him go."

There is a man working at a high level at the Gardens, who knows Ballard as well as anyone, and is convinced that Ballard does not want the team to win for fear that it might surpass Ballard himself in popularity. Indeed, Ballard has always been the number one attraction at the Gardens, with his team the sideshow. Each day, Ballard has an employee in his office clip every newspaper article in which his name appears. It doesn't matter what has been said, how vicious the attack, it's clipped, read, and then pasted into his scrapbook.

The Leafs receive the most coverage in April during the playoffs–if they're in the playoffs. And not surprisingly, this is when Ballard works his hardest to get attention. He poses for pictures with his players. He provides stories for the reporters. He tells them about plans to paint the arena and how it's going to cost him $1.5 million. He gives his views on the opposing team as well as his own. Columns are written about him, but not the players.

In the 1987 playoffs, the Leafs upset the Blues in the first round and then won the first game of the divisional final against Detroit. The next day, the story should have been about the amazing performance of the team after a dormant winter. Instead Ballard leaked the story that he had secretly signed McNamara to a four-year contract several months earlier. That turned out to be the big news, the story everybody was talking about. It wasn't about a player or the team. It was about Ballard and his most recent dubious executive decision.

Ballard's consuming need for publicity is one of several childish characteristics. Like the little boy who has to be the centre of attention, Ballard, within the framework of his environment, controls and manipulates the media so that he's the focus. If his team were a winner, it would not be as easy to upstage his general manager, his coach, and his players. Collectively, they would become a bigger story than Ballard.

Within Ballard's system there is no place for the fans. Ballard has shown continuously during his ownership that he has no regard for what is best for the supporters of hockey and his team. Metropolitan Toronto is sometimes called the hockey hotbed of the world. It has more people–children and adults–participating in organized hockey than any other city in the world. Over the years, the fans have been patient and loyal in their support. But they have received nothing in return. Fans would have preferred to see the Leafs in a division with Montreal when the league realigned in 1981, but instead, Ballard, as a favour to his friend Bruce Norris, the owner of the Red Wings, went into the Norris Division.

Not only have Toronto fans been denied a competitive team, they have been excluded from some of the finest international hockey events ever to be staged. This is because of Ballard's hatred of the Soviet Union and his feuds with Alan Eagleson.

For the most part, the Toronto fans have been placid through all of this. Ballard still gets a full house, or close to it, every night. This is mainly because 80 per cent of the 12,500 season's tickets belong to corporations, which give their tickets away to clients who may or may not show up. Either way, the seat is paid for. There is the occasional protest; for instance, a few years ago a group of people manufactured bumper stickers that read, "The cancer is at the top" and "Hate the Leafs Fan Club." But to most of the people who attend the games, Ballard is still a celebrity. Children and adults come over to him in his bunker and ask for his autograph. On his birthdays, the newspapers carry affectionate profiles, with a picture, of course.

Some journalists in Montreal feel it would be different in that city if the Canadiens had been afflicted with an owner such as Ballard. For one thing, the Canadiens do not have the same large number of corporate season's tickets holders. Also, the fans stay away when the team isn't winning. This would force the owner to sell the team or make it competitive. And if he didn't the media and the fans would likely run him out of town, figuratively of course, but perhaps literally, too. But in Toronto the Good, the capital of conservative Ontario, where citizens politely defer to authoritarian figures, the hockey fans wait and suffer silently.

Although it can be argued either way just how much Ballard really wants a winner, no one can dispute that he has done a bang-up job of ruining the hockey team, whatever his motivation. Looking back, it almost seems as if he had a plan: first, to cut all ties to the past, to the glory years. Gradually the players forget or, in the case of the younger ones, never learn about the club's history. There is no link to, and thus no responsibility to carry on, the team's tradition, because as far as players are concerned there is no tradition. There is just Ballard.

This is obviously the way he wants it. Although the Leafs have won 11 Stanley Cups, there are no championship banners hanging in the arena. There are no retired sweaters in view. While other organizations such as Montreal, Detroit, Chicago, Boston, and Philadelphia have alumni clubs, the Leafs have nothing. On several occasions, former Leaf players have asked Ballard if they could have a room set aside, but he has turned them down flat every time. Jackie Hamilton, who played in the 1940s, says, "We've tried for 20 years, but he wouldn't do it. When you're gone, you're shit." Ace Bailey says: "Old-timers aren't welcome at the Gardens."

Former Leafs are saddened by the downfall of the team. Some of them are disgusted. "They say he's been successful and has made lots of money," Bob Baun says. "But to me, part of that success should have been money spent on the team."

Elwin Morris, who played in Toronto during the 1940s, says, "When he goes to sleep at night, he doesn't think about his hockey team. He thinks about his money in the bank."

Said Day, "It upsets me. Even now I'll watch a game on TV and I don't like what I see, so I turn it off."

From Ted Kennedy: "Whatever happened, he soured. He soured on people and on life in general and decided he was going to make a lot of money. It's really sad the way the club has gone. It really is . . ."

"Like everyone else, I'm suffering," Howie Meeker says. "Suffering and waiting for them to come out of it."

The best contrast to the Leafs is the Canadiens, the other original member of the NHL. The club flaunts the history of Les Glorieux. Former players are encouraged to return to the Forum and also visit the dressing room. A lounge is set aside for the alumni. In the dressing room, plaques with rosters of every team line the walls. There are portraits of all the Hall of Famers. Courtnall, after he was traded, said, "They're proud of every team they've ever had. And they honour all the players who did great things. It's just a great organization. It's nice to be in here. It's a nice feeling. In here, there's a feeling of tradition and of winning and of pride."

He didn't feel that in Toronto. Nor does anyone, really. There is no past in evidence to grab onto, which might be a reason for there being little leadership on the team. In Montreal, Courtnall noticed that veterans Bob Gainey and Larry Robinson would help to prepare the team for games. Courtnall saw little of that in Toronto, where there were few role models and no traditions to uphold. It isn't that the Leafs have forgotten how to win. They have never learned.

In some ways the team actually reflects the personality of the owner–undisciplined, unstable, unpredictable. Some of the reporters covering the team call the players "headless, heartless, and hopeless." But when the owner doesn't care, it is difficult for the players to have pride and be motivated, to have "character."

After Harry Sinden hired a psychologist to work with the Bruins, he said he didn't think a psychologist was really needed. But by bringing him in, he felt he was letting his players know that everything possible was being made available to them to help them succeed. It was one less excuse for losing. Over the years, the players on the Leafs have been given many excuses to lose.

It is often debated whether Ballard really does interfere in the running of the team. Brophy, and before him, Nykoluk, had insisted that Ballard leave them alone, that he not interfere, and that he be generally supportive. And it is true that Ballard would never think of telling a coach what lines to use, or who to dress and who to sit out. He doesn't know enough about the game. As a rule, he doesn't meddle in trades, although in the past he has vetoed proposed deals involving players to whom he was particularly close–including Salming and Turnbull.

But trades, as a rule, are only marginally important in the building of a strong franchise. Where Ballard does interfere is in two more critical areas–spending and hiring. And that is where his interference has been most damaging.

Right now, the two best-run franchises in the NHL might be Calgary and Montreal. It's probably not a coincidence that both general managers started in the Canadiens organization when Sam Pollock was running the hockey operation. Serge Savard, the managing director of the Canadiens, was a product of the club's development system in the 1960s. After a long and illustrious career as a player, he assumed his present job in 1983. Cliff Fletcher worked with Pollock for 10 years in the 1950s and 1960s in managing, coaching, and scouting, before joining the St. Louis Blues and then the Atlanta Flames as general manager. Today, he is also president of the Calgary Flames.

Fletcher and Savard believe in spending money to provide a top-quality product, because a good product will make the club more money through attendance and sales of licensed products, such as souvenirs and clothing. "If you look at any successful company," Savard says, "it is probably committed to research and development. A successful hockey club is no different. The research is your scouting and the development is your coaching –minor-league coaching and the coaching of the NHL club."

Both organizations have large scouting staffs. For the 1988–89 season, the Canadiens employed eight full-time scouts, plus three part-timers for a total of eleven. The Flames had more, with eight full-time people and seven part-timers for a complement of fifteen. The Leafs, on the other hand, used one amateur scout, Floyd Smith, and one pro scout, Dick Duff. Because of Johnny Bower's age, he works only in the Toronto area and not every day. They are the full-time people. There are three of them. Helping are five part-timers, one of whom, Frank Curry, doesn't do much anymore.

The scouting budget for the Flames over a season is about $800,000. This includes salaries, travel many times over to the hockey regions in the United States and Europe, as well as accommodation. The cost to the Canadiens would be comparable. Given the size of the Leafs' staff, they would spend in the area of $200,000 on scouting over a season, easily the smallest amount of any team in the league.

Why does Ballard refuse to allow his general manager to hire more scouts? Money is the obvious reason, but keep in mind also that Ballard doesn't want strangers coming into the organization. He likes having the old gang around, which is why he agreed to hire Armstrong as a scout. Armstrong, of course, had to give up scouting because he was pressed into coaching the team.

Ballard's lean, money-making machine, which happens to produce inferior teams, is a stark contrast to the modern organizations in Calgary and Montreal. With the Flames, for example, there is Fletcher at the top, as president and general manager. Al Coates is the assistant to the president. Then there is an assistant general manager, Al MacNeil, whose main responsibility is the pro scouting staff and the minor-league team. In addition to the administrative staff, there is a chief scout, Gerry Blair, and a co-ordinator of scouting, Ian McKenzie.

The Canadiens have different titles for their hockey people, but the organization is just as well staffed. Jacques Lemaire is assistant to the managing director. André Boudrias is the director of recruitment and general manager of the minor-league team. Claude Ruel is director of player development and a special scout. The chief scout is Doug Robinson. In Toronto there is nothing like this.

When the Flames and the Canadiens prepare for the June draft, each club will have as many as 15 people assessing the prospects. About half of the these people will have seen the top 30 or 35 players several times. And the Leafs? In the spring of 1989, with the team owning 4 picks in the top 25–3 first-rounders and a high second–only one man, Smith, had seen all of the best prospects.

Said a scout in March 1989: "I feel sorry for Smitty, because he's by himself. He will make the decision on who the Leafs pick and he will have nobody to help him do it. I personally enjoy arguing over a certain player with the other guys and then coming to a decision. He can't do that."

The Canadiens and the Flames, of course, have done better at the draft than the Leafs over the past several years, despite Toronto's consistently picking higher.

It is too early to tell what will come out of the 1988 draft. But let's look at what the three teams have done from 1981 to 1987. In those years, Calgary has not picked any higher than twelfth. Montreal has selected higher than twelfth in only two drafts. The Leafs, however, have never been lower than seventh. Let's assess the drafting of the three teams from the second round and back.

Since 1981 Calgary has taken, among others, Joe Nieuwenyk, the rookie of the year in 1988, Brett Hull, the leading scorer for the

St. Louis Blues in 1988-89, Gary Suter, the rookie of the year in 1986, Mike Vernon, the Flames' first-string goaltender, as well as Theoren Fleury, Jiri Hrdina, Brian Bradley, Perry Berezan, and Dale DeGray.

Montreal, in the second round or lower, has drafted Chris Chelios, one of the leading defencemen in the league, Stephane Richer, a 50-goal scorer in 1987-88, Patrick Roy, the team's first-string goaltender and playoff MVP in 1986, as well as Claude Lemieux, Brent Gilchrist, Sergio Momesso, Eric Desjardins, Jyrkki Lumme, John Kordic, Steve Rooney, and Tom Kurvers.

Using the same criteria–1981 to 1987, second round and back–the Leaf draftees have included Leeman, Wregget, Bester, Gill, Jeff Reese, Jeff Jackson, Daniel Marois, Darryl Shannon, and Peter Ihnacak. Of that group, Leeman and Bester are the best. Leeman was the team's top right winger in 1988-89 and Bester the first-string goaltender. Marois, Reese, and Shannon show promise. The remainder at this point are either fringe players or players with questionable potential.

When we look at the players the Leafs have taken with their high first-round draft choices, we run into the problem of measuring development against the quality of the selections. Would Nylund have progressed more quickly on another team? Would Iafrate be a better defenceman today if he had spent two years in junior hockey rather than joining the Leafs immediately? How much of a difference would good coaching have meant to Jim Benning and Russ Courtnall? Courtnall answered that question to a degree, when he went to Montreal and said he had learned more there in two weeks than during two years with Brophy.

Player development might be the most important element of a successful organization. If the players aren't taught or adequately prepared, they are immediately handicapped. Their progress is slow or almost nonexistent.

Except for Neilson's two seasons and the two years Maloney was behind the bench, the Leaf players have received very little teaching and almost no game preparation. In the 1980s, most clubs moved to a two-assistant system of coaching. Some, such as Detroit, Vancouver, and Winnipeg, have three assistants. Only the Leafs and the Hartford Whalers are still limited to one.

In most clubs the second assistant focusses on game preparation–editing film and instructing the players on what to expect from the opposition. Some teams, such as Detroit, Chicago, Buffalo, and

Philadelphia, place an assistant in the press box with a computer to record hits, giveaways, turnovers, checks, scoring chances, and other data pertaining to games.

But there is more to player development than coaching. Fletcher says: "Development involves video, it involves psychologists, nutritionists. It involves everything it takes to put a better product on the ice." The Flames, for example, have a man on staff whose sole job is to edit videotape. The club has a video library of more than 250 game tapes. A nutritionist advises players, particularly the young, single players, on a proper diet. Some clubs have held cooking classes for their rookies. Ballard would laugh.

The training staff of the Canadiens consists of an athletic therapist, an assistant therapist, a head trainer, and two assistant trainers–plus a fitness consultant. Some teams, including the Edmonton Oilers, employ a massage therapist. The Leafs have none of this.

So, you can laugh at the Leafs. You can rage at them for being gutless, for lacking character, and for not caring. And too many of them appear to be guilty of all these things. But rather than pilloried, the Icons of Ineptitude are to be pitied, for playing in an archaic organization and for what the organization has made them.

19

What's Gonna Happen

to the Leafs?

Despite the inferior product, the Toronto Maple Leafs remain the jewel of all professional sports franchises in Canada. The Leafs lead the field simply because they are located in the wealthiest and most populated region of a northern country where hockey is the number one sport. The club has a fabled history, and has tremendous marketing and concessions potential. The only thing it doesn't do is win. But that doesn't matter, because the Gardens sells out on most nights, anyway.

Paul Beeston, the president of the American League's Blue Jays who compete with the Leafs for the sports dollar in Toronto, says, "The Leafs are probably the best sports franchise in Canada on the basis of what they have put on the ice and what they have been able to draw. My kids are diehard Leaf fans. They're 13 and 10, and they have never gone through a winning season with the Leafs. But they can't go to the Gardens enough. They can't listen to the radio enough. They watch them on TV. It's a phenomenon."

In most cities a team as bad as the Leafs would have undergone ownership changes. They might have been forced to move. They might have even folded. But in Toronto, the country's largest municipality and financial capital, the team consistently generates huge revenues.

For the fiscal year ending 31 May 1988 Maple Leaf Gardens Ltd. reported profits of $2.5 million on gross revenue of $39.6 million. In the 1988-89 season, the team played to 97.9 per cent capacity, with

29 of the 40 home games sellouts. The *Globe*'s *Report on Business Magazine* noted in 1988 that for the fiscal year ending in May 1987, MLG ranked second among Canada's leading businesses in return on capital over the previous five years (72.98 per cent return), and eleventh in 1987 (58.89 per cent).

The Leafs can't match the gate receipts of winning teams, such as the Flames, which play in larger arenas. In 1985–86, for example, according to confidential league figures, the Flames earned $12.6 million from ticket sales, while the Leafs generated only $9.3 million. That's because the Olympic Saddledome has a capacity of 19,626, while the Gardens is filled at 16,182. The owner of the Leafs, on the other hand, doesn't pay rent.

But in television revenue, the Leafs earn more than any team in the league. It's estimated to be in the $4 million-a-year range from a deal in which Molson Breweries of Canada Ltd. purchases the Leafs' Canadian television rights and then sells them off to broadcast entities such as CBC's "Hockey Night in Canada," The Sports Network, and the Global Television Network. That contract with Molson runs until 1994. In addition to television money, the Leafs earn about $750,000 a year in rink board advertising. The space at the Gardens is bought by Molson and then sold to TV advertisers.

The poor performance of the Leafs resulted in a declining midweek audience when the independent Hamilton television station, CHCH, owned the rights. Viewership in the late 1970s, when the Leafs had two above-average seasons, was as high as 1.1 million per game, according to CHCH, but then slipped to as low as 300,000 in 1987–88. When Global made its deal in 1988, it felt the Leafs would make more because of the network's larger audience.

Although Molson has been concerned for several years about the diminishing competitiveness of the Leafs, Frank Selke, the former director of hockey for Molstar Communications, a division of Molson that produces NHL games, says the team's ineptitude is not a major problem for advertisers. The real shift in audience numbers is determined by the opponent. The glamour teams, Montreal, Calgary, and Los Angeles with Gretzky, draw the crowds. The Hartford Whalers do not. "For the advertisers, southern Ontario is where it's at," Selke says. "And that happens to be where Harold Ballard is at."

Ballard is usually given the credit for the skyrocketing profits of MLG Ltd. In the 1960s, he sold ads all over the arena, increased the seating capacity, and promoted more events. From 1962 to the end of 1964, shares increased from $30 to $68 before splitting five for one in 1965. He is also hailed as a great promoter, but over the past 20 years he seems to have lost his touch. He couldn't promote the Hamilton Tiger-Cats of the Canadian Football League, which he sold in early 1989 after losing millions. And arguably the Leafs are a financial success despite Ballard, not because of him. Journalist Frank Orr once said: "Ballard couldn't promote the second coming, with the original cast."

Indeed, people in the sports and entertainment industry say the two areas where MLG Ltd. falls short are marketing and promotions, and concessions. The Blue Jays have been brilliant in the marketing of licensed products. The logo is seen everywhere and is on everything, from T-shirts to coffee mugs to toques. The club has a souvenir shop downtown. When one of the Blue Jays players does a commercial or poses for an ad, the club wants him wearing the Blue Jays uniform. "It's a great advertising tool," Beeston says. "There's nothing better than seeing a kid get up in the morning with a Blue Jay T-shirt on."

The Leafs, on the other hand, have failed to keep up with the competition in the marketing of their logo or licensed clothing products. While clubs such as the Flyers and the Canadiens offer a wide assortment of quality apparel, including knitted sweaters and winter jackets, Leaf products are limited in variety and not of good quality, league executives say. Ballard actually discourages the use of the logo, unless, of course, he gets a fat piece of the action.

When two enamel murals depicting the rivalry between the Leafs and the Canadiens were installed at Toronto's College Street subway station, Ballard tried to put a stop to it, because he hadn't given his approval to use the Leaf logo.

In 1988-89, Wendel Clark did a snow-shovelling commercial without wearing his uniform. The Blues Jays' Lloyd Moseby, who had a small part, was wearing his. Said an advertising executive, "Can you imagine having your star hockey player on a public service campaign about shovelling snow off your walks without him having his uniform on? To me, that doesn't make much sense. That's advertising you can't buy. You have the Leaf logo there. You hammer that."

Ballard has shown no interest in promoting the game, never mind his team. When the club was asked to set aside five minutes before a game so Mario Lemieux could be presented with a plaque as Canada's male athlete of the year, it refused, citing a policy of

Ballard's which stipulates that only Leafs can be honoured at the Gardens–and very few of them have, it might be added. Public relations people from other NHL teams were appalled when they heard about it. The Flames were more than happy to oblige when Lemieux visited the Saddledome.

With the sale of the Tiger-Cats and the Toronto Marlboros in 1989, MLG Ltd. now consists of the Leafs; the farm team in Newmarket (the Saints), which loses money but is expected to because it is a player-development tool; Davis Printing in Mississauga, which prints tickets to Gardens events; and the concessions division. Over the years, Ballard has expanded the Gardens' concessions by getting contracts to service Ivor Wynne Stadium in Hamilton and Varsity Stadium in Toronto. But anyone who has visited a concessions stand at the Gardens will tell you the food is not good.

An NHL executive said, "Whatever he makes in concessions isn't enough. They have the most horseshit concessions in the league. For a guy who loves to make money, they're in the dinosaur age, as far as concessions are concerned. They could probably quadruple their concessions revenue by getting into the modern age."

Perhaps because of the money made from the gate and television, MLG feels no strong need to upgrade concessions and promotions. Why spend money marketing a team that comes close to selling out? One reason would be to peddle more souvenirs and clothes. Another would be to achieve 100 per cent capacity instead of 97.9 per cent, taking into consideration that the turnstile count has been down for several years, which is usually a sign that sales will eventually decrease too.

The most compelling reason might be to prepare for the future. What if the NFL does move into Toronto? What if another arena is built and an NBA franchise is acquired. Where does that leave the poor old Leafs, an antiquated organization that has shown little regard for the Toronto sports fans?

"All it will take is a .500 season, and they're back to numero uno," Beeston says. "You cannot negate the fact we're in a hockey climate in a hockey-hungry town. I mean this is Toronto, Ontario. So many good players have come out of this area. There are such good hockey programs in this area. I suspect everybody dreams of going on the ice and being a Walter Mitty and turning the team around."

Many have dreamed of turning the organization around. But to do that you need control. Those that have attempted to buy MLG include singer Anne Murray, The Toronto Sun Publishing Corp., and John Labatt Ltd.–and, of course, there was Gobuty's failed attempt.

The price of the Gardens, of course, would be high. The worth of MLG stock on paper was in the range of $98 million to $109 million between November 1988 and March 1989, with the stock running between $33.50 and $42 a share. But that's a low figure. The Gardens site itself could go for anything between $100 and $200 million. The smaller Mutual Street Arena, where the Leafs played in the 1920s, has been sold for a reported $37 million and the Gardens is a much more desirable location. The hockey club by itself is worth about $50 million.

But in evaluating MLG there are other factors to consider. One is the effect that the SkyDome, the new stadium with the retractable roof, will have on business. Industry analysts believe that the Gardens value as an entertainment venue will be hurt by the entrance of the SkyDome into the market, but perhaps not as much as some have estimated. The Gardens is now air-conditioned, and the cost of booking into the SkyDome is not likely to be cheap. So the arena will probably function quite profitably as a less expensive alternative, along the lines of Massey Hall in relation to Roy Thomson Hall.

A larger concern is the designation of the Gardens as a historical site. This was done in May 1989 by Toronto city council under the Ontario Heritage Act, despite protestations from Ballard, who called the council members "communists." Any changes to the Gardens must now be approved by the city. If the arena can't be torn down, the value of MLG will drop because of the limitations. Said an NHL executive: "What the city has done is create a monster. Anyone interested in buying it has a terrible problem with it supposedly being declared an historical site. That could change the value of it by $30 to $60 million. I mean, who the hell would know what to pay for it?"

For prospective owners of Maple Leaf Gardens Ltd., the key to opening the door is control of the holding company Harold E. Ballard Ltd., which owns about 80.3 per cent of MLG stock. HEB was incorporated in 1944 and grew to the dominant ownership position of MLG in the 1960s and early 1970s. In 1967, HEB owned 19.9 per cent of MLG, while Bassett's Telegram Publishing Co. Ltd. had 19.5 per cent, and Stafford Smythe's CDDS-Tan Ltd. held 20.1 per cent.

By 1970 HEB held the largest number of shares, 20.5 per cent, followed by CDDS-Tan with 20.1 per cent, and Telegram Publishing with 19.7 per cent. Over the next two years a series of buyouts left HEB in sole control. In August 1971 Bassett sold his shares to Smythe and Ballard, with Smythe picking up 98,110 shares for $2.9 million and Ballard 111,636 for $3.3 million. Two months later, Smythe died, and in February 1972, Ballard, through HEB, arranged to purchase at $30 a share all MLG holdings–worth about $7.4 million–belonging to the Smythe estate and CDDS-Tan. That gave HEB 513,832 of the total 735,580 MLG shares issued, or 71 per cent.

It has been generally assumed that Ballard owned HEB and as a result was a man with whom to deal if a group or a company wished to buy the Gardens. But in fact, Ballard owned virtually nothing of HEB until January 1989 when he bought out his daughter Mary Elizabeth's shares. He wasn't in a position to sell the Gardens, because he didn't own it.

This arrangement was the result of the restructuring of HEB in December 1966, when 97 of the original 200 issued shares were withdrawn and the remaining 103 divided equally among the three Ballard children, each receiving 34, with Ballard apparently getting the extra share for tax purposes. Ballard owned all 400,000 of the preferred shares, which had a par value of $10 each, or $4 million. The preferred shares provided Ballard with dividends with a set value of $240,000 a year. Revenue to HEB from MLG's dividends, however, eventually amounted to more than $1 million annually. In 1988, for example, it was $1,040,854. He retained control of HEB through a voting trust agreement with his children. This basically empowered Ballard to run the holding company and thus control MLG until his death. He also personally owned 9.5 per cent of MLG stock.

Such holding companies, with the children owning the common shares, were quite common until Canada's tax laws eliminated estate taxes in 1972. The companies were called "estate freezes," because they enabled heirs to avoid succession duties and estate taxes. Harold Jr. says it was his mother's idea to restructure HEB. She knew in 1966 that she had cancer, and according to Harold Jr. one of the last things she told him before she died in 1969 was to hang onto his shares. "She looked at me and said, 'Don't sign anything. What's yours is yours,' " Harold Jr. said.

In the beginning this arrangement worked fairly well. Ballard, through his voting trust, managed HEB and thus controlled MLG. The dividends from HEB's 71 per cent of MLG went to him, presumably in the form of a salary as chief executive officer of HEB, and then were used to pay off the massive loans he had taken out in 1971 and 1972 to pay for the shares he had purchased from Bassett ($3.3 million) and Smythe ($7.4 million). The relationship with his children was at times stormy, but there was no entrenched animosity on either side until after 1982.

But in 1980, there occurred another problem. Interest rates were skyrocketing and Ballard still owed $8.8 million on his loans. He had a major cash flow problem, in that his bank debt and service charges exceeded the dividend income of HEB from MLG shares. Said a source close to Ballard: "Interest rates were 22 per cent and H.E. was in a bind. He still owed about nine [million dollars]. So he went to Molson and did a deal. They would pay his interest and over a set number of years they would end up with an option to buy x number of shares. It works out to about 20 per cent. Not 20 per cent of HEB, but 20 per cent of the Gardens stock. It's a case of buying a chunk of stock out of HEB Limited."

The key components of the 1980 deal were as follows:

a.) Molson agreed to pay the interest on the HEB debt for a 10-year period, expiring 31 October 1990.

b.) HEB agreed to reduce the principle amount of debt by at least $600,000 a year.

c.) Molson, in return for the interest payments, received a nontransferable option to acquire from HEB 147,115 shares in MLG or 19.99 per cent of the issued stock. The option is exercisable within 30 days after 31 October 1990 and is for a price of $10,000.

d.) Molson received a right of first refusal on the remaining MLG shares owned by HEB, which amount to 50.75 per cent of the MLG stock.

Amazingly, given Ballard's blathering, this deal was kept a secret until late 1988 when rumours started about Molson's taking over MLG and a sale being imminent. Ballard, however, had nothing to sell, except for his personally owned MLG shares. The children owned HEB. By this time Ballard was not speaking to any of his children and was regularly denouncing them in the media. He also seemed fearful that the children might expel him from HEB even though he was assured control of the company until his death.

In an attempt to consolidate his holdings Ballard informed Bill in the fall of 1988 that he wanted to buy out his share of HEB. Bill snubbed his father's offer and responded by saying he'd buy out his father instead. On 12 November, Ballard thought he had a deal with Harold Jr. in which he would pay his son $15.5 million for his 34 shares. Instead, a lawyer for Bill Ballard showed up at Ballard's office to inform him that Bill had an option on Harold Jr.'s shares and Harold Jr. would not be selling.

Bill had purchased, for an amount believed to be $100,000, from Harold Jr. a right of first refusal on his HEB shares, which was good until 30 June 1989. Harold Jr. had fallen into financial difficulty, mainly because he rarely worked. He had held a part-time job at Davis Printing, the Gardens subsidiary, but even that disappeared after he gave an interview to Mary O'Connell of CBC Radio's "Sunday Morning" in which he told of his father's sticking his finger in a light socket when he was five years old. The electrical shock startled Harold Jr. He jumped, knocked his head against a table, and started to cry. When Dorothy ran into the room Ballard told her he was just "giving the kid some juice." O'Connell asked Harold Jr. what he had learned from the incident and he said it taught him not to be an electrician when he grew up. When word of Harold Jr.'s interview got back to his father he was immediately fired from Davis Printing.

When Mary Elizabeth learned of Ballard's attempt to buy out Harold Jr., she had a lawyer contact Ballard. She despised Yolanda, no longer spoke to her father, and viewed the selling of her shares as the final severance. On 20 January 1989, she sold her 34 shares to her father for $15.5 million. To get the money, Ballard once again went to Molson, which lent him the money at commercial rates. Finally, Ballard had an ownership position in HEB.

Following Ballard's purchase, the rumours of a Molson takeover increased. Bill Watters, the hockey agent, remembers a conversation with Ballard, who is a good friend, during which Ballard asked him about a job offer Watters had received from the Quebec Nordiques to work as assistant to the president and owner, Marcel Aubut. "You're too good to work for those frogs," Ballard told Watters. "Stick around here, there'll be something for you. [Gord] Stellick's a nice fellow, but he can't do the job. He won't be back next year."

Ballard then told Watters that he had a good chance of replacing

Stellick as general manager of the Leafs, but that he would have to talk to Molson because they were going to take over the arena and the hockey club. This never happened, of course, but according to a Gardens source Ballard was prepared, at one point, to sell his share of HEB (33 per cent from the stock bought from his daughter) and also allow Molson the option on another 19.9 per cent from the 1980 agreement. However, the source says Molson "low-balled" Ballard in negotiations, offering only $28 a share for MLG stock, when shares were trading at around $40. This infuriated Ballard–but not nearly as much as information he was to receive a few months later.

Publicly, Molson has always said it wasn't interested in taking over MLG. It already owns the Canadiens, and NHL bylaws stipulate that one company cannot have ownership positions in more than one team. But in December 1988 Norman Seagram, the president of Molson, went to New York and advised league president John Ziegler of the company's option on the Gardens stock. Then, in the late spring of 1989 Ballard heard the rumour that Molson was negotiating with Bill and Harold Jr. to buy their shares in HEB and effectively take control that way. According to the information Ballard received, Toronto developer and money broker Eddie Cogan had approached Mickey Cohen, the chief executive officer of Molson, and had told him that he had obtained the shares of both sons, and that a deal was possible. Rosanne Rocchi also says that she was approached, as was Donald Crump, by Molson, about Ballard's shares.

According to insiders Molson was sick of Ballard's inept management of the Leafs and also the events in his personal life which only added to the sense of incompetence at the Gardens. A more competitive team would mean higher advertising rates on television, which would put money in Molson's pocket.

Molson's attempt to take over HEB did not go unchallenged. Ballard fought back, and quite effectively, it seemed, at least at first. In mid-June at the NHL's annual congress in Minneapolis he told the league's board of governors that Molson was attempting to "steal" the team. The NHL agreed to investigate the apparent takeover attempt, and then, when Ballard arrived back in Toronto he prepared to battle the insurgents. On 20 June he executed two basic manoeuvres. With the help of Rocchi, he convinced Harold Jr. to sell his HEB shares to him for $21 million. A large percentage of Harold Jr.'s shares were subsequently cancelled. Ballard also sold HEB his personal shares in MLG (9.5 per cent of MLG or 350,320 shares). As payment, Ballard received additional shares from HEB. With the restructuring of the company Bill Ballard's ownership position was reduced from 33 per cent to 31.78 per cent. Ballard owned the remaining 68.22 per cent of the stock.

It appeared a brilliant move. In a period of a year, Ballard had moved from owning nothing in HEB to holding a strong majority of the company shares. Even if Molson did exercise its option in 1990 on the 19.9 per cent of Gardens stock held by HEB, Ballard would still be left with about 60 per cent of HEB.

But as Ballard toasted his victory in his Gardens office with Rocchi, there loomed another threat. Bill Ballard was preparing to challenge the sale of Harold Jr.'s shares. He still held right of first refusal on those shares and he did not receive the opportunity to exercise that option. If he is able to nullify the sale and buy the shares himself, suddenly he would be the principal owner of HEB with enough clout to insist on being on the board of directors and perhaps even to challenge his father's control of the company.

But whatever battles are fought in the future, both Bill Ballard and Molson are in excellent positions to take over the company when Ballard dies, regardless of what is stipulated in his will. With Molson in a position to purchase 19.9 of MLG in 1990 and also having right of first refusal on any more of Ballard's shares that come available, Molson should be able to determine the future ownership of MLG. Molson's major concern, of course, is John Labatt Ltd., the rival brewery. Molson does not want Labatt's getting a piece of the company. When Labatt's bought 45 per cent of Bill Ballard's company CPI for about $20 million in 1987, industry insiders felt it overpaid but was willing to do so in order to gain a foothold at the Gardens. For Labatt's, which already owns 45 per cent of the Blue Jays, to also have an ownership position with the Leafs would be a marketing coup.

But Molson will do everything it can to block Labbatt's, probably by becoming at least a minority owner of the Leafs. One answer to the problem of Molson owning shares in two NHL teams might be the merger between Molson and Carling O'Keefe Breweries Ltd., which is owned by Elders IXL Ltd. of Australia. The Canadiens are not included in the merger and presumably will remain part of Molson Cos. Ltd. of Montreal. The new company is to be called simply Molson Breweries and under that aegis the Leafs could fall.

The other option would be to simply sell the Canadiens. Although the Montreal club has more prestige than the Leafs in terms of what has been accomplished over the past 20 years, there is more money to be made in Toronto, where the ticket-buying public supports professional sports franchises much more enthusiastically than in Montreal. When the Canadiens fall out of first place in their division, attendance drops off by two thousand almost immediately. In Toronto, a new Leaf owner would almost assuredly tear down the Gardens, if approval could be obtained from the city, and replace the arena with another structure, perhaps a condominium. A new Gardens in another location would be built large enough to seat 22,000. A well-run and moderately successful Leaf team would sell out in such an arena most nights. Another reason for choosing the Leafs ahead of the Canadiens is the television revenue. The advertising dollar is higher in Toronto, because of the large population and the wealth of southern Ontario.

Ballard will no doubt look after Yolanda in his will. Most feel that whatever she gets, she has earned for living with him as long as she has. Gardens sources say she will get the condominium at the corner of Carlton and Jarvis streets. When Ballard bought it about five years ago it cost him $150,000 and today it's worth about twice that. It is believed that Ballard has set up a trust fund which would pay Yolanda $150,000 a year. She may want more and successfully challenge the will, given the number of years she has lived with Ballard. If Yolanda does not get the money from Ballard's share of HEB, minus the bank debt of course, it is likely to go to charity. This is what Ballard has said he would do all along, and it makes sense. It would be his ultimate ego trip, albeit a posthumous one. He would go down in Canadian sports history as the great benefactor. His name would be attached to a huge charity trust fund and he would be remembered and revered in perpetuity.

A.B. (After Ballard) will be a challenge for whomever takes over the Leaf organization, but Ballard's management won't be a tough act to follow. There is a broken team to fix and a tarnished image to shine. Here are the things that should be done.

Separate the Leafs from MLG by giving the team its own board of directors. On the board include former Leafs such as Kennedy, Kelly, Mahovlich, Baun, and Sittler. Bring back the presence of a Smythe by putting Stafford's son, Tom, a Toronto businessman, on the board. Make Ace Bailey, Hap Day, and Bob Davidson honorary directors. This is an advisory group and also a link with the past.

Hire a president who understands what the Leafs mean to hockey fans. He in turn finds a general manager with sound hockey instincts and administrative skills. Under him would be an assistant general manager and also a director of player personnel.

Hire three super scouts whose mandate is to evaluate the top junior players in North America and Europe. Two full-time scouts should be based in western Canada, two in Ontario, one in Quebec, and two in the United States, in the Mid-West and New England. In Europe there would be one full-time scout and a network of three stringers. Two professional scouts are retained, one for the NHL and another for the minor-pro leagues.

There would be a head coach, with three assistants, one of them to teach, another to look after game preparation, and the third to be responsible for player conditioning. One of the assistants records game data on a computer, so the staff knows exactly what each player is doing in terms of hits, giveaways, checks, and scoring chances. Build a video library and hire a librarian to edit and compile game tapes.

Add other support groups. Hire a qualified medical trainer, as well as a physiotherapist, an athletic therapist, a massage therapist, a team psychologist, and a nutritionist. An alumni club is started and the players are given a hospitality room at the arena, which is open on the evenings of games and available for dinners and parties. You encourage former players to return, and welcome them to the dressing room after games.

A film and a book on the history of the club are commissioned. The film is viewed by every player and the book is required reading. The club's past is celebrated by bringing back all former players for a gala dinner attended by guests and the members of the present team.

Changes are made in the dressing room. Plaques commemorating the 11 Stanley Cup champion Leaf teams are placed on the wall. A portrait of every Leaf Hall of Famer is included, along with a list of his accomplishments. Banners signifying the 11 Cup titles are hung from the top of the arena.

Return to the traditional Leaf uniform. The only team of the original six to wear a radically different uniform from the 1960s is the Leafs, probably because Ballard wanted to put his personal stamp on the team. He did, and it stands for incompetence. So make the logo a little larger and a little leafier. Restore the double stripe on the sleeve and body of the sweater. Put the three stripes back on the socks.

Someday some of these things will happen. The cloud will lift and another era will begin. Fans will go to a game on Saturday night and the team will win. In the winter we will talk about the players and their great achievements, instead of the owner and his failures. And in the spring, children will sneak downstairs or stay up late to watch their team fight for the Stanley Cup. There will be new heroes, just like Day, Conacher, Horner, Apps, Kennedy, and Armstrong before them. The gloom will disappear but the lessons learned from the past will not be forgotten.

Postscript

On Friday, 11 August 1989, Gord Stellick resigned as general manager of the Toronto Maple Leafs. He reached the decision the previous Sunday when an attack on him by Harold Ballard had been reported by Milt Dunnell in the *Star*. In this one, Ballard told Dunnell he intended to hire another general manager, which, of course, was news to Stellick. "I'm afraid Stellick is too young and still has too much to learn," Ballard said. "He was the youngest general manager in the NHL when we appointed him and we may have expected too much."

Featured prominently in Dunnell's story was Stellick's controversial trade of Russ Courtnall, which Dunnell described as one of the worst in the history of the franchise. Dunnell quoted a nameless Gardens director as saying he got sick to his stomach and lost his breakfast when he heard of the trade.

Stellick went to work that week hoping something would happen to change his mind. Nothing did. Ballard continued to put him down. In a follow-up story, the *Sun* reported Ballard as saying: "Stellick could be gone tomorrow if I could find someone else to do the job. Stellick's a nice kid, but nice kids don't win." At work, Stellick was told he was no longer to be included in decisions relating to hockey. Instead, Ballard said he would rely on the advice of George Armstrong. When Mike Kitchen was hired as an assistant coach a week earlier, Ballard insisted that Armstrong make the announcement, just as he had made sure that Armstrong selected the Leaf choices at the NHL draft in June.

For 14 years Stellick had been a loyal friend to Ballard and a tireless worker. Ballard had said more than once that he loved him like a son. But now the old man was humiliating him in public and at work. Stellick couldn't understand what he had done to deserve it. Bill Ballard, who viewed all of this from a distance, knew there didn't need to be a reason. "When Harold started calling Gord a son I knew he was in trouble," Bill said ruefully.

At one point, Harold Ballard told Stellick he was upset because he hadn't achieved "results" with the team. But Ballard had put severe restrictions on what Stellick could do and how much he could spend. He hadn't even been allowed to hire his own coach.

It was suspected that Ballard was jealous of the attention his general manager had received in the media. Months earlier, in December, after Stellick had finally convinced Ballard to dismiss John Brophy, Stellick immediately called a news conference to announce the move.

But then Ballard changed his mind. Instead of firing Brophy, he wanted him to take a 30-day vacation, and then return to coach the team. The idea of a head coach being ordered to leave his team for a month and then return to coach was ludicrous. But that's what Ballard wanted and he was incensed when Stellick sent out a release stating that Brophy had been let go. Ballard called Stellick and said, "You couldn't wait to tell the fucking media, could you?"

"What was I supposed to do?" asked Stellick.

"If you want to keep your job just do what you're told."

Stellick would have announced his resignation on the Tuesday of his final week. But the deadline for contract offers to players entering their option year was Thursday, 10 August, and Stellick wanted to be sure that the contracts were sent out.

That night he attended a Canadian Football League game at the SkyDome with his brother Bob. After the game, he went to the Gardens, let himself in, and cleaned out his desk, leaving at 2:30 a.m. Gord was back at the Gardens at nine that morning, although he wasn't sure Ballard would see him.

During the summer, Yolanda and Harold had been spending most of the days at the Georgian Bay cottage–but not the nights. Bill had a cottage nearby, and Yolanda and Harold were obsessed with the idea of Bill suddenly appearing in the middle of the night and harming them.

Bob Stellick was already in the hockey office when Gord arrived. He told his brother that he should attempt to see Ballard as soon as possible. "Hit him with it now," Bob said. "Don't wait."

Gord put in a call to Ballard, but Yolanda, who now was screening all of Ballard's calls, answered the phone. "Don't bring up anything serious," Yolanda said. "He hasn't had his insulin shot or any medication. I don't want Harold to be shocked."

Yolanda had always professed to be a supporter of Gord and Bob. The Stellicks' father had emigrated from Czechoslovakia, and Yolanda had said she was of Czechoslovak descent. Several times, Yolanda had told people in the hockey office that she had "saved the Czech brothers' asses" by sticking up for them. Stellick can remember Yolanda at one point during the winter coming to him in tears, saying, "Gordon, I've saved you. Harold was ready to fire you but I talked to him and now everything is okay!"

Stellick was worried about being overly emotional when he met Ballard. But any desire to stay with the club, any affection for Ballard, had been driven out of him. "This is not my team anymore," he said to himself and to his friends that week. As he walked into the semi-darkness of Ballard's office, he recalled the events of the past several months.

When Yolanda saw him, she quickly crossed herself, ran up to him and said dramatically, "Gordon, I've been praying for you!"

Stellick viewed the strange scene and thought, "Holy mackerel. Why did this take so long?"

Ballard was surprised over Stellick's resignation; Armstrong was shocked. A source in the hockey office said later: "George turned as white as a ghost when he heard." Of most concern to Armstrong was the prospect of Ballard's insisting that he take Stellick's place. Armstrong had neither the knowledge nor the inclination to be general manager.

Stellick handled the news conference well. He didn't denounce Ballard, although, when asked to comment on Ballard's remarks, he did say, "I thought public floggings were banned in Canada." He was barely able to conceal his contempt for Dunnell, who had diligently reported Ballard's putdowns without once calling Stellick for a reaction, or mentioning in his column that public statements undermining coaches and managers were a major reason for the instability of the organization and failure of the team. It was unthinkable, of course, for Dunnell to criticize his powerful friend.

The people in the media were sympathetic towards Stellick but nobody pitied him. It was a dignified departure. He was without a job but he had not lost his integrity. Wayne Parrish in the *Sun* described his tenure as "grace under massive bombardment." Of Ballard, he wrote, "the stupidity, the intemperance and monstrous incomprehension of the demented old coot." Jim Proudfoot of the *Star* noted that Ballard "reserves for himself the exclusive right to carry on with the destruction of hockey's greatest franchise. Nobody is permitted to interfere."

The front office changes did not end with Stellick's departure. Ballard regretted Stellick's decision to leave, and spent part of his days immediately after the resignation sitting alone in Stellick's empty office. When Ballard interviewed Frank Bonello, who was the director of the NHL's Central Scouting Bureau, for the vacant managing post, Bonello told him Armstrong would have to be replaced. Bonello said it was clear Armstrong did not want the job and should not have it. Alan Eagleson said the same thing when Ballard called him about managing the team. Armstrong's unacceptability as coach was what Stellick had been trying to convey to Ballard for several months. A few days after Stellick's resignation, Ballard finally did remove Armstrong from the coaching position.

With training camp less than a month away, the club seemed to be in chaos, without either a coach or a general manager. In the *Star*, Proudfoot argued that Ballard's ownership could no longer be tolerated and that the league should step in and demand that he sell the team. No one expected that to happen. And, of course, Ballard's directors of Maple Leaf Gardens Ltd. voiced not the mildest admonishment.

There was no mad rush for the GM's job. Bonello wanted too much money, as well as the kind of control held by other general managers in the NHL. Eagleson turned down the offer to manage the team. Predictably, Ballard took the easy way out. He promoted Floyd Smith, the chief scout, to general manager. Smith is an old friend. He'll do as he's told. Ballard will feel comfortable having him around. Smith, in turn, recommended Doug Carpenter for coach, and Carpenter was hired. But he brings with him baggage that will leave him vulnerable to attacks from Ballard. He is a former school teacher and he is considered a student of the game. These are factors that will likely alienate the owner before long.

During the turmoil with the Leafs, Ballard braced for another battle, this one with his son Bill. On 2 August Bill and his business partner, Michael Cohl, filed a $70 million law suit against Ballard and associates, challenging the June transfer of shares in Harold E. Ballard Ltd. from Harold Jr. to his father.

Bill Ballard and Cohl claimed that they had the right of first refusal on Harold Jr.'s one-third interest in HEB's common shares, but were not allowed to exercise the option. Named in the suit were Ballard, HEB Ltd., Harold Jr., and HEB directors Donald Crump and Donald Giffin. Bill Ballard and Cohl asked that Harold Jr.'s shares, which he had sold to his father for $21 million, be delivered to them for $20 million. If they were not, the partners were asking for damages of $70 million.

With Bill already owning a third of HEB's common shares, possession of Harold Jr.'s shares would put him and Cohl in a position to take over MLG and hand Ballard his most significant and perhaps last defeat.

The June sale of Harold Jr.'s shares to his father brought an end to the once strong relationship between Harold Jr. and Bill. Harold Jr. had maintained a low profile following the sale of his stock. But on 19 August the three Toronto newspapers reported on their front pages that he had been charged with breaking into his father's house on Montgomery Road in Etobicoke–the same house in which Bill and his family had lived for several years until moving out in 1988–and making off with some furniture and hockey memorabilia. Harold Jr. was charged with assault after he allegedly resisted arrest. Sergeant Russell Ruddock of 22 Division was quoted in the *Sun* as saying, "He choked us, grabbed our ties and ripped my partner's shirt off his back. He flatly refused to accept he was being arrested." Both officers were treated for minor injuries at the Queensway General Hospital.

Harold spent the night in a holding cell and arrived at Old City Hall in a paddy wagon the next morning, handcuffed to several other prisoners. As part of his bail conditions, he was told to stay away from his father and Yolanda, as well as the Gardens and the Montgomery Road house. Harold Jr.'s appearance had changed. He had put on a considerable amount of weight and shaved his head. During his court appearance, he made faces and winked at a woman he recognized. When Provincial Court judge John Murphy mentioned the name of Yolanda Ballard, Harold cupped his hand to his ear and shook his head, saying "Yolanda?" as if to indicate that he hadn't heard her last name correctly. As he left the court, he mugged for the reporters and grabbed his friend Marty O'Neill, who had posted Harold's $1000 bail. When Yolanda was told of the charge, she said, "I'm not surprised."

Milestones

in Leaf History

1917   The National Hockey League begins with four
       teams, the Montreal Canadiens, the Montreal
       Wanderers, the Ottawa Senators, and the Toronto
       Arenas.

1919   The Arenas are renamed the St. Patricks in the
       hope of drawing support from the large Irish
       community in Toronto.

1927
February   In financial difficulty, the St. Pats are sold to a
       group of Toronto businessmen headed by Conn
       Smythe. The team is renamed the Toronto Maple
       Leafs.

1930   Before the start of the season, Smythe purchases
       King Clancy, a star defenceman with the Ottawa
       Senators, for $35,000 and sends the Senators two
       players, forward Eric Pettinger and defenceman
       Art Smith.

1931
November   Maple Leaf Gardens opens after being built in a
       period of five months at a cost of $1.5 million. A
       capacity crowd of 13,542 attends the first game,
       which the Leafs lose 2-1 to the Chicago
       Blackhawks.

1933

January Foster Hewitt's play-by-play of Leaf games goes nation-wide on the General Motors Saturday night radio broadcasts. Hewitt's sign-on becomes, "Hello Canada and hockey fans in the United States and Newfoundland."

December Ace Bailey's career comes to an end when he is knocked to the ice by Eddie Shore in a game against the Bruins in the Boston Garden. Bailey suffers a fractured skull and almost dies on the operating table. Bailey's sweater, number 6, is retired.

1942

April In defeating the Detroit Red Wings, the Leafs become the first and only NHL team to fall behind 3-0 in a best-of-7 Stanley Cup final, then come back to win 4 consecutive games.

1949

April The Leafs win their third consecutive Stanley Cup, sweeping Detroit in 4 games.

1951

April The Leafs win their sixth Cup in 10 years, defeating the Montreal Canadiens 4 games to 1.

August A plane carrying Leaf defenceman Bill Barilko on a fishing trip in northern Ontario crashes. Barilko, who had scored the Cup winning goal in overtime against Montreal, is killed. He is the second Leaf whose sweater (number 5) is retired.

1961

November Controlling interest in the club is purchased by the partnership of Stafford Smythe, Conn Smythe's eldest son; John W. Bassett, the publisher of the Toronto *Telegram*; and Harold E. Ballard, a Toronto businessman and sportsman.

1964

April The Leafs win their third consecutive Stanley Cup, defeating Detroit 4 games to 3. Punch Imlach becomes the first and only man to coach and manage 3 consecutive Cup winners.

1967

May The Leafs win their fourth Cup in 6 years, defeating the Canadiens in 6 games.

1972

February Harold Ballard assumes majority ownership of the club.

1981

December Darryl Sittler becomes the first Leaf captain to demand a trade.

1982

January Sittler is sent to the Philadelphia Flyers for a high-school player, centre Rich Costello, and two draft choices.

1985

June The Leafs receive the top pick in the NHL's entry (amateur) draft for the first time since the inception of the draft in 1969. The Leafs, who earned the right to select first by finishing last overall in the league, take defenceman/left winger Wendel Clark of the Saskatoon Blades.

1989

May Maple Leaf Gardens is declared a historical site by Toronto city council under the Ontario Heritage Act.

CUPS

AND ACHIEVEMENTS

1920-21   The Toronto St. Patricks finish first in the National Hockey League with 15 wins and 9 losses.

Cecil H. (Babe) Dye, a right winger, is the top goal scorer in the NHL with 35 goals in 24 games.

1922-23   Babe Dye leads the league in goals with 26 in 22 games.

1924-25   Babe Dye leads the league in goals with 38 in 29 games.

1928-29   Irwin W. (Ace) Bailey, a left winger, wins league scoring championship with 32 points (22 goals and 10 assists) in 44 games.

1930-31   Defenceman F. M. (King) Clancy is selected to the league's inaugural all-star team.

1931-32   The Leafs capture the Stanley Cup, sweeping the New York Rangers in 3 games.

Left Winger Harvey (Busher) Jackson wins the scoring championship with 28 goals and 25 assists for 53 points in 48 games. Centre Joe Primeau is awarded the Lady Byng Trophy, given to the player who exhibits the best type of sportsmanship and gentlemanly conduct combined with a high standard of playing ability.

Four members of the Leafs are all-stars. Jackson is the first team left winger. Charlie Conacher, a right winger, and Clancy are on the second team. Dick Irwin is the second team coach.

1932-33   The Leafs finish first in the Canadian Division with a record of 24 wins, 18 losses, and 6 ties.

Clancy, Conacher, Jackson, and Irvin are selected to the NHL's second all-star team.

1933-34   The Leafs finish first in the Canadian Division and have the best record in the NHL (26-13-9).

Conacher wins the scoring championship with 32 goals and 20 assists for 52 points in 42 games.

Five members of the Leafs are all-stars. Conacher, Clancy, and Jackson are on the first-team. Primeau and Irvin, as coach, are selected for the second.

1934-35   The Leafs finish with the best record in the league again, 30 wins, 14 losses, and 4 ties.

Conacher repeats as scoring champion, with 36 goals and 21 assists for 57 points in 47 games.

Conacher and Jackson are first-team all-stars. Irvin is on the second team.

1935-36   Conacher is a first-team all-star. Centre Bill Thoms is on the second team.

1936-37   Centre Syl Apps wins the Calder Trophy as the best rookie in the league.

Jackson is selected to the first all-star team.

1937-38   The Leafs finish first in the Canadian Division with 24 wins, 15 losses, and 9 ties.

Right winger Gordie Drillon is the scoring champion with 26 goals and 26 assists for 52 points in 48 games. He also wins the Lady Byng Trophy.

Drillon is a first-team all-star. Apps is on the second team.

1938-39   Apps and Drillon make the first all-star team.

1940-41   Turk Broda wins the Vezina Trophy as the top goaltender in the league.

Broda, left winger David (Sweeney) Schriner, and defenceman Wally Stanowski are first-team all-stars. Apps is on the second team.

1941-42   The Leafs win the Stanley Cup, defeating Detroit 4 games to 3.

Apps wins the Lady Byng Trophy.

Broda, Drillon, and Bucko McDonald, a defenceman, are second-team all-stars.

1942-43   Gaye Stewart, a left winger, wins the Calder Trophy.

Right winger Lorne Carr is a first-team all-star. Apps is on the second team.

1943-44   Walter (Babe) Pratt, a defenceman, wins the Hart Trophy as the league's most valuable player. Gus Bodnar, a centre, takes the Calder Trophy.

Pratt and Carr are on the first all-star team. Goaltender Paul Bibeault and coach Hap Day are on the second team.

1944-45   The Leafs win the Stanley Cup, defeating Detroit 4 games to 3.

Goaltender Frank McCool wins the Calder Trophy.

Pratt is on the second all-star team.

1945-46   Gaye Stewart is on the first all-star team.

1946-47   The Leafs win the Stanley Cup, defeating the Montreal Canadiens 4 games to 2.

Howie Meeker, a right winger, is awarded the Calder Trophy.

1947-48   The Leafs finish with the best record in the league (32 victories, 15 losses, and 13 ties). They win the Stanley Cup, defeating Detroit in 4 games straight.

Broda wins the Vezina Trophy as the league's top goaltender.

Broda is selected to the first all-star team.

1948-49   The Leafs win the Stanley Cup, defeating Detroit in 4 games straight.

1949-50   Defenceman Gus Mortson is a first-team all-star. Centre Ted Kennedy is on the second team.

1950-51   The Leafs win the Stanley Cup, defeating Montreal 4 games to 1.

Left winger Sid Smith, defenceman Jim Thomson, and Kennedy are on the second all-star team.

1951-52   Smith wins the Lady Byng Trophy.

Thomson and Smith are second-team all-stars.

1953-54   Harry Lumley wins the Vezina Trophy.

Lumley is a first-team all-star. Kennedy and defenceman Tim Horton are on the second team.

1954-55   Kennedy wins the Hart Trophy. Smith takes the Lady Byng.

Lumley and Smith are on the first all-star team.

1955-56   Centre Todd Sloan is on the second all-star team.

1957-58   Frank Mahovlich wins the Calder Trophy.

1959-60   Defenceman Allan Stanley is selected to the second all-star team.

1960-61   Johnny Bower wins the Vezina Trophy. Centre
          Dave Keon takes the Calder. Centre Red Kelly
          wins the Lady Byng.

          Bower and Mahovlich are first-team all-stars.
          Stanley is on the second team.

1961-62   The Leafs win the Stanley Cup, defeating Chicago
          4 games to 2.

          Keon wins the Lady Byng Trophy.

          Mahovlich and Keon are second-team all-stars,
          along with defenceman Carl Brewer.

1962-63   The Leafs finish first in the league with 35 wins,
          23 losses, and 12 ties in 70 games. They win the
          Stanley Cup, defeating Detroit 4 games to 1.

          Defenceman Kent Douglas wins the Calder
          Trophy. Keon takes the Lady Byng.

          Brewer and Mahovlich are first-team all-stars.
          Horton is on the second team.

1963-64   The Leafs win the Stanley Cup, defeating Detroit
          4 games to 3.

          Horton is a first-team all-star. Mahovlich is on the
          second team.

1964-65   Bower and Terry Sawchuk win the Vezina
          Trophy.

          Brewer and Mahovlich are second-team all-stars.

1965-66   Left winger Brit Selby wins the Calder Trophy.

          Stanley and Mahovlich are second-team all-stars.

1966-67   The Leafs win the Stanley Cup, defeating
          Montreal 4 games to 2.

          Keon is awarded the Conn Smythe Trophy as the
          most valuable player of the playoffs.

          Horton is a second-team all-star.

1967-68   Horton is a first-team all-star.

1968-69 Horton is a first-team all-star.

1970-71 Goaltender Jacques Plante and Keon are
         second-team all-stars.

1974-75 Defenceman Borje Salming is a second-team
         all-star.

1975-76 Salming is a second-team all-star.

1976-77 Salming is a first-team all-star. Right winger
         Lanny McDonald is a second-team all-star.

1977-78 Salming and centre Darryl Sittler are second-team
         all-stars.

1978-79 Salming is a second-team all-star.

1979-80 Salming is a second-team all-star.

CAPTAINS, COACHES, MANAGERS

1927-28   After heading a group that buys the Toronto St. Patricks, Conn Smythe renames the team the Toronto Maple Leafs and appoints himself coach and manager.

Alex Romeril, a former amateur hockey player in Toronto, briefly holds the position of manager.

Defenceman Hap Day is named captain.

1929-30   Frank Selke, an electrician by trade but a long-time hockey coach, manager, and organizer, is hired full-time as Smythe's assistant in September 1929.

1930-31   Part way through the season, Smythe resigns as coach and brings in Art Duncan, a former defenceman.

1931-32   Early in the season, Smythe fires Duncan and hires Dick Irvin, who had coached the Chicago Blackhawks the previous season.

1937-38   Charlie Conacher is appointed captain after Day is traded to the New York Americans.

1938-39 Red Horner follows Conacher as captain after Conacher's trade to Detroit.

1940-41 Hap Day is hired as coach after Irvin is told by Smythe to take the coaching job with the Montreal Canadiens.

Syl Apps replaces Horner as captain after Horner's retirement.

1943-44 Bob Davidson takes over as captain when Apps leaves the team to join the Canadian armed forces in the Second World War.

1945-46 Selke resigns as Smythe's assistant and takes over as manager of the Canadiens.

Apps rejoins the team and assumes the captaincy.

1948-49 Apps retires and is replaced as captain by Ted Kennedy.

1950-51 Day retires as coach and takes on the responsibilities of manager, although Smythe is still the manager in title. Joe Primeau is the new coach.

1953-54 King Clancy is appointed coach, replacing Primeau, who retires.

1955-56 Kennedy retires and is replaced as captain by Sid Smith.

1956-57 Day resigns his position as Smythe's assistant, and then Smythe steps down as manager. In his place is a hockey committee comprised of Gardens shareholders and headed by Smythe's son, Stafford.

Howie Meeker replaces Clancy behind the bench; Clancy stays in the organization.

Smith retires, and Kennedy, who makes a comeback, shares the captaincy with Jim Thomson.

1957-58 Billy Reay is hired as coach to replace Meeker, who is fired.

George Armstrong is named captain, replacing Kennedy, who retires, and Thomson, who is traded to Chicago.

1958-59 Punch Imlach is hired as assistant general manager. A few months later, he is appointed manager. His first important decision is to fire Reay and appoint himself coach.

1969-70 Imlach is fired as coach and general manager. Jim Gregory is named general manager and John MacLellan coach.

Armstrong retires and is replaced by Dave Keon as captain.

1973-74 Red Kelly is named coach, replacing MacLellan who stays in the organization.

1974-75 Darryl Sittler replaces Keon as captain after Keon leaves the team to join the World Hockey Association.

1977-78 Roger Neilson is hired as coach, replacing Kelly, who is fired.

1979-80 Imlach returns as general manager.

Neilson is fired and Floyd Smith is the new coach. Gregory is fired.

After Lanny McDonald is traded, Sittler renounces the captaincy, but takes it back at the beginning of the next season.

1980-81 Joe Crozier takes over behind the bench, replacing Smith, who stays in the organization. A few months later, Crozier is fired and replaced by Mike Nykoluk.

1981-82 Imlach is dismissed and replaced by scout Gerry McNamara.

Sittler demands a trade and is eventually sent to the Philadelphia Flyers. Rick Vaive replaces Sittler as captain.

1984-85   Nykoluk is fired and replaced by assistant coach Dan Maloney.

1985-86   Vaive is stripped of the captaincy after missing a morning practice. The position is left open.

1986-87   Maloney resigns as coach after refusing a one-year contract. He is replaced by John Brophy.

1987-88   McNamara is fired as general manager, and replaced by an interim management group made up of assistant general manager Gord Stellick, scout Dick Duff, and Brophy. At the end of the season, Stellick is appointed general manager.

1988-89   Brophy is fired a few months into the season and replaced on an interim basis by George Armstrong, a scout. At the end of the season, Armstrong agrees to stay as coach and is given the title of director of player personnel.

1989-90   In August 1989 Stellick resigns as general manager. Floyd Smith is promoted to take Stellick's place.

Armstrong is removed as coach in August, before the season even begins. Doug Carpenter of the Quebec Nordiques is hired in his place.

OWNERSHIP
HISTORY

1895

1 February   Conn (Constantine Falkland Cary) Smythe is born in Toronto to journalist Albert Smythe, and his wife, Polly (Mary).

1903

30 July   Edwin Harold Ballard (Harold E. Ballard) is born in Toronto to Sidney Ballard, a machinist and manufacturer of ice skates, and his wife, Mary.

1915

25 August   John White Bassett is born in Ottawa to John White Bassett, Sr., a journalist and later a newspaper executive, and his wife, Marion.

1921

15 March   Stafford Smythe is born in Toronto to Conn Smythe, a businessman and sportsman, and his wife, Irene.

1927

February   Conn Smythe heads a group of investors including financier John Paris (Jack) Bickell to purchase the Toronto St. Patricks of the National Hockey League for $200,000. Smythe assumes the position of manager and coach, and changes the name to the Maple Leafs.

1931   Maple Leaf Gardens Ltd., which includes the
        Maple Leaf team and the Gardens, is
        incorporated. It has authorized capital of
        100,000 seven per cent, noncumulative,
        participating shares, par value $10, and 50,000
        common shares, no par value, of which 80,000
        preferred and 36,779 common shares were issued.
        The Gardens is built in five months for $1.5
        million and opens in November.

1932
October Ballard takes control of his first hockey team as
         coach and manager of the National Sea Fleas of
         the Ontario senior league. The Sea Fleas had won
         the national championship, the Allan Cup, the
         previous season. The team fails to make the
         playoffs and then embarks on a European tour in
         the late winter of 1933. At the world hockey
         championship in Prague, Ballard's team becomes
         the first Canadian squad to fail to win the gold
         medal, losing to a U.S. team in the final game.

1936   A year after retiring, Sidney Ballard dies of lead
        poisoning, the result of many years of working
        with lead at his machine and skate shop. He dies
        a millionaire, and Harold, the only child, inherits
        the business. Ballard operates on a smaller scale,
        repairing and selling sewing machinery for the
        garment trade. He continues to work part-time in
        amateur hockey.

1941
September Conn Smythe, a major in the Canadian Army,
           forms the 30th Battery as part of the 7th Toronto
           Regiment, Royal Canadian Artillery, Canadian
           Active Army (the Sportsmen's Battalion).

1944   Harold E. Ballard (HEB) Ltd. is incorporated as
        Ballard's personal holding company. Two hundred
        shares are issued.

        The Sportsmen's Battalion leaves for Europe. In
        July Smythe is hit by shrapnel in an air attack at
        Caen and is hospitalized. He returns home in
        September.

1947

November   Conn Smythe wins a battle for control of Maple Leaf Gardens Ltd. against two directors, Ed Bickle, a stockbroker, and Bill MacBrien, an insurance executive. Backed by Percy Gardiner, a financier and one of the wealthiest men in Canada, Smythe buys 30,000 shares from Gardiner at $10 a share, giving him about 30 per cent interest in MLG (50,000 shares), and enabling him to take over as president.

1961

November   Stafford Smythe, Harold Ballard, and John Bassett, the publisher of the Toronto *Telegram,* all of whom are MLG directors, borrow about $2 million to purchase 45,000 of Conn Smythe's shares. Combined with their own holdings, the three partners control about 60 percent of MLG. They agree that in the event of the death of any of the partners, the surviving partners have the option to buy the deceased's shares.

Stafford Smythe is appointed president of the company. Ballard is executive vice-president in charge of the Gardens. Bassett is chairman of the company's board of directors. Conn Smythe retains 5100 MLG shares and stays on as a director. He has an office, a secretary, the use of a car, and is paid $15,000 annually.

1966

March   Upon hearing that Ballard has booked a fight at the Gardens between Ernie Terrell and Muhammed Ali, an opponent of the United States involvement in the Vietnam War, Conn Smythe resigns from the board and requests that his shares be purchased.

December   HEB is restructed with 97 of the original 200 shares withdrawn and the remainign 103 divided equally among the three children, each receiving 34, with Ballard apparently getting the single remaining share for tax purposes. Ballard owns all of the 400,000 preferred shares and retains control of the company through a voting trust agreement with his children. It gives him control of the company until his death.

1967   As of October, there are a total of 735,580 shares
        in MLG. Harold E. Ballard Ltd., which is Ballard's
        personal holding company, owns 146,070 shares
        (19.9 per cent). Bassett's company, The Telegram
        Publishing Co. Ltd., owns 143,695 (19.5 per cent),
        and Stafford Smythe's company, CDDS-Tan
        Investments Ltd., owns 148,500 shares (20.1
        per cent).

1968
October The Department of National Revenue begins an
        investigation of MLG. The Royal Canadian
        Mounted Police enter the Gardens with search
        warrants and seize company documents. Federal
        authorities also search the homes of Ballard
        and Smythe. Bassett chooses to resign from the
        Leaf hockey committee, but remains chairman of
        the board.

1969
June   MLG directors meet to decide whether Stafford
        Smythe and Ballard should stay as president and
        vice-president of the company. Only 15 of the 23
        directors attend. A secret vote ends in a 7–7 tie,
        which leaves Bassett, as chairman, to cast the
        deciding ballot. He votes to remove Smythe and
        Ballard.
            The result is a bitter falling out between Bassett
        and his two partners, and a battle for control of
        the company. In 1969, CDDS-Tan owns 148,500
        shares (20.1 per cent); HEB 146,070 shares (19.9
        per cent); and Telegram Publishing 145,000 shares
        (19.7 per cent).

December Ballard's wife, Dorothy, dies of cancer, leaving
        Ballard and three grown children, Mary Elizabeth,
        Bill, and Harold Jr.

1970   As of November, HEB owns 150 525 MLG shares
        (20.5 per cent); Telegram Publishing 145,000
        shares (19.7 per cent); CDDS-Tan 148,500 (20.1
        per cent). Ballard owns 1030 personal shares;
        Smythe 4935 shares.

| December | Ballard and Smythe succeed at a shareholders' meeting in ousting Bassett and the other Gardens directors who had voted to remove them. Smythe and Ballard are reinstated as president and vice-president of the company. |

1971

| July | A year-long police investigation results in charges of theft and fraud against Smythe and Ballard. They are charged jointly with theft of $146,000 in cash and securities. Smythe is charged with defrauding MLG of $249,000. Ballard is charged with defrauding MLG of $82,000. |

| August | Bassett admits defeat in his bid to take over control of MLG and sells a total of 182,840 shares at $30 a share, for $5.5 million. Smythe buys 98,110 of Bassett's shares for $2.9 million. Ballard buys 111,636 shares for about $3.3 million. |

| October | Just days before Stafford Smythe is to stand trial, he dies in hospital of stomach cancer. |

A few weeks later, Ballard is appointed president of MLG.

1972

| February | Ballard, through HEB, arranges to purchase all of the MLG holdings (251,545 shares) owned or controlled by CDDS-Tan and the estate of Stafford Smythe, at a cost of about $7.4 million, giving him 513,832 shares of the total of 735,580 common shares issued. |

The estate controlled or owned 103,045 shares. CDDS-Tan owned or controlled 148,500. Ballard's offer of $30 a share was accepted by the executors of Smythe's estate and by the principal officers of CDDS-Tan on 4 February.

HEB, which was incorporated in 1944, owns about 71 per cent of MLG. Ballard personally owns 2230 MLG shares. HEB is structured in such a way that Ballard's three children own all of the common shares, which are equivalent to 71 per cent of MLG, while Ballard owns the 400,000 preferred shares with a par value of $4 million, giving him the voting majority in the company and managerial control.

| *May, June* | Ballard stands trial on 49 counts of fraud and theft involving a total of $205,000. He is found guilty on 47 counts. |
| *October* | Ballard is sentenced to three three-year terms to run concurrently. He is taken to Milhaven Prison and placed in a minimum security unit called Bath.
In Ballard's absence, his son Bill, who graduated from Osgoode Hall Law School that spring, runs the Gardens as vice-president. |

1973

| *Summer* | Ballard is released from Bath late in the summer and taken to a halfway house in Toronto; shortly after he is placed on parole. |
| *August* | Bill Ballard and partners Michael Cohl and David Wolinsky form Concert Productions International (CPI), a concert and event promotions company, as an MLG subsidiary. In 1974, the partners buy the company from MLG. |

| **1976** | After disagreements with his father, Bill Ballard quits as vice-president of the Gardens and joins CPI on a full-time basis. |

1980

| *November* | Conn Smythe dies. |

Ballard still owes $8.8 million on the bank loans used to buy out his two partners and is in financial difficulty because of high interest rates. Ballard seeks help from Molson Cos. Ltd., which agrees to pay the interest on the bank debt in return for options on MLG shares. Molson receives an option to acquire from HEB 19.99 per cent of the MLG stock. The option is exercisable within 30 days after 31 October 1990. Molson also has the right of first refusal on the remaining MLG shares owned by HEB.

1982

Summer   Ballard meets Yolanda MacMillan and their long
relationship begins.

1987

August   Yolanda MacMillan legally changes her name to
Ballard.

October   Ballard guarantees a $2.5 million bank loan from
the National Bank of Canada for his friend,
Michael Gobuty, a businessman in financial
difficulty. A few weeks later, Gobuty and Ballard
are sued for the value of the unpaid loan.

1988

July   Ballard survives a quintuple heart bypass at
Toronto General Hospital.

September   Bill Ballard is charged with assaulting Yolanda
Ballard in his father's office. He pleads not guilty
and is publicly supported by his brother and
sister.

As of September 1988, MLG capital stock consists
of 3,677,900 common shares, with about 2450
registered shareholders. Harold Ballard controls
directly and indirectly 2,952,455 or 80.28 per cent
of the outstanding common shares. Ballard
personally owns about 9.5 per cent of MLG stock,
with the other 71 per cent (2,602,135 shares)
owned by HEB.

1989

January   Ballard's daughter, Mary Elizabeth, sells her
one-third interest in the common shares of HEB
to her father for an estimated $18 million. Molson
loans Ballard the money for the buyout and takes
ownership of the shares if there is a default on
the payments.

June   Ballard announces that he has bought out the 34
shares in HEB belonging to Harold Jr. for $21
million. Some of the shares are cancelled. Ballard
also sells his personal holdings of 9.5 per cent of
MLG stock to HEB for payment in HEB common
shares. As a result, Harold Ballard and Bill Ballard
are the sole owners of HEB, with Ballard owning
68.22 per cent and Bill 31.78 per cent.

August   Bill Ballard and Michael Cohl file a lawsuit to challenge the sale of Harold Jr.'s shares in HEB to his father, claiming that they were denied their right of first refusal on Harold Jr.'s shares. Bill Ballard and Cohl ask for Harold Jr.'s shares to be delivered to them for $20 million. If they succeed they will be in a position to take over control of Maple Leaf Gardens Ltd. Failing that, they seek damages of $70 million.

INDEX

Hull, Bobby, 50, 78
Hull, Brett, 238
Hunter, Dale, 222
Hutchison, Dave, 88

Iafrate, Al, 154, 155, 160, 213, 223, 239
Ihnacak, Miroslav, 173
Ihnacak, Peter, 116, 154, 173, 239
Imlach, George (Punch), background, 41; character, 53; health, 55, 85, 90, 93, 115; and media, 53, 84, 88; joins Toronto Maple Leaf organization, 41; as assistant GM, 41-42; as coach, 24, 42-46, 51-56, 85; as GM, 7, 42-43, 53-55, 85-93, 115, 117, 123, 141, 156; as Sabres' GM, 84; and Harold Ballard, 91, 93, 121-22, 175; and Carl Brewer, 53-54; and King Clancy, 146; and Alan Eagleson, 85-87; and Red Kelly, 45-46; and Frank Mahovlich, 46, 51-55; and Darryl Sittler, 86-89; and Conn Smythe, 42-44; and Stafford Smythe, 41, 85
Irvin, Dick, 15, 19, 23, 24, 29, 30, 31
Irwin, Candice, 130, 202, 204
Irwin, Robert, 103, 106, 109, 130, 203, 204, 205
Ivan, Tommy, 50-51

Jackson, Harvey (Busher), 12-13, 15, 20, 23
Jackson, Jeff, 239
James, Val, 160, 213
Jarvis, Doug, 82
Jeffries, T. D., 63
Jennings, Bill, 79
Johansen, Trevor, 79
John Labatt Ltd., 181, 245, 250
Johnson, Ching, 10
Johnston, Eddie, 100

Jones, Jimmy, 79
Jones, Ron, 131-32, 201, 206
Joshi, Suneel, 141

Kaihla, Paul, 177, 179
Kaszycki, Mike, 122, 164
Keenan, Mike, 221
Kelly, Red, 43, 45-46, 52-57, 73-74, 144, 145, 222, 251
Kennedy, Theodore (Teeder, Ted), 24, 25, 28-33, 235, 251, 253
Keon, Dave, 39, 40, 46, 47, 52, 53, 56, 57, 72, 73, 74
Kerr, John, Judge, 224
Kid Line, 12-13, 23
Kiley, Mike, 229
Kinnear, Guy, 227
Kitchen, Mike, 255
Klein, Doris, 26
Knox, Northrup, 84-85
Knox, Seymour, 84-85
Kordic, John, 220, 223, 239
Kotsopoulos, Chris, 155, 212
Kravitz, Bob, 118
Krimson, 180
Kurri, Jari, 78
Kurvers, Tom, 239

Labatt's. See John Labatt Ltd.
Lach, Elmer, 29, 30, 33
Lafleur, Guy, 62
LaFontaine, Pat, 170
Landon, Larry, 121
Landry, Tom, 24
Lanz, Rick, 218
Lariviere, Garry, 6, 215, 221, 222
Larsen, Peter, 179, 180
Laughlin, Craig, 217
Lawton, Brian, 151
Laxdal, Derek, 164
Leeman, Gary, 154, 213, 228, 239
Lemaire, Jacques, 238
Lemieux, Claude, 239
Lemieux, Mario, 151, 243-44
Ley, Rick, 71, 72
Lloyd Bag Corporation, 107-8

Merenda, Sal, 203, 204, 205
Metro Junior A Hockey League, 40
Metz, Don, 32
Metz, Nick, 30, 32
Miami Heart Institute, 191
Mikita, Stan, 50
Miller, Thomson, Sedgewick, Lewis and Healy, 190, 193
Molson Breweries of Canada Ltd., 242, 247–250
Molson Cos. Ltd., 250
Molstar Communications, 242
Momesso, Sergio, 239
Montreal Canadiens, 16, 26, 29–31, 37, 41, 55–56, 61–62, 67–68, 160, 235–38, 240, 243, 250–51
Montreal Maroons, 12, 16, 26
Montreal Wanderers, 9
Moore, Dickie, 55
Moore, Ross, 104
Morris, Elwin, 30, 235
Morrison, Jim, 41–42
Morrison, Scott, 148, 164, 169
Mortson, Gus, 32
Mr. Hockey, 16
Muni, Craig, 117, 173, 215
Murdoch, Bob, 221
Murdoch, Don, 80
Murray and Thompson Sports Representatives and Advisors, 161
Murray, Anne, 245
Murray, Bob, 164
Murzyn, Dana, 151, 152
Mutual Street Arena, 14, 16

Nanne, Lou, 126, 169
National Bank of Canada, 188–90, 192, 197
National Hockey League (NHL), founded, 9; first all-star game, 20; reduced to seven teams, 26; effect of Second World War on, 27–30; players' rights, 29; sponsorship, 39, 162, 164;

1967 expansion, 61; entry draft, 67; merger with WHA, 73; involvement in European market, 78; waiver draft, 120; and the media, 126, 148, 149; and ownership bylaws, 249
National Hockey League Central Scouting Bureau, 121, 152, 258
National Hockey League Players Association (NHLPA), 54, 85–86, 149, 162
National Sea Fleas, 16, 68–69
Neely, Bob, 72, 73
Neil McNeil High School, 40
Neilson, Roger, 74–79, 81–84, 98–102, 115, 144, 145, 154–56, 168, 239
Nevin, Bob, 40, 46, 51, 52
Newhouse, F. J., 111
New Jersey Devils, 232
Newport Sports, 141
Newsday, 147
New York Americans, 26
New York Rangers, 10, 16, 17, 28, 52, 79, 80
Nidoo, L. M. Dr., 226
Nieuwenyk, Joe, 238
Nilan, Chris, 225
Nilsson, Ulf, 78–80
Norris, Bruce, 234
Norris Division, 2, 4, 234
Norris, Jim, 61
Northgate Hotel Ltd., 63
Nykoluk, Danny, 91, 126
Nykoluk, Mike, 91–92, 116–17, 120–28, 139, 144, 153, 232, 236
Nylund, Gary, 154, 155, 160–64, 170–72, 239

Obodiac, Emma, 130–31, 135–36
Obodiac, Stan, 129–31, 134–36, 142, 148, 215
O'Connell, Mary, 248
Olczyk, Ed, 163, 172, 219–20, 228
O'Leary, Jim, 164
Olmstead, Bert, 43, 47

Olympic Saddledome, 242
O'Neill, Marty, 259
Ontario Heritage Act, 245
Ontario Hockey Association
  (OHA), 16, 40, 68-69, 75
Ontario Racing Commission, 194
Ontario Securities Commission,
  198
Orr, Frank, 138, 141
Ottawa Senators, 9, 13, 26

Paiement, Wilf, 88, 92
Palango, Paul, 126
Palmateer, Mike, 79, 81, 85, 86,
  87, 140
Palmer, Paul, 140
Pappin, Jim, 55
Parent, Bernie, 71-72
Parrish, Wayne, 126, 165, 168,
  257
Passmore, C. M., 18
Patrick, Lester, 12
Patterson, Gerry, 140
Pearson, Scott, 200
Peterborough Petes, 75
Peterson, Brent, 82
Philadelphia *Inquirer,* 127
Pilote, Pierre, 50
Pinder, Herb, 218
Plante, Jacques, 47
Poddubny, Walt, 116, 155
Poile, Bud, 33
Polano, Nick, 125
Pollock, Sam, 68, 237
Powell, Clayton, 64
Pratt, Walter (Babe), 28, 30, 31,
  32
Price, Waterhouse and Company,
  62
Primeau, Joe, 11-13, 16, 23, 34,
  37, 221
Professional Hockey Writers
  Association, 148
Pronovost, Marcel, 84
Proudfoot, Jim, 165, 258

Pulford, Bob, 39, 40, 47, 52-53,
  57, 155
Puskas, Louis, 108, 109

Quebec Aces, 41
Quenneville, Joe, 88
Quinn, Pat, 232

Rachlin, Allen, 208-9
Raft, George, 18
Ramsay, Craig, 84
Ramsay, Donald, 138
Rare Jewel, 13
Reaume, Marc, 46
Reay, Billy, 41-43
Reber, Thomas, 188, 192
Reese, Jeff, 239
Reeve, Ted, 27
Regan, Larry, 45
Reid, Dave, 217
Report on Business Magazine, 242
Richard, Henri, 45, 56
Richard, Maurice (Rocket), 26,
  29, 30, 32, 47, 59
Richardson, Luke, 223
Richer, Stephane, 239
Riverdale Mercuries, 39
Roach, John Ross, 12, 16
Robert Amell and Co., 40
Robinson, Doug, 238
Robinson, Larry, 62, 151, 236
Rocchi, Rosanne, 193, 197, 207,
  209, 250
Rochester Americans, 59, 61
Rodden, Mike, 13
Rollins, Al, 34
Romain, Joseph, 11
Roman, Steve, 201
Ronberg, Gary, 127
Rooney, Steve, 239
Ross and MacDonald, 14
Ross, Art, 17
Rousseau, Bobby, 56
Roy, Patrick, 239
Royal Canadian Mounted Police,
  62
Ruddock, Russell, Sergeant, 259
Ruel, Claude, 238